PRAISE FOR YES IS THE ANSWER

One of Esquire's *summer reads for 2013*

"As with chess, Progressive Rock is commonly assumed by outsiders to be a sexless, all-male realm of wasted intellect. Many of the essayists in *Yes Is the Answer* operate under this belief. If you're a Prog fan, opening the book can be like stumbling into Monty Python's Department of Abuse."

—*Los Angeles Times*

"There are some fancy names attached but one of the craziest essays I've read on anything in a long time was by a Spanish writer named Rodrigo Fresán, which begins with The Arcade Fire, and talks a great deal about A *Clockwork Orange* and makes the crazy-but-possibly-true comparison that "Comfortably Numb" is to "A Day in the Life" as Nathan Zuckerman is to Holden Caulfield. He wrote it in Spanish but, luckily, it was translated. I think one would like it even if one hates Yes and ELP (and [has] never heard of Soft Machine)."

—*The Nation*

"What's especially tired about this trope in popular versions of Rock history is that it assumes that its practitioners and fans didn't acknowledge the pomposity and silliness of Prog. It overlooks the fact that pomposity and silliness were the point of Prog, and that these qualities could be as exciting and valid as three-chord songs played by sociopathic misanthropes. At least that's the case made with... persuasiveness by the new book *Yes Is the Answer*."

—*Grantland*

"Most of these essays are highly personal and only glancingly about the music. But everyone had a good time, and that's what matters most."

—*The Oregonian*

"The book—a tribute to what Weingarten identifies in the introduction as Prog Rock's grandeur, its mushy mysticism, its blissed-out mystery—is a high point in a renaissance that's been building: a reverential 2009 BBC documentary (*Prog [Rock] Britannia*), a magazine (*Classic Prog*), and a growing number of festivals, including Prog Angeles, organized by Cornell and featuring members of Weezer and others. Tastemaking online music journal *Pitchfork* drops the P-word on an almost weekly basis in describing some impossibly cool band's music, from metal monsters Mastodon to French electronic duo Justice—an admission, finally, that someone was listening. And there is the full-on revival of the band responsible for a concept album about hemispheres of the brain: Rush. As Nirvana's Dave Grohl said in his speech inducting Rush into the Rock and Roll Hall of Fame, 'There's one mystery that eclipses them all: when the f–k did Rush become cool?'"

—*Maclean's*

"You would have to look long and hard to find someone who felt less warmly about the movement known as progressive rock as your humble blogger... Why, then, can't I put down this new book, *Yes is the Answer*, a collection of writers on prog?"

—*The Misread City*

"Editors Marc Weingarten and Tyson Cornell have gathered twenty writers who discuss how those mathematical soundtracks for D&D all-nighters impacted their lives with humbleness and wit."

—*Psychobabble*

"Owning up to one's own affinity for any Prog Rock after reading *Yes Is The Answer* (mine being Floyd's Meddle) is up to you."

—*AntiGravity Magazine*

"This is the kind of book you've been waiting your whole life for and you may not have even known it. Rather than an historical account of the rise and fall of Progressive Rock, *Yes Is the Answer* features essays from a number of musicians, critics, and authors who reflect not just on the genre, but the ways in which it has shaped (or misshaped) their lives. This goes beyond an analysis of favorite Yes, Gentle Giant, or Todd Rundgren albums, it's about, as is so often the case, what happens once those albums have entered our orbits. Some of these essays are touching, haunting, beautiful, others are funny or even in their way frightening. Some are all of those things and more. And reading this from cover to cover is an absolute pleasure."

—PopMatters

"Any time I get the chance to read a book about Progressive Rock of the 70s—and it's positive; in fact, lovingly penned—I am all for it."

—Vintage Rock

"For music fans that have only ever found solace in their headphones, *Yes is the Answer* will provide charming, intelligent, and occasionally emotional glimpses at how others experience and interpret their favorite groups."

—Decoder Magazine

"If you're interested in essays about how music effects our lives in count-less ways, about the scene in the late '60s through the early '80s, about growing up and burning out, coming to terms with age, this is a good read with some sad bits, some angry bits, and a lot of very funny bits."

—In The Mouth of Dorkness

"In many cases, it's the very love of Prog that becomes the backdrop of fraught adolescence, most notably in Tom Junod's 'Out, Angel Out,' which details how Peter Gabriel, during his turn in Genesis and then upon his defection from the band, gave the writer a kindred spirit."

—Las Vegas City Life

"Lovers of Progressive Rock legends like King Crimson, Genesis, or Emerson, Lake & Palmer should check out *Yes is the Answer*."

—The Rumpus

YĪTA

YES IS

THE ANSWER

AND OTHER PROG ROCK TALES

edited by Marc Weingarten & Tyson Cornell

A Barnacle Book Rare Bird Books

New York Los Angeles

THIS IS A GENUINE BARNACLE BOOK

A Barnacle Book | Rare Bird Books
453 South Spring Street, Suite 531
Los Angeles, CA 90013
abarnaclebook.com
rarebirdbooks.com

Printed in Canada
Set in Goudy Old Style
Distributed in the U.S. by Publishers Group West
Interior illustrations by Alexandra Infante
Full spread illustration by Mattias Adolfsson

10 9 8 7 6 5 4 3 2 1

Paperback ISBN: 978-1-940207-13-1

Publisher's Cataloging-in-Publication data

Yes is the answer: and other prog rock tales / edited by Marc Weingarten and
Tyson Cornell.
   p. cm.
   ISBN 978-0-9854902-0-1

1. Progressive rock music—History and criticism. 2. Rock music—History and
criticism. 3. Rock music—Analysis, appreciation. I. Weingarten, Marc. II. Cornell,
Tyson. III. Title.

ML3534 .Y47 2013
781.66 —dc23

For Absent Friends

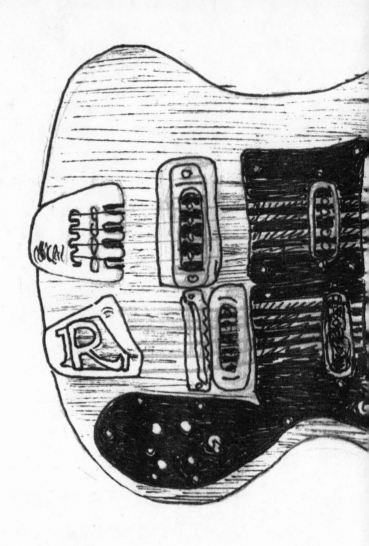

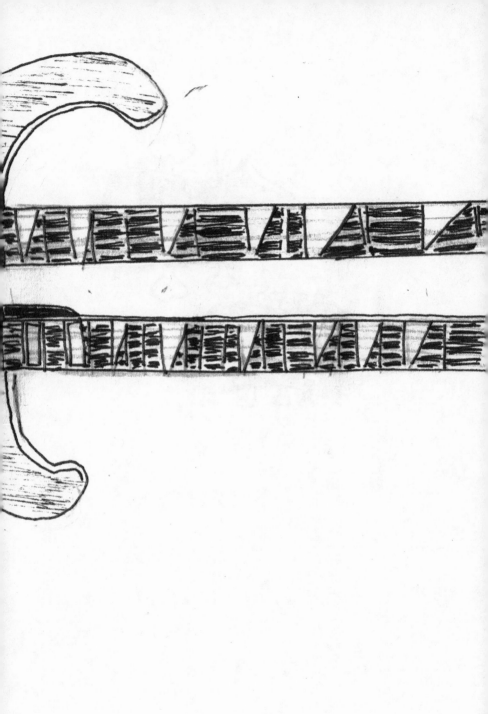

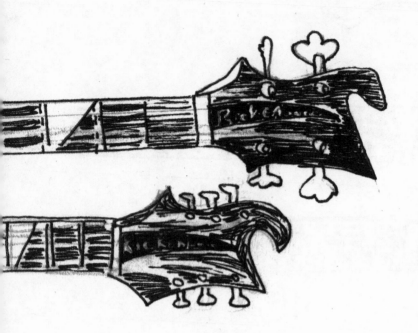

Projecting our images

in space and in time

YES IS THE ANSWER

Disclaimer: Some of the essays in this book are prolix and self-indulgent. These are essays about Prog Rock. This is as it should be.

CONTENTS

YES IS THE ANSWER: AN INTRODUCTION

THE HATERS WEREN'T ALL wrong, of course. Prog *was* ridiculous. But never underestimate a young boy's finely honed sense of irony. We loved some of this stuff precisely because it was overblown. It's kind of like when Evel Knievel jumped over thirty cars—you mean, he did *that*? We would laugh at some passages, marvel at others—it was all part of the ongoing conversation about Prog.

And yes, it was pretentious. That's why we liked Prog Rock; it strived for something beyond what we were hearing on AM radio. We didn't give a damn about rock's first principles, all that three chords and the truth business; give us Prog Rock's grandeur, its mushy mysticism, its blissed-out mystery. When you're a certain kind of cloistered fifteen year old male, you're looking for music to lay out an alternative universe much the same way that Tolkien, weed, and comic books did. Prog delivered the goods like nothing else. At least for me.

I didn't care much for comics. I had Prog musicians with their codpieces, their Mylar capes, and white leather boots. They *were* superheroes, and their talent infused them with special powers. When you're a young boy looking up at a man with flowing blond hair negotiating a groaning bank of very complicated circuitry, it's like you've come face to face with some kind of earthly God. Or Thor with a Moog.

Prog was most certainly not monolithic. Yes's cosmic Technicolor Dream was not even in the same area code as King Crimson's dark, distorted vision. And don't even get me started on Genesis, a band whose eccentricity and Ambrose Bierce-ian worldview made them every bit as weird as Captain Beefheart.

Prog was indulgent, sure, but it wasn't aimless noodling. That was Jazz Fusion, which ditched good songwriting for chops, man. Jazz Fusion fans were douchebags, anyway, the kind of kids that grokked on instrumental gear and got hard-ons during their long Saturday afternoons in guitar shops, ogling over Ovation double-necks. We were *deep* into the music, the gestalt of it. Who cares if the lyrics were terrible? I was more of a formalist in those days. It was about the way Prog washed over you, opened an aperture to a new headspace you had never inhabited before.

Prog Rock fans were a select tribe of fellow travelers, and we were defensive about cultural Jihadists who had besmirched our beloved music with that Fusion tar brush. Besides, most enemies of Prog didn't really listen to it. We were protective of our music, because it was *ours*. The uninitiated didn't *get* Prog, so we clung ever tighter to it.

Reading the essays in this book, you will be prone to believe that Prog Rock was exclusively for the young, and fixed in a specific cultural moment: the post-*Sgt. Pepper*, pre-Punk seventies. Which is true. And for many of our contributors, Prog was a passing fancy. Even some of its greatest practitioners have given it up, as evidenced by the fact that King Crimson's Robert Fripp and Bill Bruford have both retired from public performance. But no one among us here has forsaken the thrills that Prog Rock has given us and continues to give us: that transportive frisson as we stared intently at Roger Dean's sci-fi landscapes while grooving to "Astral Traveler."

If you have this book in your hands, surely you've been there, too.

—Marc Weingarten, March 2013

HERE COMES THE KNIFE

by SETH GREENLAND

This will be our reply to violence: to make music more intensely, more beautifully, more devotedly than ever before.

—Leonard Bernstein

THE DAGGER FLASHED IN a streak of white light before plunging toward its target. Silver rings on the assailant's tapered fingers. A thin wrist extruding through a frilly cuff. Two thousand rapt witnesses. The point of the blade thrust between the E and the F keys and the notes continued to drone through the old theater. My friends and I were seated in the fourth row of the Fillmore East in New York and Keith Emerson had just stabbed his Hammond organ like some kind of rock and roll Jack the Ripper. My twelve year old eyes shot out of my head like they were on springs. Because we were kids and not old enough to attend a satanic rite like this on our own, my parents had brought us, and now their mouths were agape in scandalized suburban astonishment. Keith Emerson of the mod clothes, Prince Valiant haircut, and unthreatening leading man looks was a murderous dandy! What kind of lunacy were my parents exposing their charges to? We were witnessing the wild birth pangs of a genre.

Emerson, Lake & Palmer were still in the future. This was The Nice, a virtuoso English Prog trio—not that we had heard the word *Prog*—and they were my favorite band in the world. Consisting of Emerson, bassist Lee Jackson, and drummer Brian Davison, they had just sacked their guitarist Davy O'List and were touring as a trio to support their first album, *Thoughts of Emerlist Davjack*. They were opening for Ten Years After, a band led by the manic-fingered British guitarist Alvin Lee that played a steroidal version of Chicago blues. Ten Years After sounded like Muddy Waters on a three-day meth binge. The Nice didn't sound like anything we had ever heard. They were our kind of band.

First, some context: This was before Prog grew bloviated and pretentious, before the elves and "faeries" (Faeries? Are you locked in an Andrew Marvell poem? It's f-a-i-r-i-e-s!) took over. Before it became what Spīnal Tap so nimbly skewered. This is back when Prog first arrived and hit rock fans—few of whom were familiar with composers like Stockhausen or John Cage—the way Stravinsky's *Le Sacre du Printemps* gobsmacked that classical audience in 1913. The early Prog practitioners cast a spell similar to that of the Romantic poets a century before Stravinsky's provocation. Like Keats and Shelley, they were young artists who wanted to upend bourgeois expectations by reimagining classical forms. This was not something our seventh grade brains were capable of articulating, but we were fascinated by the new sounds, the lyrics that accompanied them, and the wholly original sonic world Prog rockers were creating, a reimagining of Beethoven and his ilk in a way that made those bewigged worthies somehow relevant in a post-Beatles world.

Most of the Pop music we knew consisted of love songs and our young palates had become jaded. Prog opened a Huxleyan door. Songs about space travel, other realms of reality, and madness; those were things to argue about and extol over our fifty-cent lunches in the school cafeteria, to engage with alone as you lay awake at night dreaming of a girl who probably had pictures of the Bee Gees on her bedroom wall.

What kind of twelve year old goes to a Nice show? The story starts, as so many do, with piano lessons. Mr. Gould came to my house every Tuesday. He was in his fifties and always wore a gray suit and a dark tie. He had a receding hairline and saggy jowls and when he demonstrated anything on the keyboard his fingers bounced like ten tiny ballerinas. Once, he showed me a picture of a pet capuchin monkey perched on his head. It was the only non-pianistic insight into the man I ever received. He was teaching me to play the light Pop music of the time, songs like "Windy" by The Association and Paul Mauriat's "Love Is Blue." If I was not going to wrestle with classical music—and that was about as likely as being kidnapped by aliens—these were the numbers that Mr. Gould was willing to teach.

While I was practicing scales and "Judy In Disguise" by John Fred and his Playboy Band, something else was afoot. I played organ in a garage band with a group of guys and our artistic avatar, our tastemaker, the musical mind from which all things flowed, was our drummer, a kid named Bones: tight chinos, an untucked button-front shirt and a drum attack like his idol, Keith Moon. Bones was a wisp of a person who possessed the certainty of a mountain.

Along with being the most talented musician in our friend group, at twelve he was a music snob and serious anglophile with a preternatural connection to what was going on in England. He turned us on to bands like the Small Faces, the Move, and the superbly named Dave Dee, Dozy, Beaky, Mick & Tich. It was in his second floor bedroom on a leafy street one gray autumn day that he fixed me with a portentous stare and said: "You have to hear this." Then he dropped the needle on *The Piper At The Gates Of Dawn*. People were listening to Jefferson Airplane then, to The Young Rascals, to Motown. It wasn't like there was no good music around, but Pink Floyd was a sonic message beamed from another planet, a declaration of insanity (little did we know the fate awaiting their founding member Syd Barrett) that shook our insular TV dinner, homework, and bedtime world. They were an uncontrolled slide down to a Stygian realm we could not have imagined. Their instruments were familiar, what you usually heard in a rock band back then: guitar, drums, and organ. But this was an organ that didn't sound like the tinny—although admittedly cool-looking—Vox we heard on Dave Clark Five records or the Farfisa Sam the Sham and The Pharaohs used on "Woolly Bully." The organ that Rick Wright was playing on songs like "Interstellar Overdrive" had a darker, more threatening tone, an altogether more powerful one that rumbled from the deepest bowels of the earth so when the song ended it made you nervously glance around the room to make sure everything was still the same. Its effect was one of awe and disturbance, its implications nothing less than religious. To Mr. Gould's piano student, this was even more appealing than his monkey.

Impressed and slightly unnerved, I asked Bones what else he had that sounded like Pink Floyd and from his voluminous shelf of vinyl came The Nice. I held *The Thoughts of Emerlist Davjack* in my hand and looked at the photograph of the band on the cover. There were four of them and they were cool and English, a tautology for me in those days. Bones announced that their guitar player had gotten the heave-ho and they were now an organ-dominated trio. An organ trio? I was dubious. Isn't that the kind of act that plays Doris Day songs in the lounge of the Holiday Inn you stayed at with your mom and dad on the family trip to Amish country? "No," Bones said. "They're not that kind of organ trio."

Then he handed me *Ars Longa Vita Brevis*—of course, he had both their albums. How Bones had come by this band was a mystery, but with music he was remarkably omniscient for someone yet to experience puberty—and we put it on and sat back to listen. There was no shortage of organists back in the late sixties. The list of bands that had an organ player would fill the rest of this page. And they all stood around in the background and played as if they were studying with Mr. Gould. Their parts were usually simple harmonies, the keyboard equivalent of the sha-la-las heard on so many doo-wop recordings. Sure, Matthew Fisher played the evocative organ melody that kicked off Procol Harum's "A Whiter Shade Of Pale," but they were a quintet and you had the sense that he was being let out of his cage to play that bit, only to be shoved back in when it was over. The Zombies' Rod Argent played some jazzy organ parts, but he stepped out in front on rare occasions.

There was a song on *Ars Longa Vita Brevis* called "Rondo," an organ showpiece where Emerson's keyboard pyrotechnics easily equal those of Ray Manzarek on the roughly contemporaneous "Light My Fire." The song is a rock reimagining of jazz pianist Dave Brubeck's "Blue Rondo A La Turk," and Emerson's whirling dervish version claims it for the rock canon. As I listened my pulse accelerated. *You could do this with an organ? Why had no one told me this before?* Immediately upon hearing it I had to play the song again. Then I went home, sat down at the piano, and—sausage-fingered—tried to master it.

When you are in junior high and want to be a rock star, you imagine yourself enacting the roles of your heroes. As Mick Jagger, you caper around the stage making love to the microphone, impregnating the audience with your eyes. As Jimi Hendrix, you rip sonic worlds from the strings of your Stratocaster, then spray it with lighter fluid, toss a match, and bask in the heat of your brilliance. But an organist was out of luck because there were no heroes, no role models. Yes, there were Jimmy McGriff and the great Booker T. Jones, but these were not players who connected with suburban adolescents. So it was impossible to fantasize about being an organist. It would have been like fantasizing about being a librarian. While it was an entirely respectable endeavor, the imaginary life of the young organist who quietly yearned for the spotlight was dominated by visions of learning how to play the guitar.

The Nice changed the equation. Emerson had studied classical music growing up, and Bach and Bartok infused his playing. Add to that what he was stealing from the jazz world, and he was combining it all into something wholly original and, to me, awe-inspiring. Cascades of notes, great washes of tones, total command of the sound and the stage. In Keith Emerson, the organ had its Eric Clapton, Jimmy Page, and Jeff Beck all rolled into one.

For me, it was never again as exciting as that first moment in the world of Progressive Rock. There were some good bands and some great songs, but when Punk came along and beat Prog to death with a club, I was not among the mourners. It had descended into a Mannerist phase and gotten silly. I had stopped listening to it. While the importance of King Crimson and their contemporaries in rock history is generally acknowledged, after The Clash and Elvis Costello arrived, it was hard to hear *In The Court of the Crimson King* without an indulgent smile at the vagaries of youthful taste.

And then one day more than forty years later, in a resonant echo of my parents at the Fillmore, I am with my teenage son at the Hollywood Bowl where we are waiting for his favorite band to take the stage. It's a warm summer night and the Bowl is full to bursting. The stage is dark. The unusually attentive audience is thrumming in anticipation. My son, a far more talented musician than I, has been anticipating this evening for months. He leans forward and stares straight ahead, willing his heroes to appear. Then the lights burst on blasting a hole in the darkness and Radiohead begins to play. Their pulsing, hypnotic sound fills the Bowl and my head and it is transporting and wholly original—it can't be anything but Radiohead—and yet deeply indebted to what came before. This melding of classical and jazz and electronica, charged with a relentless forward thrust is the legacy of bands like The Nice.

Radiohead ranged through their catalogue and delivered an inspired set, and the Hollywood Bowl was the perfect place to see them, but I wish Johnny Greenwood had stabbed his keyboard.

Seth Greenland is the author of three novels, most recently The Angry Buddhist. *His play* Jungle Rot *won the Kennedy Center/American Express Fund For New American Plays Award and the American Theater Critics Association Award. He was a writer/producer on the HBO drama series* Big Love.

Out, Angels Out
by Tom Junod

Is Peter Gabriel the God that is referred to in Genesis?
—Old-Fashioned Mort Goldman

I HAVE A CONFESSION TO make: I don't know the meaning of the cover art from Peter Gabriel's first solo album. More to the point, I never did. I say this—admit this—because in college, I made myself something of a reputation as the One Who Knew. People used to come to my dorm room to get high and ask me, as though I were some kind of seer. They'd hang out for a while, then find the record in a pile and pull out the sleeve, the one with the spooky picture of Gabriel peering out the lowered window of a dark car, his eyes aglow, as silvered and inhuman as the stars in the sky. "Okay, you know what this means?"

"Yeah."

"Well...?"

I'd just smile, swami-style, and burn another bowl. I never told them. I *succeeded* in not telling them, succeeded in conveying the impression that they somehow weren't worthy of the knowledge I possessed. I even got away with quoting Peter himself, from the great and holy *The Lamb Lies Down On Broadway*, which happened to be the double album I always used for cleaning pot. "I'd rather trust a man who doesn't shout what he's found," I'd say. "There's no need to sound if you're homeward bound." Of course, I wasn't shouting what I'd found, only that I'd found it, so I was hardly in position to lord my enlightenment over anyone, much less suggest that they didn't deserve to be privy to knowledge they hadn't yet earned. But that's why I pulled off my pose to the extent I did.

I never really had to convince anyone that I had a secret store of knowledge about Peter Gabriel.

I just had to convince them that I'd endured some kind of trial to get it.

I GREW UP PROG, which is to say that I grew up on Long Island, stoned and semi-smart, sensitive and without any real prospects for getting laid. I listened to music in vehement reaction against the disco that came from the city, the Southern Rock that made my classmates talk and dress like they came from the country, and the proto-Punk Rock that violated my suburban notions of class and quality. We lived *nice*, in a house with French provincial furniture covered in plastic, and the music that I chose to listen to was as elaborate and artificial as one of my mom's divans. I realize now that I wasn't rebelling by holing up inside my room and blasting music that must have sounded, to my parents, like Gregorian chants; I was showing off, to them and everyone else. I was trying to prove that I could appreciate what they couldn't—concept albums and songs that took up an entire album side. Prog was the intellectual protest music of a kid who had never read a proper book, the "religious experience" favored by a Catholic schoolboy who'd stopped going to church, the romantic aria of a kid who had not only never heard an opera but who had also never been kissed. It was masturbatory, literally. American culture had already pigeonholed rock music as a teenaged way of saying, *you don't understand me*; Prog Rock announced a different kind of alienation, a way of saying, *you don't even understand my music*. I wanted my parents to like Prog; to recognize that Rick Wakeman was a better keyboard player than Roger Whitaker; to know that the music their son listened to behind his closed door contained literary references and "classical motifs." But all my parents knew, when they saw the Roger Dean posters on my wall and heard the sonic overkill of *Relayer*, was that I was on drugs.

And I was. I was on drugs, and the music on my stereo corresponded to the drugs I was on. Led Zeppelin: booze skimmed from the bottles in my father's bar. Yes: weed. Genesis: better weed. Indeed, I started listening to Genesis when I went from hanging around with Catholic-school kids to hanging around with public-schoolers—when my allegiances migrated from the kids who bought pot to the kids who sold it. These were the burnouts who gave each other nicknames about how burnt out they were. A guy named Chris had become "Crisp"; a guy named Walburton, "What's Burnin'?" There was Bernie Spacey, whose real name I never knew. Then there was a kid, half-Irish, half-Italian, with a haircut like a Roman emperor—O'Rippio. He was the Genesis freak. He had seen them in New York City, for the historic *Lamb* tour, and now possessed the bristling zeal of a convert. He would go along with us when we went to the movie theater in Amityville that showed *Yessongs* on Friday nights—smoking pot in front of the *Amityville Horror* house along the way—but he wore an almost parental air, as though we were children whose unformed tastes he tolerated, until he had the chance to talk about Genesis. Then his voice would change. It would deepen, and gain an oracular authority. He would sometimes hold up a professorial index finger as he talked. He'd grow expansive and cagey at the same time—he'd make you ask about what he was determined to say. "What's so great about Genesis?" you'd ask, and he'd first give you a closed-lipped and almost pitying smile, and then intone a single word, the name of an angel: "Gabriel."

What can I say? I bought it. I wanted what O'Rippio had, not just knowledge but a style informed by knowledge, and so I bought his bullshit, and then I took my bike to Sam Goody and bought *Selling England By The Pound*. I played it for the first time that night, on headphones, afraid of what I—what my parents—might hear. What kind of secrets did this "Gabriel" possess, and what could I learn from him? Sure enough, with the opening line he sent me to the dictionary. "Can you tell me where my country lies? / cried the unifaun to his true love's eyes"—well, what the fuck was a unifaun? And, on the second side, who was Father Tiresias? I had no clue. I was used to Prog bands spouting a lot of highfalutin nonsense about *Topographic Oceans* and "Karn Evil 9," but the nonstop grandeur of Yes and ELP told me what to think about the stuff that didn't make sense—told me, indeed, that it was grand. Genesis offered no shortage of either grandeur or nonsense, but its music was harder to locate emotionally. *Selling England* was an album that took as its subject the concept of "Englishness," about which I knew nothing, and cared even less. For God's sake, it even ended, in "Aisle of Plenty," with a dirge-like litany of English grocery store prices. It was eccentric and obscure, with its one trifling afterthought of a love song sung by, of all people, the drummer. And yet *Selling England By The Pound* did what no Prog record had ever done: it made me sad. "Aisle of Plenty" might have been about an old English lady wandering around a supermarket, but to this day when I hear its trickling minor-key opening—and the words, "Still alone in o-hell-o, see the deadly nightshade grow," sung in a high broken whisper—I think, yes, that's what my adolescence sounded like, out there on Long Island, if only in the deserted cathedral of my headphoned brain.

See, we don't get to choose our blues, especially when we're young. Our blues choose us, and Genesis chose me. Hell, *Gabriel* chose me. True, like all good Prog bands, Genesis never deigned to play so much as a blues lick in any of its extended instrumental workouts; but Peter Gabriel had the distinction of being the only Prog frontman with any blues in his voice, or, for that matter, any rock and roll. It was just a special kind of blues and a special kind of rock and roll. Why did I instantly identify with Peter Gabriel more than I'd ever identified with Greg Lake or the Andersons, Jon and Ian? Easy—Gabriel was more fucked up. He wasn't a hero, romantic, or otherwise. He shaved his hair down the middle of his head in a kind of obverse Mohawk. He wore costumes. He was theatrical, but he wasn't, like, *Glam* or anything. He was equally funny and dour—"mordant" is the word I'd use now. He sang elaborate fairy tales about sexual frustration. He trafficked in rage and a creepiness that passed for menace. He did me the great favor of making me feel uncomfortable. The rest of the English Prog singers sounded, well, English, like choirboys channeling Merlin the Magician. Gabriel didn't even sound exactly like himself. He didn't have a voice; he had voices—"it's all *octaves*," quoth O'Rippio—and they all had the advantage of being instantly recognizable. Oh, he was English, all right, and so one of his voices was pretty enough for the acoustic interludes that Genesis loved to play before Tony Banks broke out the Mellotron. But Gabriel also had a talent for antic mimicry, and he had a falsetto, and he had, whenever he needed it, maybe the best rasp in all of rock music, not just Prog. It wasn't even a rasp—Rod Stewart had a rasp. Gabriel had a voice that emerged from way down deep in his throat, and could go from barking violence to willful ugliness to something that went beyond beauty because beauty wasn't what it was gunning for. No rock singer since Jim Morrison had soared higher with a lower voice, and there was always, in Genesis, a conflict between the gorgeous swelling fussiness of a lot of the music and the pre-ravaged voice that pitched every song towards darkness. It wasn't that Peter Gabriel sounded like a guy who ran around on stage dressed like a flower; it was that even when he was riding some impossible crescendo–and even when he was running around on stage dressed like a flower–he sounded the way blues singers sounded, like he might have been a hundred years old.

I wanted to sound like that, but not as a singer: I didn't sing. I wanted to look like that, but not in costume: I spent every day in Earth Shoes and Levi's corduroys. I wanted to be able to communicate what Gabriel communicated, that innate understanding of darkness. But first I had to understand. I wanted to be Gabriel, but first I had to figure out what he was singing about–to unravel the meaning of his songs. Amazingly, I wasn't alone in this. We used to go to that pagan place–the woods–to smoke pot, but also to decipher Genesis songs, particularly their religious content. We were all ruined Catholics, but our exposure to the stew of numerological obsession, English anti-clericalism, and references to the apocryphal books of the Bible contained in *Selling England*, *Foxtrot*, and *The Lamb* turned us into something else–yes, I was a Teenaged Gnostic. I had never heard the word "apocalypse" until Genesis rendered it in 9/8 on "Supper's Ready," but now that I had I couldn't get enough of it. I wanted to find out why "666 is no longer alone" and who Gog and Magog were and where I might find the New Jerusalem. Alas, the one guy who knew wasn't telling: O'Rippio. He had seen Genesis perform "Supper's Ready" as an encore after they did the *The Lamb Lies Down On Broadway* in its entirety. He had seen Gabriel don a crown of thorns at the beginning of the song and emerge in white raiment at the end. *A crown of thorns! White raiment!* O'Rippio not only knew; he *said* he knew. He told us he knew. "Supper's Ready" occupied a central place in the oeuvre of Gabriel-era Genesis because it occupied the whole second side of *Foxtrot* and because it starts out sounding like a proper love song and ends up describing the marriage of Good and Evil. I got that– but was there more? Was there something I was missing, a meaning only O'Rippio knew? He wouldn't say. He'd get that thin smile on his face and start using that imperious oracular voice he'd copied from Gabriel himself. When people yelled out requests at Genesis concerts, Gabriel would pretend to listen, then drop his voice and say: *Wrong.* And that's what O'Rippio said now, in the same dismissive voice. He knew the meaning of "Supper's Ready," and I didn't. He *possessed* the meaning of "Supper's Ready," and I never would, unless I agreed to fight him for it.

Well, not fight. Box. O'Rippio wanted to box me. He wanted to box me as a condition of disclosure. I was sort of the jock of the burnouts, the high school football player, the quarterback; I lifted weights, and I went to town on the heavy bag hanging in my garage when I was really wasted. But O'Rippio boxed. He learned to box in a boy's club, he competed in the Golden Gloves, and he knew how to feint and how to slip punches. He had the same kind of knowledge about boxing that he had about "Supper's Ready." But in this case, I had knowledge, too. O'Rippio said that he only wanted to spar—you know...put on the gloves...mess around a little bit. But I knew that he wanted to beat the shit out of me. I knew he was *going* to beat the shit out of me if I took him up on his offer. So I took a shortcut to the Gabrielesque knowledge I was looking for. I chickened out, and instead of boxing O'Rippio I dropped acid with my friend Rael.

I'D HEARD OF RAEL before I became his friend. Everybody in town had. He was a legendary wiseass who'd become a legendary head. He had a rep—as a guy who got busted in, like, third grade for calling a cop "the fuzz," and now as a guy who could get you wacky weed. He was the last person I expected to see among the burnouts in the woods, but there he was, searching for meaning like everyone else by searching for the meanings of Genesis songs.

His name wasn't really Rael. Rael, of course, was the hero of *The Lamb Lies Down On Broadway.* But I'll call him Rael because he had some of the same characteristics—he was a little bit wilder than the rest of us, a little crazier, a little funnier, a little more violent. He drove faster and got into more fights. He actually chased girls. He was the only one who dressed disco, in tight shirts and pressed pants and shoes with chunk heels, and he was definitely the only one who liked to dance. Thing was, he danced to Prog. All alone, he danced to "Cinema Show," to "Back in N.Y.C.," to "Apocalypse in 9/8," even to King Crimson's "Red." He had a big reel-to-reel tape player in his room, and once when I went to visit him he was dancing, with his big Mouseketeer headphones clapped on his ears, to a live version of Yes's "Gates of Delirium." How could anyone dance to "Gates of Delirium"? But he wasn't just dancing, he was in a state of ecstasy, and he rewound the tape and squeezed the headphones over my ears to show me why. "Listen to that!"

"Listen to what?"

"The bass!"

"Okay..."

"He made a mistake! Chris Squire made a mistake! You can't hear that? Listen again! *That's a fucking mistake!*"

No, I didn't notice the bright beam of mania shining forth from his eyes like an image from a Prog album cover. To me, Rael was just, you know, excitable, and his excitability is what made us friends—he pushed me where I wouldn't normally go. He got me into fights and he got me into acid. He had a theory about *The Lamb*, that it was about acid, that Gabriel's Rael was tripping as he went out into early morning Manhattan, ocean winds blowing on the land. He'd subjected the whole double album to an elaborate textual exegesis, and he could prove that all its imagery corresponded to the features of daily life in New York City, lysergically transformed. He could even prove that Rael took a shit, on the third side, in "The Lamia" ("'the Lamia of the pool'? That's shit!"). I'd been preparing to drop acid by reading Carlos Castaneda and Baba Ram Dass, and had been looking for an equivalent of Castaneda's "Don Juan," my own spirit guide. Now, through my friend Rael's tutelage, I'd found him. I'd drop acid, and my spirit guide would be Peter Gabriel.

We did it at the summer house my parents owned, in the deserted days after I graduated high school and waited to start my summer job as a dishwasher. Mom and Dad let me use the house for a weekend, and I packed the steaks, the Heinekens, the weed, and the windowpane. I went with Rael and some other burnouts, along with a cassette player and a tape of Genesis recorded from *King Biscuit Flower Hour*. We put the windowpane on our tongues in the late afternoon, with Rael quoting from *The Lamb*: "Something inside me has just begun, Lord knows what I have done..." Then we smoked a bowl, and went to the dock of the bay to watch the sunset.

It never ended. The sunset never *ended*, man, and it wasn't orange or red, it was purple, and it turned the water the color and viscosity of purple Jell-O, right before it sets and it's halfway between warm and cold. It offered a spectacle, but more than that, it offered an inkling, a presentiment that my life might actually turn out all right, if only because I had no power over it, if only because all the power was out *there*, in the purple Jell-O magnitude of a sunset that never went away, and to this day lingers in my mind—no, my being— like the retinal stain of a flashbulb. I felt peaceful, facing, for probably the first time since puberty, the possibility of peace. But Rael was ecstatic, exultant, as twisty and alive as a downed wire, bopping around the dock in 9/8 while quoting from "Supper's Ready": "That's it, Tommy, that's it! That's what he means! 'Shedding ever changing colors! In the darkness of the fading light!'" He pointed to the sun. "*That's* the 'Supper of the mighty one'!"

O'Rippio wouldn't tell me the meaning of "Supper's Ready" because he didn't think I was "ready for it," and because he wanted to kick my ass. Well, fuck O'Rippio, and the intercessory role he fancied for himself. I didn't need a priest. I didn't even need to know the meaning of "Supper's Ready" because I had *experienced* the meaning of "Supper's Ready," and it, like the rest of my life, had been right there in front of me all along.

I went to college in upstate New York after the summer. I followed a girl I was in love with but who wasn't in love with me—my high school dream girl; the measure of my ardor; the fruitless search I believed would offer the resolution to all my fruitless searches. She remained uninterested in anything but friendship but perhaps she was no longer my ideal audience, for what interested me now was a *new* audience, and the possibility of transformation. From the stoner second-stringer of my Catholic high school emerged the state college Seeker, the haunted philosopher with the stereo loud enough to promulgate *The Lamb* and "Supper's Ready" and, God help me, Crimson's *Larks' Tongues In Aspic* to the entire campus. I specialized in the late night rap session, the protracted paean to the oneness of being, the post-bong espousal of the principles of Eastern mysticism—and to my amazement, nobody called me on it. I'd wanted to turn myself into a Gabrielesque figure, and here, though I still wore Levi corduroys and Earth Shoes and didn't have a girlfriend, I had the opportunity to do so.

I even had a plan for completing the transformation. Since my new life had begun when I took acid with my friend Rael, I now had to take more acid with my friend Rael. Since my rebirth had followed the blueprint found in the lyrics that Gabriel had written for Genesis, I now had to see what he had to say in the lyrics he was writing for himself, because by the time I'd gone to college, Gabriel, of course, had "gone solo." A loaded phrase, that—sort of the opposite of the dreaded "gone disco." But Gabriel had earned it. He'd left Genesis just as I'd come to love Genesis, and published his reasons in a letter to *Melody Maker*. I had a clipping of the letter. I studied my clipping of the letter. A rock star's renunciation of rock stardom, it bore the title of a perfect Prog record: "Out, Angels Out—an investigation." As a piece of writing, it managed to be both direct and playful, personal and philosophical, foregoing score settling for apocalyptic intimations: "I believe the world has soon to go through a difficult period of changes," Gabriel had written. "I'm excited by some of the areas coming through to the surface which seem to have been hidden away in people's minds. I want to explore and be prepared to be open and flexible enough to respond, not tied into the old hierarchy..."

You see? Gabriel was experiencing what I was experiencing! He was transforming himself as I was transforming myself! He was getting out, in order to open himself up—in order to ready himself for the birth of the world he helped bring into being. Oh, it's hard now to appreciate the extent of the powers I ascribed to him, or of the belief I burdened him with. To me, "Out, Angels Out" counted not as a press release or letter but as a *document*, nothing less than the beginning of the future. Genesis had survived his departure—I had seen them in New York, with Phil Collins at the microphone and Bill Bruford on the drums—but there was nothing they could *teach* me anymore. What did I expect Gabriel to teach me, in his incarnation as a solo artist? I didn't know. All I knew was my plan: I would come home for Christmas. I would spend Christmas with my parents and then take their car to Florida with Rael and a couple of other friends. I would trip again, and then when I came home I would get tickets to Peter Gabriel's first solo show, rumored to be imminent. I would go to the show, listen to what Gabriel had to say, and emerge as nothing less than a completely new human being.

And strangely enough, despite the absurdity of my expectations, that's how it all worked out. We took my parents' Buick to Florida and stayed for a few days just north of Miami, in the condominium where my father kept his mistress. Then we drove down to Key West and at a bar called the Green Parrot bought some acid from a guy who looked like a pirate. We dropped the acid with *The Lamb* playing on a cassette recorder, and the "enossification"—Brian Eno's playful synthesizer treatment of Gabriel's vocals—shading places on the record it had never shaded before...shading, indeed, *everything.* It was January 1977. We were staying in a cabin at a motor court in Key West, Florida, and it was night, and it was cold. "Something inside me has just begun, Lord knows what I have done," Rael said, once again, but this time the sunset had already ended, and what didn't stop, what never stopped, were the guttural groans and skirling shrieks emanating from the cassette player. The whole world had been enossified and sounded like a chewing maw, and we put on our thin coats against the cold and went out in it.

Rael had been right all along. *The Lamb* was about a trip of some kind—a really bad one. "Fly On A Windshield"? That was us. "The Grand Parade Of Lifeless Packaging"? That was, um, *them.* And where were we? "In The Cage." In a panic, we went down to the dock where tourists gathered to watch the sunset. A woman stood in the dark, staring at a docked pleasure boat. Older than us, much older, indeed what my father would call "a pro," she had straggly brown hair, and wore a thin raincoat. "Big boat, eh, boys?" she said, then turned around...to reveal a face split down the middle, half smooth and shining, half lost to pockmarks and a living, molting port wine stain. "Yeah, big boat!" Rael said, pulling me away. "Big fucking boat! Wonder women, you can draw your blinds! Don't look at me, I'm not your kind..."

We stumbled down the street, wondering what had hit us. I had expected the trip to be something out of *Be Here Now* or *A Separate Reality* or *The Impersonal Life*—all the chestnuts of chemically enhanced cosmic devotion that I read in high school and still read when stoned in college. Instead, it felt like a story I'd read for freshman English, "Young Goodman Brown." Where was the oneness of the universe? Where was the beneficence? Then I stopped at an enormous cactus, studded with an infinity of thorns, its crooked arms enveloping the world. I fell down in front of it. I *kneeled*. God had created that cactus as surely as he had created that melting purple Jell-O sunset...which meant that he had created ugliness just as sure as he had created beauty...which meant that he had created evil just as surely as he created good...which meant that he had created his *own* crown of thorns. I might have been a teenaged Gnostic but I was also the product of twelve years of Catholic education, and my supper, at last, was ready, in the realization that the fallen world could not be redeemed because the fallen world could not be transcended—because the fallen world was all there was. The cactus, along with every other living thing, had its own sound, an alternating threnody of hunger and digestion, and Rael had to restrain me from impaling myself upon it. A police cruiser pulled up with its own brutish Enossification, its own metal machine music, and a cop rolled down the window.

"He okay?"

"Yeah," Rael said. "He's okay. Everything's okay. The whole *world's* okay..."

We wound up going to the concrete pier that marked the southernmost point of the continental United States. We sat there all night, the slapping sea the color of milk, an endless expanse of divine indifference. Before dawn a ravaged homeless man with a pointy beard walked out on the pier to ask us what we were doing and when he left we agreed he was the devil and threw all our money and pot into the water. Then we went back to the motor court where our other friends had slept. They were hungry. We went out to the Perkins' Pancake House where we watched people "eat without a sound," as Gabriel put it on *Selling England*. We began the drive back to New York, and that night, in the dark of I-95, I wrote my first poems: one an apology to my mother; another a long reflection about Key West, both of them in doggerel. Rael wrote out the lyrics of "Supper's Ready" again and again on the back of a brown paper bag.

I GOT THE GABRIEL tickets in February, as soon as they went on sale, and possessing them was like possessing a hoard of gold in a country with a worthless currency, or perhaps more properly a check from a dead father. The second semester of my freshman year in college had begun, and I had gone from being intriguingly dark to seriously weird. After dinner, I'd kick my roommate out of my room, close the door, sit on my bed and croon the bovine omni-syllable of the spiritually desperate: om. I'd be *om-ing*, a verb coined by my baffled suitemates who'd gather on the other side of the door and listen. An example of its proper usage:

"Let's get stoned."

"Can't. My dope's in the room and Tom kicked me out."

"What's he doing in there?"

"He's om-ing."

"Shit. Again?"

I was waiting for Gabriel to tell me what to do next. I was also waiting to see Rael again, since he alone knew what had happened in Key West, and so on the afternoon I got the tickets, I called him. His mother answered. Her voice quaked.

"Tommy, what is *Punge?*"

"What?"

"What is *Punge?*" She sounded desperate now.

"I don't know what you're talking about..."

In fact, I knew exactly what she was talking about. This is how Prog I was: during high school, my friends and I spoke in a different language, a highly inflected variant of English derived, in part, from *The Hobbit*, and called, of course, The Lang. I didn't invent it; they did. But with an improvisatory genius inspired by the necessity of hiding adolescent activities from their parents—fighting, drinking, shoplifting, having sex, smoking cigarettes, smoking pot. The Lang had words for all those categories. It sounded like a winsome Scottish brogue, and not everybody could speak it, but I was fluent enough to have acquired a Lang name I could have used as my Prog name: Totus. Rael didn't speak The Lang, but he'd picked up some basics, and now his mother began to weep as she demanded to know the meaning of one of its core words.

"Tommy, please. You have to tell me. What is *Punge?*'"

"It's pot," I said. And it was: Punge, derived from the textbook descriptions of marijuana's "pungent aroma."

"That's all?" she asked.

"That's all."

"Then what did you two do when you went to Florida? What did you take?"

"We took LSD."

"Oh, God."

"What's happened?"

She inhaled, and made a sound like an involuntary scream. "My boy," she said. "Today, my boy tried to do away with his father. And then two policemen."

A certain part of my life ended at that moment. *Do away with*: the formal diction and almost euphemistic quality of that phrase made the awful fact of what she was trying to describe specific and inescapable. I woke up, maybe even grew up.

"Is...?"

"He's alive," she said. "Everybody is, thank God. But Tommy"— she exhaled now—"you have to come down here. You have to tell everyone what happened. You have to tell everybody it wasn't *him*, it was the drugs that you boys took..."

And I did. A few weeks later, I took a bus to Long Island, and gave an affidavit to Rael's lawyer about dropping acid and waking up to a world red in tooth and claw. I found out then that the trip had never stopped for Rael—that he had never come down. The auditory hallucinations, in particular, had continued, the terrible groans and growls of a world comprised of creatures either eating or being eaten. They haunted him, they tortured him, and they lent credence to his conviction that the devil not only walked the earth but took the shape of many men, including his father. Rael tried to drown them out by singing the lyrics of Genesis songs but one day when his father yelled at him to pipe down he chased his father around the house with a shotgun and when his father hid behind a locked door he pressed the shotgun up against the door and pulled the trigger. The door exploded, but his father had ducked in anticipation, and saved his own life. His mother called the police, but when Rael heard the sirens he got into his car and rammed the approaching cruiser in an ecstasy of acceleration, all the while singing the lyrics of "Supper's Ready" at the top of his lungs. He smashed his face and went to the hospital in an ambulance and now faced three counts of attempted murder, one for his father and two for the cops. I gave the lawyer a statement, along with the paper bag upon which Rael had written lyrics and reflections on the way home from Florida.

Then I went to see Peter Gabriel's first concert as a solo artist, knowing that in some way he had driven one of my best friends stark raving mad.

THE CONCERT WAS ON March 5, 1977, at the Capitol Theater in Passaic, New Jersey, a famous dump right outside New York City. I went with a friend from high school, The Lang speaker who'd dubbed me Totus and whose own Lang name was—and still is!—Wy. The band Television opened. We'd never heard of them, and their reception from the crowd indicated what kind of crowd it was. For all its decrepitude, the Capitol Theater pioneered an unfamiliar technology; two huge screens flanked the stage and showed a live video of the concert in black and white. Even people in the back of the house could see the faces of the performers, and so we had a chance to see Television's Tom Verlaine, the band's skinny, pale, and almost cadaverous frontman as he played his measly little Telecaster and sang in a quivery voice that sounded like Patti Smith. What the fuck was this? Punk Rock? Was this fucking *Punk Rock*? Never mind that Verlaine's tunings and harmonics really were "progressive"—where were the keyboards? The Mellotron? The multiple guitars and the big ass drum kit? Where was Gabriel? A certain kind of anxiety had settled in because we had come to see something old and something new at the same time...and because we all expected and feared change. Gabriel had just released the first solo album, but the few people who'd heard it didn't know what to make of it, with its hodgepodge of songs and styles. We didn't think he'd give us something that sounded like Genesis. But he better not give us something like *this*—he better not be giving us fucking Punk Rock. The crowd gathered at the Capitol was a Prog crowd, not to mention a foretaste of the ossified "Classic Rock" audience of the near future. We wanted big. We sneered at small. The huge black-and-white images of Television dwarfed the actual members of the band, with their Garage Rock equipment and their bare bones sound and their keening unschooled lead singer. They did their first song, eliciting a little stutter of silence. Then—

"Fuck you!"

"You suck!"

"Get the fuck off the stage!"

"Faggots!"

I had never seen or heard anything like it. They were getting booed off the stage—literally—and the video screens only magnified their terror. Verlaine's face looked like an elongated painting of a face, like something out of Munch but with the screaming mouth replaced by huge eyes filling with tears. I couldn't take it, and went with Wy to the lobby. There we waited until Television finally fled and the lights went up. Now I was more nervous than ever. What could Peter Gabriel do to satisfy this crowd? What could he do to satisfy me? It didn't matter if he wore a costume, it didn't matter if he freaking levitated—I had a friend in jail, and I wanted him to say something about it. Hell, I wanted him to tell me what to do…and then the lights went down and we ran inside.

He wasn't wearing a costume, and he wasn't levitating. He was sitting at a piano, under a spotlight. He wore street clothes, and a haircut that betrayed the hand of a "stylist" just over his ears. He might as well have been a civilian, until he began to sing "Here Comes The Flood." In "Out, Angels," he had alluded to his belief that the world must undergo some kind of apocalyptic trial; now, in a tender voice, he delivered an ode to end times:

> Don't be afraid to cry at what you see
> The act is gone, there's only you and me
> And if we break before the dawn
> We'll use up what we used to be…

So…he knew. He knew what had happened in Key West, and then what happened on Long Island, with Rael. Except that I knew he didn't. In his solo incarnation, Peter Gabriel had refused something—the temptation to be more than who you are that forms the vital heart of Prog Rock. Sure, there is plenty of Prog on Gabriel's first solo album, with its programmed synthesizers and its treated vocals, and there was plenty of Prog at the Capitol Theater, with guitar high priest Robert Fripp playing behind a black curtain as "Dusty Rhodes," and Gabriel himself marching around like a Monty Python character on "Moribund the Burgemeister." But he had borrowed some of his band members from Lou Reed's *Rock and Roll Animal* lineup; he covered a soul song, in Marvin Gaye's "Ain't That Peculiar" and a rock and roll song, in The Kinks' "All Day and All of the Night"; he sang about lust in "Modern Love" in a way that Ian Hunter might have understood; he sang a blues song; and he sang, in "Solsbury Hill," the acoustic song shaping up as a radio hit; and even when he sang *The Lamb's* "Back in N.Y.C." for an encore—sang it in costume, in a black leather jacket—he sang it as if to reclaim it for the rock and roll gods. But he wasn't quite a rock and roll god himself; indeed, there was something slightly diminished about him, something almost fallen, in the way of angels. But he did nothing less than save my life that night, because he did have something to say to me, after all. He might have fallen; he might no longer be the "angel standing in the sun" heralding the reconciliation of good and evil at the end of "Supper's Ready." But it was because he was fallen that he was finally free.

I NEVER OM-ED AGAIN. I went back up to school, and went back to hanging out with my friends. We partied, and *Peter Gabriel*—supposedly called "Car," though I've never met anyone who uses that title—became our party album. I played it every night, on my big Cerwin-Vega speakers, and even sang along with "Solsbury Hill," banging my heart, boom boom boom, on cue. It's an overplayed punchline now, but "Solsbury Hill" was *my* song in the second semester of my freshman year in college, the anthem of someone who'd given up trying to reduce the universe to a single vibrating syllable and set out to make himself a writer. "To keep in silence I resigned / My friends would think I was a nut / Turning water into wine / Open doors would soon be shut…"

Not only was my door now open; one day, a girl from down the hall walked through it. I knew her from the study lounge. She was an English major. I used to ask her what she was reading. One book featured a guy holding a basketball on the cover; I asked, "Uh, is that, like, a book about sports or something?" She answered, "Well, sort of," and told me about John Updike and Rabbit Angstrom. Now she liked "Solsbury Hill," and would come down to my room to listen to it. She was almost as tall as me; she had blonde hair; she wore no makeup and yet had bright color in her cheeks and suggestive color in her lips; she wore t-shirts advertising her Finnish descent; she had a northern and almost Tartar cast to her eyes, with folds of skin pulled down ever so slightly over the outside corners; her eyes changed color according to mood, alternating between a streaky blue-green and an encompassing winter-sea gray; she had a small pointy nose, and she smelled better than any human being I'd ever known. Most of all, she didn't leave the room when I started talking about philosophy, and on March 17, 1977, I ran into her downtown, at a bar celebrating St. Patty's Day. When her friends got up to leave, she stayed behind, and we started talking, oh, about her own nagging philosophical concern: where the universe ended. We went to bar after bar, managing somehow to keep the conversation going; then we decided to walk together back to campus, and it took us six hours. Twelve days after seeing the first show of Peter Gabriel's solo career, I was in love. The next day, she came to my room and we listened to "Solsbury Hill" again, but the anthem that had belonged to me now belonged to us, a song of escape claimed as a song of return. We tried keeping our relationship secret for no reason I can remember, but one night one of her roommates saw us sitting on my bed listening again to "Solsbury Hill"—yes, "my heart going boom boom boom"—and asked, "Oh, is that your song? How cute."

PETER GABRIEL HAS MADE nine solo recordings, in addition to three live albums and two soundtracks. The first four solo records were, in the manner of George Foreman's children, all called *Peter Gabriel*, though, for marketing purposes, online music services call them *Car, Scratch, Melt,* and *Security*, from the images on their Hipgnosis-designed album covers. These gave way to three records with two-letter names: *So, Us,* and *Up,* the last of which came out in 2002, and is Gabriel's last record of original material. On his two most recent records, Gabriel has sung songs either written by other people or by himself earlier in his career. He has won six Grammys and five MTV Awards; has lent a song to a cinematic moment considered "iconic" by an entire generation of Americans; has dated a movie star; and is the only Prog Rock star who has gone on to a rock star career after breaking with a Prog Rock band. He is such a big star—such an international citizen with interests in a world-music label and a questing record of philanthropy—that many people don't look at him as a Prog musician at all but rather as a musician who succeeded in leaving Prog behind.

One thing he most certainly is: a musician with excellent timing. He is known primarily for two things: musically, for incorporating "world beats" into his songs, building them from percussion samples that grew out of his acquaintance with musicians from non-Western countries; visually, for extending his preoccupation with the theatrical potential of rock music—what made him unique as frontman for Genesis—to the emerging language of video. As it happens, both coincided with the rise of the compact disc and music television, the two transformative Reagan-era technologies that drove the music industry's boom before its internet bust. People too young to grow up with him on the turntable grew up with him on the television, and the stop-action video for his biggest hit, "Sledgehammer," is supposedly the most played video in the history of MTV. His eccentricities, if not his obsessions, found an audience, and even when his audience waned, he found himself with something more permanent: prestige. Indeed, when you create a "Peter Gabriel" station on Pandora, you also create a Sting station, a Paul Simon station, a post-Roxy Brian Ferry station, a David Byrne station, a U2 station, even a Phil Collins station—a station dedicated not so much to music as to discernment, or what might be called "adventurous lifestyle enhancement."

When Bret Easton Ellis set out to satirize the materialistic nihilism of his Wall Street serial killer in *American Psycho*, he had him write three long appreciations of post-Gabriel Genesis. Could he have done the same with Gabriel himself? Could he have used "Peter Gabriel" as handy shorthand, as a byword for brand names, as a measure of meaningless musical thread-counts? Gabriel, after all, never lived down his Prog Rock pedigree any more than Genesis did. Even at the peak of his success, he was never a critical favorite. And even when he was admired, he was never particularly cool. Yet he never became a joke, like Phil Collins. Or merely luxe, like Sting. There are two reasons for this. The first is his voice. It's not just too good to laugh at; it's suggestive of experience too deep to laugh at. It punctures his pretensions even as it serves as their vehicle. It has always drawn from a strange store of dignity, even when he dressed in costumes equipped with stuffed phalluses, and even when you hear "Games Without Frontiers" or "Shock The Monkey" on classic rock radio for the 237th time. With that voice, he could, as the old saying goes, "sing the phone book"—a talent that has come in handy now that, on *New Blood*, he's doing the rock star equivalent of singing the phone book and covering songs from his own catalogue with orchestral accompaniment.

The second reason is Prog itself. He is not the one who left Prog behind—Phil Collins did that. Genesis did that, but never Gabriel. He never became a joke, because he stayed true to what initially *made* him a joke, at least to critics. Even when he sang the occasional Pop song, he wasn't poppy. He never even wrote a proper love song until he wrote "In Your Eyes" for *So*, and it's a breakthrough love song because it's a Prog love song, entirely consistent with the grand and grandiose concerns of "Supper's Ready." John Cusack made the song iconic when he played it from a boom box in *Say Anything*, but he wouldn't have played the song at all if the song hadn't said this: "In your eyes / I see the doorway / to a thousand churches / the resolution / of all my fruitless searches..." If it's not quite a religious song, it's still, like a lot of Prog, spiritual in its concerns and in its very overreachingness. Yes, Prog is music of adolescence, an education for the not properly educated. Your enthusiasm for it can come to seem embarrassing in retrospect, like an epic crush on a girl who never so much as knew your name. But yearning offers an education all its own: the fruitless search informs the search that comes to fruition, and the constancy of the epic crush is what prepares you for the constancy required by marriage and parenthood. Prog is all about yearning, which is why it's so big, and why it's often so overblown. But Peter Gabriel somehow found a way to express Prog yearning in a post-Prog career, and in so doing he not only found a way to preserve the Prog strain in popular music (look no further than the music of sometime collaborators Kate Bush and Sinead O'Connor), but also to preserve the feeling of Prog in adult life.

Listen, for instance to "Come Talk to Me," from *Us*. It's about his estrangement from his daughter, and his efforts to bridge that estrangement. Not exactly a Prog concern; but it begins with the ominous rumble of what sounds like a pipe organ, and then the plangent and martial cry of bagpipes. It's totally overblown, totally over the top—and there's a part of you that thinks, *No wonder his daughter won't talk to him.* But I have a daughter now, and when we've gotten into fights, I have been surprised to hear the organ rumble, and to listen to the martial bagpipes blow.

WE NEVER KNEW WHAT kind of car it was on the cover of the first Peter Gabriel album. All we knew was that it was a sedan, that it was a sickly blue, that it was wet, and that Peter Gabriel was sitting inside of it. On the front cover, he's pressed close to the windshield, and his eyes are closed. On the back, he's staring out of the closed vent window; he looks forlorn. On the inner sleeve, he's rolled the window down, but his eyes are lost in shadows; flip it over, and his pupils come alive and go dead at the same time—they're silver and faceted, and he looks like a space alien in that terrible moment when the space alien reveals who he really is.

Did I ever know the meaning of that cover? Sort of. The album itself included a song called "Humdrum," with the line, "From the white star / came the bright car"—well, that was it, right? The cover was about that line, and that line was about energy. The energy that burns in the white star is the same as the energy that burns in the bright car; the energy that burns in the bright car is the same as the energy that burns in Peter Gabriel's eyes—and that energy, inhuman and beyond good and evil, is all we know of God. Something like that. But a few days before I graduated from college, a friend said, "So I guess you're not going to tell me the meaning of the *Peter Gabriel* cover, are you?"

"Nah," I said. And why would I? I'd built a mystique out of my supposed mastery of meaning, and after all this time I couldn't very well say that it was about "energy." Besides, I'd fought for that meaning, lame as it was, and by now the fight itself meant more than *Peter Gabriel* ever did; indeed, it *was* the meaning. I was alive. My friend Rael had gotten out of jail, and then a mental hospital, but he couldn't listen to Gabriel or even Genesis anymore because when he did he still heard the sounds that had driven him crazy. A couple of years earlier, Gabriel had given a concert at my college, but I didn't think of inviting Rael; I went instead with my girl who liked Gabriel's music and hoped that he would play "Solsbury

Hill." He was touring in support of his second record, *Peter Gabriel*, which we referred to as *Peter Gabriel 2*. The record had come out in the summer of 1978, and Gabriel came in the fall. That night, it snowed, freakishly; we had to wait for him. We waited five hours in the college gymnasium, listening to Steely Dan's *Aja* over the loudspeakers, again and again, so many times that I have trouble listening to *Aja* to this day. People left, expecting the concert to be canceled. But Gabriel showed, and he played, to a half-filled house. He had short, cropped hair. He wore tight white jeans, bounded around the stage in sneakers, and sang a lot of his songs with a punky snarl. Then he disappeared from the stage, and showed up in the back of the gymnasium. I'd read about this—I'd read that he disappeared and then "materialized" in the middle of the crowd, and I wondered what kind of powers he possessed. Now I saw that what he possessed was a new technology—a cordless microphone. He sang into it and he walked amongst us. We'd been sitting on the floor, in front. The crowd parted and closed around him, as he came toward us. Finally, there he was, right next to me, right next to us, a smallish man, his face and neck shiny with sweat. I didn't grab his hand, or try to touch him. But my girlfriend leaned over, and with a sudden flourish, almost a sudden violence, grabbed him around the shoulder, and pulled him to her. She kissed him.

And then she married me.

Tom Junod has been a writer-at-large for Esquire *for the last fifteen years. He has written about everything from Mister Rogers to President Obama's drone war, and his story about a photograph taken on 9/11, "The Falling Man," has been named one of the seven best articles in* Esquire's *history. He lives in Atlanta, GA, with his wife and daughter, and remains embarrassed not just that he recently went to see the "Gabriel-authorized" recreation of the original* Lamb Lies Down On Broadway *show by the Genesis tribute band The Musical Box, but that he was one of the guys— and they were all guys—singing along.*

Your Magic Christmas Tree
by Peter Case

Oh, will your magic Christmas tree be shining gently all around?
—"Chinese White" (Mike Heron)

The Incredible String Band weren't the inspiration, nor the Beatles. I lay my attraction to the LSD juggernaut straight away to Madison Avenue's *Time* magazine. It was late spring, 1969, the year I turned fifteen, and got out of the ninth grade. *Time*'s descriptions of trips made the psychedelic world sound so beautiful, and a lot of us had become filled with anticipation and desire.

My friend Jeff and I were feeling its power, for the first time, in the yard outside his parents' split-level tract home, in the middle class Forest Glen housing development sub-division of Hamburg, New York. I was lying on the lawn along the side of the house, and my girlfriend, Marianne, came riding up the sidewalk on a purple Sting-Ray bicycle with a white banana seat. "The little long-haired girl," one of my pals used to smirk and call her, when she first transferred in from the Jesuit school in Buffalo. Now she was wearing cut-off mod striped shorts, some kind of teenage short sleeve blouse, and her straight brown hair spilled over her back and down both sides of her face. She rode right up to me, across the grass, then stopped and peered at me through tiny wire rim glasses, looking very sad. And she was angry with me. I was stretched full, flat out on the ground, face toward the sun, and I couldn't stop laughing. She stayed for a minute or two, but we weren't communicating, so she rode off, shaking her head. "You always said you wouldn't do this," she said, right before she split. She looked like she was gonna cry.

Jeff and I decided to pull ourselves together and began to trundle into town, walking down a long and busy high road called Sunset Drive, then over to Mike Bannister and Jon Duffett's place, known to all the kids in town as "The Apartment," the first and only hippie pad around, where we all used to hang. It was a gray garage apartment behind a two-story house on well-named Pleasant

Avenue, a few doors from the old brick school building, right in the center of the village.

Bannister and Duffett were my heroes. They were several years older, and had seen the world, surviving on their own terms. It seemed to me like they lived on Mount Olympus. I'd see them walking around the village, in a crowd, with long hair, scarves and sashes, looking like gypsies, and beautiful girls by their sides in like-wise colorful clothes with cigarettes dangling from all lips beneath shades, all in rag tag hippie wear, though Western dapperness was Bannister's thing. Seeing them was like sighting an outlaw version of the Beatles walking by your house on their way crosstown for some kicks. Just watching them going by was sort of a high. I was sitting on my parents steps as they passed, so I got their attention by blowing some train licks on the blues harmonica, and the procession stopped. Hello. We all became friends, and soon found out we listened to the same music.

> "Oh Lord, live and learn
> I see your face and know you"
> —"See Your Face and I Know You" (Williamson)

THESE WERE THE FIRST other Incredible String Band fans I'd met. Mike Bannister was a true rolling stone, and so was Duffett. They were nineteen and eighteen, respectively. Mike was a drummer, and looked like a cross between Brian Jones and Eeyore. He had played for a while in a popular and loud local garage band called the Novas, and was a founding member of a rebellious high school gang called the Fountain Club, which really pulled off some insane and locally legendary hijinks. Once, using jump ropes, they tied an abusive gym teacher to the lockers. I loved that story. Mike also belonged to a dirty-water street-fraternity called Club 69 who built their own patchwork clubhouse in the woods by the Eighteen Mile Creek, a shack covered in tarpaper with beds and a refrigerator for their beer. There was nothing too bright about that place. It was a teenage Punch and Judy show, but Mike had picked up some subtle-ty since then, and jettisoned that crowd. He had a more thoughtful manner now.

Maybe it was Jon's influence. Jon was a folkie, kind of a young beat-generation type and a teenage wino, a slim, dark-haired handsome kid, who had traveled the breadth of the country already, hitching rides and jumping empty boxcars all the way to and from California in 1967. He played an ancient beat-up Martin guitar somebody had laid on him, and was a fan of Dylan, Donovan, Dave Van Ronk, and Memphis Slim. I knew and loved all these artists too, though I was three years younger than him, and pretty green. We soon started writing songs together, and performing around the area at basement coffeehouses, freaked-out parties, even church group meetings.

Michael and John's place was quite small, and seemed even smaller when it was packed with stoned kids making out and listening to records, the usual story in sixty-nine and seventy. I spent some of the most formative hours of my youth in that pad, in various attitudes and mental states. Some of those hours went by in a second, others seemed to last an eternity, and we all knew the local police had the joint under surveillance. Soon shakedowns were common, along with the occasional full sheriff's raid.

> *"Whatever you think, it's more than that"*
> —"Job's Tears" (Williamson)

MIKE HERON AND ROBIN Williamson were Scottish, from Edinburgh. They looked like gypsy time wanderers from the nineteenth century, and played exotic musical instruments no one in rock had ever seen before. They were called the Incredible String Band and every record had a different lineup. They'd started out playing Uncle Dave Macon and Carter Family songs, and immediately began to create their own style. After their first album was released the trio became a duo, as legend has it, after their banjo-man made a trip to Afghanistan and disappeared for ten years. One of the guitarists, Robin Williamson, also vanished—took his advance money and, with his girlfriend, Licorice, set off for Morocco. He came back months later playing an instrument he'd found there called the Gimbri, a fiddle with a mystically insinuating whine, and they used it all over the next records, as well as the sitar and tablas from

India, the Arabian oud, the Irish pennywhistle, thumb pianos from Nigeria, and good old funky guitars played in odd tunings, with banjos and harmonicas grounding and rounding out the sound. Robin was a virtuoso penny whistler, and a top-drawer a cappella balladeer in the traditional Scottish fashion. He had perfect pitch and a unworldly voice, capable of soaring, leaping or spinning on a driven nail. He spoke more than a few languages fluently, and told stories that'd make a bear hold his breath. His partner Mike was a psychedelicized Beat Combo refugee, and together they were magical because they were fearless, and had a great appreciation for chance events. They were courting ancient wisdom, unraveling the mysteries of music, and shooting high dice with Pop music and epic poetry, something Bob Dylan recognized and mentioned at the time in the folk journal *Sing Out*:

Q: Do you think [the Beatles] are more British or International?

> They're British I suppose, but you can't say they've carried on with their poetic legacy, whereas the Incredible String Band who wrote this "October Song"...that was quite good.

Q: As a finished song—or did it reach you?

> As a finished song it's quite good.

It was their aspirations that characterize their music as something that would soon be called Progressive in other quarters, though it was a word they never used. They were on a higher, more creative track than nearly anything else in music, and were shattering audiences' reliance and expectation on the common forms of song. Verse/bridge/chorus went bye-bye...form was directed purely by content; they did what ever they felt like doing whenever they felt like doing it! And it was powerful.

Already a big chart hit in the U.K. with their third LP, *The Hangman's Beautiful Daughter*, the String Band were introduced to American teenagers by the writers of *Hit Parader*, which, way back in the sixties, was probably the first great rock magazine ever, delving deep into music way off the beaten track (and I've been waiting in vain for years to see reprints). Their pictures showed them to be charismatic and intense-looking attractive "stars" in their own way. They were completely different from anything else on the scene, and, I'd say, completely original.

All of their mad music was in pursuit of something high and strange and I think it can be pretty well-defined in this description of Emmanuel Swedenborg, "the wonderful Restorer of the long lost Secret" (from a book I read recently about William Blake):

> "There were ancient truths to be revealed...that which for many Ages has been lost to the World... And what was this long lost secret? It is the opening of the gate. It is the sure knowledge that nature and the material world are the vessels of eternity."[1]

OK, MAYBE I WAS so ripped I didn't know what they were talking about.

And, on the first day of summer, as my friend Jeff and I walked along the shoulder of the road, deep-breathing poisonous exhaust fumes and nearly getting run down by trucks, I was mesmerized by the sight of the roadside flowers, all red, blue, and yellow, glowing brighter than neon signs. And the trees were breathing, waving above us, the green leaves swirling in a mass, inhaling and exhaling as we walked by below. And the lyrics to these songs kept playing in my head.

> "For rulers like to lay down laws,
> And rebels like to break them,
> And the poor priests like to walk in chains,
> And God likes to forsake them"
>   —"October Song" (Robin Williamson)

BUT BY THE END of that summer, I was pretty much out of my mind. I began to experience a lot of problems. Somehow I'd lost my depth perception. It was just gone one day. I could be overcome at any time by strange feelings and huge terrors. And I felt like I was emotionally ripped open all the time, not angry or anything simple like

---

1   From *Blake: A Biography* by Peter Ackroyd

that, but more like a blaze in my chest, and a rollercoaster feeling in the pit of my stomach. My heart hurt from just contemplating the quotidian details of life. All feelings were extremely intense. The fact and idea of death was making me sick. I was in despair, and not just a little bit. I felt like my tongue was hanging out, black. It was then that a seemingly wise and older friend, who was all of twenty-three, who had just come back from far away, and a college down South, suggested that I was having a spiritual awakening, and all my mad symptoms were a good sign. I'd never thought of that! He said that people who went through spells like I was having were often destined to be truly religious people. Not like organized religion, he said. He said my subconscious was kicking off the fetters of my repressive upbringing, the look-but-don't-touch, absurd and lonesome dues and don'ts of my schooling, and suggested that I read, for companionable knowledge and entertainment, the eighteenth century English poet William Blake. So I started to do just that, and found it helped, and even though I couldn't understand all of it, I kept feeling drawn to it. It was exciting at times, and also could be very soothing. And *Wee Tam and the Big Huge* by ISB was on the crummy old record player in the corner, and it was on A LOT.

I DROPPED OUT OF the tenth grade that fall. By then, I could barely function, even amongst the freaks. When I first heard the String Band's *Changing Horses* LP it was on a trip to the country with friends. They were taking turns walking me about out in the gardens, and then we returned to the house and listened to this record, the ISB, now a four piece on the cover with their girlfriends, Licorice and Rose, were singing a goofy psychedelic boogie-woogie about a pig named Big Ted.

I lost track of them for a while after that. Life got better for me, after it got worse, but it took long time, and I didn't even hear of them again for several years.

> "...if you let the pigs decide it,
> They will put you in the sty"
>
> —"No Sleep Blues" (Williamson)

As it turned out, the Incredible String Band and the popular culture developed in opposite directions—the String Band were literate, melodic, and insanely inventive. Heron, coming from a Beat Combo background, was the tunesmith who crafted most of the catchiest songs, while Robin Williamson's best numbers were like spells. All the arrangements were magical and floating, at times spinning upside down, and often springing loose like a mad music box, with two guitars caroming off each other, while flutes and whistles dixielanded insane counterpoint, and backward grooves were pounded out on bongos, congas, and woodblocks, until the whole thing seemed to deny gravity. And Robin's mastery of his voice and language were no joke, however hippy-dippy they appear at first twenty-first century perusal.

They were incredible all right, wowing and charming audiences in the U.K. and across the U.S. And they were supernaturally ambitious, seeing themselves as the first purveyors of what would become known as world music, as well as lyrics composed along the lines first laid down by the Beats, a philosophy summed up in the Blakean idea—first thought, best thought—a concept later popularized by Allen Ginsberg and his teacher, and worldwide authority on Buddhist meditation, Chogyam Trungpa.

Said Robin in an interview:

> "It struck me that you could write a spontaneous, free-form lyric, a la Jack Kerouac. And then you could link it up with spontaneous free-form music, drawn from the various regions of the world."

Form followed content, so, wherever you dropped the needle on the record, you'd be lost for a time. Like Progressive groups Pink Floyd or King Crimson, you had no choice but to follow the melodic breadcrumb trail out of the enchanted sound forest. And it was wonderful.

But the one thing this String Band didn't have was the BIG BEAT, the hard and fat Dionysian noise on the two and four with the passionate screaming voices and noodling electric guitar solos— the evolutionary development in sound that came to dominate all rock and Pop music at that moment, and for the next several decades.

America was being submerged in violence—both on its streets, in Southeast Asia, and other world hotspots—Great Britain was going along for the ride, and even the gentlest citizens on both sides of the water were losing their attention span. Did that have something to do with the evolution of people's tastes? The U.S. was being led by a man who was busy telling the world he wasn't a crook. The Beat was King, and the drugs and sounds kept getting heavier.

As Bob Dylan had noticed several years before, the ISB had a true poet in Robin, who could tell you of the world close to your nose in rhymes that led you to see it in a fresh way. Robin could prophesize, telling the present and the future with mythological eyes, but if the public wanted words, they demanded their singers be confessional. And as the sixties hit the end of its road, all the heroes died or disappeared, most either shot by assailants with three names, or choking to death while on pain killers. And it was hard for the culture to recognize their poets when words were used all day, everyday, across the radio, television, and in the newspapers, to confuse the populace about its actions, products, and programs.

> *"Now there comes a time to every man*
> *When he must turn his back on the crowd"*
> —"Log Cabin Home In The Sky" (Heron)

BUT I LOVED THE Incredible String Band anyway, because they went so far the other way, away from the common fixations on celebrity, away from music as sex tonic, away from teenage rock and roll problems, or even the Beatle's "Taxman"-type rock star anxiety musings, and they blazed their own trail, into dreams, to strange hidden regions of countryside and memory, to isolated hilltop villages, in the gaps between mountains, to places where they were bringing their own music, and poetry, and pursuing the quest they felt couldn't wait—the quest for God—while all the time remaining a couple of Scottish wise guys with an outlaw attitude. The String Band enacted a true rejection of the culture, were actual full-service rebels, and always did things at their own speed, in their own style. They had an original sound, and their own voices. Their songs were pitched lighter and lower than what anyone else was doing then or is doing now, far away from the usual bump and grind of the rock of any period. Don't get me wrong, I love a good bump and grind. But I learned to dig these guys early and it stuck with me. They were psychedelic Woody Guthries, Blakean men of the people, and, in fact, *Wee Tam* concludes with a tune Woody popularized: on the end of the song/suite called "Ducks On A Pond," they bust into a rousing version of "Ain't Got No Home In This World Anymore," and it's not precious, but nuts, with stomping feet, caterwauling voices, an overblown harmonica, raucous...and compares favorably to Woody and Leadbelly's rockin' team-up with Sonny Terry and Cisco Houston on the rare Stinson sessions.

There are railroad gates you have to jump if you want to dig them—traces of cuteness, an excess of the diminutive, little clouds, little hedgehogs, and caterpillars for cousins. "Maxwell's Silver Hammer" may be the worst song the Beatles ever recorded, but the ISB have a couple as bad as that in their oeuvre.

And yet, a couple rambling ragamuffin folk singing guitar players from Scotland introduced what's now called World Music into Pop. And while doing this they broke nearly every rule of musical arrangement while somehow maintaining a rootedness in the music that kept it plugged into the earth, to true feeling, spaced-out but somehow with a foot in traditional forms. They exploded folk music while somehow keeping it alive far beyond its time.

> *"When I was born I had no head*
> *My eye was single and my body was full of light"*
> —"Douglas Traherne Harding" (Heron)

I SAW THEM SOON after my arrival on the West Coast in 1973. I was on the run from my disastrous teenage life in New York, had said goodbye to my pals Banister and Duffett, and made the bus-and-train journey to California alone. I was at the start of a bold new Western Adventure, the one I'm still on. And there they were, the week I got into town, playing at San Francisco's elegant Palace of Fine Arts, to a more than half-empty theater. I was surprised to see they were electric now, with bass and drums, but I found the show to be dynamic, and Robin and new ISB member Malcolm spoke at length between songs. They were very funny, talking spontaneously about America and the coast they'd traveled the length of just the day before. One hilarious rant was a satire of Los Angeles all-night television, including an impression of a local personality, *Movies 'til Dawn* sponsor, cowpoke-turned-used-car-salesman par excellence, Cal Worthington, walking "his dog Spot" (an elephant) through the lot. This was followed by a rocking fiddle reel version of "Black Jack Davy," and when I heard that I knew they were still great.

So the next day, I went to a record shop and purchased the new album, "No Ruinous Feud," took it back to the house where I was staying, played it about twice, and completely lost interest. It wasn't terrible or anything, but the magic from the night before couldn't be found in the grooves, nor the songs.

Eighteen years later, I saw Robin play for a full house at McCabe's Guitar Shop in Santa Monica, one of the great folk clubs in the world. He played Celtic harp and guitar, sang and told stories, and was brilliant throughout. He had completely turned into the magician-poet he'd always evoked. I met him upstairs after the show. I had a baby asleep on my shoulder, and Robin said, after taking a good look: "You have a very beautiful daughter there." He was wearing red Converse low tops. I went out and bought a pair.

Dedicated to the memory of friends
Jon Duffett, 1952-2011, and Michael Bannister, 1951-2008.

Peter Case is a three-time Grammy-nominated songwriter/performer and producer. His first book, As Far As You Can Get Without A Passport, was published by Neverthemore Books in 2007. He lives in San Francisco.

Yes Is No Disgrace
by Matthew Specktor

i thank You God for this most amazing
day: for the leaping greenly spirits of trees
and for the blue dream of sky; and for everything
which is natural which is infinite which is yes
                                    —e. e. cummings

*S*O MUCH OF LIFE involves the covering up of one's tracks. The cigarette smoke you wave out the window, the stash you flush before the cops (or your parents, because let's face it, I'm talking about *teenage* life here—the one developmental stage that probably never ends) toss your room, the browser history you clear because, uh, you don't *really* like girl-on-girl porn. Sometimes you hide not just from the authorities but from yourself. Because some music, for example, was made to be played loud—has anyone ever felt a pang over rattling the windows with "Can't You Hear Me Knocking?"—where other music, well, it might be built for volume but you just can't do it without slouching in your seat and hoping—no, praying—the neighbors aren't home. Yes. Good lord, Yes. Am I really playing a Yes record? Where are my headphones...?

There's a rare shame that attaches to certain bands, and while I'm sure this topic will be broached elsewhere, over and again, in a collection of essays about Prog—the one genre (after disco and country have been thoroughly reclaimed) to which shame doesn't just attach, but which remains wholly permeated—Yes is just more squirm-inducing than most. Genesis? They had Peter Gabriel. Crimson? Fuck, they were heavier than the Sex Pistols. Van der Graaf Generator? Art Rock for people who thought David Bowie was a flyweight. But Yes? Yes? We're an inch away from the Little People of Stonehenge here.

To go on about Yes's essential, both notional *and* actual, naffness though is to miss the point. Yes was amazing, and though they lost me after a while (I can't really get with *Tales from Topographic Oceans*, and the later Rabin-era reconstitution of the band I've always hated), everything up to and including *Close to the Edge* is incredible. Well, *Time and a Word* isn't the best, but—wait, I'm not gonna qualify here. I'm going balls out to say it. I love Yes, and their greatness is truly inseparable from their ridiculousness. Or from *my* ridiculousness, which is the best gift rock and roll can ever give you. Some bands teach you who you want to be, or who you think you want to be: the worldview expressed by The Velvet Underground, no matter how fucked up, remains somehow aspirational. But Yes? They teach me something of who I am. Which is uncool to my very last breath, indulgent (who isn't?), and—both by accident and design—prone to moments of ineffable beauty. Again, who isn't?

An older kid turned me on. That was how it happened, back in the seventies. This kid, Paul, he was my neighbor, and I hated him. He was a year older than me, though, and he had authority, not of coolness (even *I* knew this redheaded dork who could barely skateboard his way out of a paper bag wasn't that), but of experience: he'd smoked pot before me; he abused me by calling me a virgin (which he was too—again, even I knew that—but at least he didn't have to scurry to a dictionary to find out what the word meant); he owned copies of *Obscured by Clouds* and *Brain Salad Surgery*. He was a regular sophisticate, in other words, while I was cutting my teeth on Aerosmith and The Nuge. I first discovered *Fragile* through him. Yeah, yeah, yeah, yeah: "Roundabout," I know, blessing and curse, the one every true Yeshead has come to hate, because it's the only Yes song most people know. Dutifully, I lifted the needle after "Cans and Brahms," which was a reliable minute-and-a-half of "what the fuck is this shit?" every time. I delved no further. Within a few years, I'd learned the reflexive Yes hatred (*Triple album, my ass! That's only cool when The Clash do it!*) common to all but the most iconoclastic members of my generational subset.

Where do I get off then claiming ownership of Yes? What the fuck do I know? Only what the last few years of obsessive reclamation have taught me, and by "obsessive reclamation" I mean reclamation of almost everything—not just Yes, but every piece of detritus stamped between my birth and 1980 or so—I ever rejected. Because I rejected a lot of things; I rejected, essentially, myself, and all these years later I can only hope to get back some ghost or dream of who I might have been, and was (Goddamn if, put that way, the sentiment doesn't begin to resemble, uh, a Yes lyric in its spatial and emotional cubism, but whatever). Yes are a time machine for me. They take me back to something that never quite existed. All the best, and least defensible, bands do.

The Yes Album was my gateway as an adult. I'd like to be cool—or, you know, defiantly even more *uncool*—and say it was *Yes* (the eponymous debut from 1969) or *Time and a Word* (1970, heavy on the oomphing Wagnerian strings), but as for most people—"most people" who ever cared about Yes—the third album is the first great one. The tripartite "Starship Trooper," in particular, was the jam: organ-dominated, heavy in the best sense (i.e. with a rich, melodic, epic *slowness* that might be relatable for anyone who ever dug, say, *Physical Graffiti*), with a nimble acoustic bridge ("b. Disillusion," repurposed from an earlier song called "For Everyone," which you can catch on a set of BBC recordings from 1969-70) that's not a million miles from Crosby, Stills & Nash if Stephen Stills were a more proficient guitarist, and then an absolutely glorious instrumental tailout ("c. Wurm") in which a heavily flanged Steve Howe just kills it, and which leaves me feeling about as joyously spaced out as any record ever has. What a song! And it's not alone on an album that also includes "I've Seen All Good People" and "Yours Is No Disgrace," both of which clock in very economically, considering, under ten minutes, both of which are hooky as hell, and both of which exhibit the band's defining—"defining," at least to non-Prog-nerds—virtues: exquisite harmony vocals, Chris Squire's insane, chunky (is that the right descriptor? They're almost...slab-like, somehow, like pieces of poured concrete) basslines, and that beautiful, churchy Hammond organ which apparently Jon Anderson did not want, since Tony Kaye was kicked out of the band, or quit, soon thereafter. In classic marked-man fashion, Kaye appears on the front of the album wearing a cast, apparently thanks to a car accident, but still, it's conspicuous.

We're going to have to talk about Jon Anderson, though, speaking of conspicuous, even as it pains me to do it. The dude's voice was...high, and much of what attaches to this band in terms of mockery can be traced back to the singer. And, shit, the lyrics, too, without either of which Yes might've been a more ignorable, but also a less risible, force. "Yesterday a morning came, a smile upon your face" is the first line of "Yours Is No Disgrace." (So far, so good: we're in CSN territory here.) "Caesar's palace, morning glory, silly human race." (Whoops, no. The catastrophic clash between "Caesar's palace" and "silly human race"—how absurdly the adjective "silly" comes across when sung by a man whose balls sound like they're in a vise, besides—makes this scan like Shelley for twelve year olds.) "On a sailing ship to nowhere, leaving any place / If the summer change to winter, yours is no disgrace."

Yep, I haven't the faintest idea what that means either, if it means anything at all. I don't require song lyrics to have meanings, and I sometimes think Iggy Pop is a better poet than Bob Dylan, but the obvious, arch, fey (yes, it's both arch *and* fey) straining after meaning, that symbolically freighted "Caesar's palace" that crops up even before we get to "mutilated armies" whose "morals disappear" later in the song, to say nothing of a "purple wolfhound" and...a bunch of other stuff: all this marks Anderson as a truly terrible lyricist, and one doesn't have to dig too much further into the catalog ("In and around the lake / mountains come out of the sky and they stand there," say, to cite the band's best known hook as a locus of prepositional, geographic, and kinetic confusion, a hectic slaw of an image that busily manages to convey almost nothing sensical at all) to find other examples. Yeah, he's abysmal. He's also—I'm just gonna say it—awesome. Once you get past the ridiculousness of the words (not a crime, in rock and roll), and the castrato-like alto tenor (probably something of a crime: it seems to me that singer dudes with high registers are mostly the object of fetishistic attention—Tim Buckley, Antony, etc.—or of some scrutiny, at least), once you're past these things it's clear he's great, anyway. He can *sing*, and more importantly, his voice suits the instrumentation: its airiness rides, just so, over the syrupy thickness of the organ, the stony and angular aggression of the bass. It's just what a band this hammeringly classical needs.

Yes were absurd from jump street. They were also a bit more conventional than you think. They covered The Byrds ("I See You") and the Beatles ("Every Little Thing") on *Yes*, in ways that were jazzy but also—hey, look, it's the "Day Tripper" riff—recognizable; they did Richie Havens and Stephen Stills on *Time and a Word*: taken together, you realize they were big into California folk rock at the beginning, just like Led Zep, and the classical pretensions came later, around the time Rick Wakeman and Steve Howe shoehorned themselves into the band. (I call them pretensions: for many people, of course, this was Yes's reason for being, which is a perfectly noble and probably more accurate view.) Those albums were good, but the band really crystallized—they became themselves—with *The Yes Album*, and *Fragile*, and *Close to the Edge*, and...depends how far you're willing to follow after that: many people love *Tales*...if they're not so doctrinaire or stupid that they simply must reject a four-song double-album out of hand; ditto *Relayer* and *Tormato*. I'm betraying my own limitations here, more than I am the band's.

Then again, what else is rock and roll supposed to do? Yes's alleged crime against the orthodoxy was...what? Pretension? Ambition? Melodicism? (God knows, every band I've ever been told to love, every sanctioned and iconic outfit since the Beatles has displayed not less than two of these qualities, the first as often and as aggressively as the others.) Or was it, rather, the sin—ha ha—of being *uncool*. The accident, perhaps, of being the right band at the wrong time. Unless it's something even better than that, which is to be the *wrong* band for all times, not an outfit like Can (who were only outre until we caught up with them) or Big Star (who made the mistake of playing short songs at a time when—God, how benighted we were—the world preferred long ones, from the likes of, well, Yes), but a band whose time will never come, simply because even when it did come, when they were selling out stadiums and maxing out their indulgences (filling a studio with hay, so that *Tales from Topographic Oceans* would have that pastoral feel) they were already preposterous.

I COULD NOTE THAT aspects of their later work seem to echo things that are at least reasonably cool (the guitar melody that kicks off "Long Distance Runaround" sounds to me a lot like Jerry Garcia), or prefigure things that are indisputably so (the next section of that song would be perfectly at home on *Remain In Light*), or even things that will be so (the very song was covered by Red House Painters!) once everybody else figures them out.

But, no. Let me, instead, submit that this is the very meaning of being alive: that we fit imperfectly with our surroundings and express ourselves mostly in the most lurching ways ("silly human race"). I won't argue that to love Yes is to love humanity, simply because that sort of grandiose overstatement seems a little Prog in itself, and besides, I don't know enough about any of it: not the band, not the records, and not even humanity. I'll limit myself, instead—limit myself even further—to saying Yes make me feel good, except when they annoy me (which they still do—"The Clap" may be a virtuoso guitar performance, but I hear it as ragtime interpreted by a hyperactive Renfair attendee). They make me feel so good, though. They make me feel like the world is opening up before me, like I'm lying on my back in my childhood bedroom staring up at the sun glazing the palm fronds outside my window, like I'm a little bit high (though maybe that's just a trick of the light) and *maybe* I'm apprehending something, signaled by those incredibly detailed Roger Dean sleeves—one part Goya, one part *Silmarillion*, I guess— that I'm still not quite getting. I might, though. I could. If I listen a little harder, and if I can get over my own embarrassment (I'm not embarrassed by the band, at this point: it's my own essential frailty and lameness that attacks me), if I can get over myself, and if I grow up, I can follow this music as far as it'll go. *Close to The Edge* and beyond, to the world that exists until it doesn't, and your longing is the only thing that remains.

Matthew Specktor is the author of the novels American Dream Machine *and* That Summertime Sound, *as well as a book of nonfiction. His writing has appeared in* The Paris Review, The Believer, Tin House, Salon, *and many other periodicals.*

Achilles' Heel
by WESLEY STACE

In Faint Praise of Lyrics in the Genre of Progressive Music; The Canterbury Scene Singled Out as an Exception

I COME NOT TO PRAISE Progressive music, nor to bury it—and certainly not to defend it or to claim that I am quite special for liking it. You like it, too: what's the big deal? As my touring partner once exclaimed in a moment of enlightenment during a very long drive as we listened, perhaps for the first time ever, to *Tales from Topographic Oceans*: "It's better than Classical music!" But if you're one of those stubborn souls whose cultural conditioning means you consider Prog too uncool, then I can only encourage you to cast aside prejudices and give a little listen. I do not consider Prog a guilty pleasure, a category in which I have no faith. My attitude to *Fragile* is the same as my attitude to *Main Course* by the Bee Gees, to Purcell's *Dido and Aeneas*, *Highway 61 Revisited*, *A Rainbow In Curved Air*, and George Formby's entire oeuvre: why *wouldn't* you like it?

The fact is you're reading this book, which presumably means that you either like Prog or you like the work of a particular contributor—or you're in the intersection of that Venn diagram: the sweet spot, as it's technically known. So I'm not going to explain a lot about the bands, and I'll describe the music as briefly as possible (because such explanation gets tedious). And though you may know a lot about Prog, you don't know anything about me, and that, I'm afraid, is my way in, because we're going back in time on a Prog pilgrimage. And, if you're British (and I am), there's only one destination for a pilgrimage—Canterbury:

> And specially, from every shires ende
> Of Engelond, to Caunterbury they wende,
> The holy blisful martir for to seke,
> That hem hath holpen, whan that they were seke
> —Geoffrey Chaucer, *The Canterbury Tales*

FROM THE AGE OF thirteen, through most of my teenage years, I attended the King's School, Canterbury, my uniform a pinstriped
suit, a wing collar, and a gown. Occasionally, I had to wield, but
never wear, a mortarboard. I studied Latin and Greek. The situa-
tion was ripe, as all teenage situations are, for meaningful identifi-
cation with a type of music that was to be mine and mine alone.

That music was not to be Progressive Rock.

Prog was everyone's older brother's music. Punk, which was already New Wave, was everyone-your-own-age's music. The year was
1978, and I was at Canterbury until 1984, or as I think of it *Street
Legal* to *Infidels*. It was, in other words, "The Religious Period." Not
mine, obviously: Bob Dylan's Religious Period (though it was I who
walked through cloisters to class, underwent confirmation at the
hand of the Archbishop of Canterbury in his Cathedral, and hung
out with my friend Tom at his house, the Deanery). In fact, it *was*
my religious period, and my God was Bob Dylan.

I arrived at King's with a large, hideously ugly poster, free with
purchase of *Bob Dylan at Budokan*, featuring my hero in silver lamé,
which I Blu-Tacked to my dormitory wall. It had been on my bedroom wall at home in Hastings and it made me feel less homesick.
Over those next years, with occasional forays into whatever contemporary music caught my ear (a bit of Two-Tone, etc.), that's what
I listened to. Once I'd run out of Dylan (who made albums spar-
ingly) or when my palate needed cleansing, I'd listen to music that
seemed germane, someone whom He had mentioned, befriended,
anointed, or covered: John Prine, David Blue, Doug Sahm, Steve
Goodman, Randy Newman, Kinky Friedman, Leonard Cohen,
Tom Waits, Townes van Zandt, whomever. If it had curly hair or it
drawled, I listened. Everything I liked about music could be delivered in a lyric and a simple tune sung with strummed accompaniment on an acoustic guitar (though the gospel confirmed you could
also go electric); I didn't need solos, makeup, or choreography (and
I certainly didn't need to dance). I had very clearly defined views,
I leaned towards the left wing, and I was an idiot: so that was an
ideal combination.

The one kind of music I disliked more than any other was Prog,
the lyrics to which were patently ridiculous (as close to meaningless
as anything could be), the solos of which were indulgent in the ex-

treme, the posters for which were science-fictiony hippie futurism, and the fans of which were hairy. At school, one particular acolyte played the electric guitar endlessly, silently, alone, broadcasting only into his own amplifier headphones, lank hair flopping about. On reflection, he was probably just practicing, but at the time it seemed like I'd walked in on him masturbating.

Someone once put on a copy of *Yesshows*, every aspect of which was repellent to me, Roger Dean inward. To make conversation, without wanting to appear patronizing about his pitiful taste in music, I idly mentioned that a particular sound was quite pretty, wondering whether it might be a harp of some kind. The owner of *Yesshows* looked at me with great disdain: "It's an electric guitar." Then he gave me a lecture on harmonics, which made me hate the music even more. Didn't he know you only have to strum and drawl to communicate?

THE IRONY IS THAT I was at school in Canterbury, which, beyond being a hothouse for my own progress (where I learned how to smoke, kiss, play the guitar, and pass exams) was home to one of the great scenes of the Progressive era.

I met an older girl, also at school (girls didn't have to wear the uniform), with a fantastic record collection. The last thing she asked before she kissed me for the first time was: "Have you heard Jimi Hendrix?" To which I responded, untruthfully, "Yes." Because I didn't want to delay the kiss with her explanation. And it was she who lent me *Triple Echo* by Soft Machine, an attractive boxed set (at a time when there were very few boxed sets beyond one's parents' monolithic library of operas) comprising a compilation of that group's finest early material.

Soft Machine offered the additional frisson of being from Canterbury. It was hard to believe that, in this antiqued cathedral town, within which I was circumscribed by precinct walls and strangled by a wing collar, there had once been an actual music scene; but here was the evidence. The first songs that caught my attention were a very beautiful slow ballad called "A Certain Kind," and a long John Peel session version of "Moon In June," for which the high-voiced lisping lead singer sung what seemed to be—but couldn't have been—extemporaneous lyrics: where he was at that actual moment (sitting behind a drum kit "here in the BBC"), chatting to his friends ("So to all our mates like Kevin / Caravan, the old Pink Floyd / Allow me to recommend 'Top Gear' / Despite its extraordinary name") and the amenities of the studio itself ("Not forgetting the extra facilities / Such as the tea machine just along the corridor"). Having yet to register postmodernism, I'd never heard anything like it: I perhaps felt it *Monty Python*-ish. When the singer's freewheeling intro segued into "Moon In June" *proper*, the music was loud and amazing; distorted keyboards that sounded more like guitars, weird time signatures—I didn't know *what* all was going on. But I liked it. The lyrics were funny, really funny; the music was heavy, and the song was long (thirteen minutes and seven seconds), probably the longest song I'd ever heard (including "Sad-Eyed Lady Of The Lowlands," which at eleven minutes and twenty-three seconds—though I could hardly bear to admit it—was boring, and a rip-off since it unnecessarily took up a whole side of *Blonde On Blonde*).

Disaster struck: I took the prized collection home, left one of the LPs on the sofa in the sun, and returned to find that record unplayably and unnaturally warped, warped in a way that did not speak well of the gram-weight of the Harvest label's vinyl at the time. The girl would clearly kill me, which would clearly kill everything. So I returned to school via London on an optimistic quest, quite typical of me at the time, to replace this out-of-print rarity. After combing all the new record stores, I miraculously found a sealed copy in a cut-out shop in a basement on Oxford Street at a beyond reasonable price, which left me with a little change from whatever money I had wangled out of my mother. With this, I bought a Virgin records two-for-one (remember when they used to do that?) of *Rock Bottom* and *Ruth Is Stranger Than Richard*, the second and third solo albums of Robert Wyatt, high-voiced lisping singer and drummer of Soft Machine. I then took the train back to Canterbury, handed over the replacement copy of *Triple Echo* to the girl (who made it clear that she thought I had done the "right thing" and that I would be rewarded, possibly soon), and tripped back to my study, spring-heeled, where I opened my Wyatts and wondered whether I should bin the ruined disc from *Triple Echo* or if I could persuade it back into shape using some reverse-warping technique.

Perhaps the reason I gravitated towards the Canterbury Scene, apart from the girl with great taste, was its good humor. Prog's Achilles' Heel—a suitably heroic metaphor—is that it demands to be taken seriously: its virtuosity, its ambition, its plus-plus-sized dimensions, its absurd humorlessness even when humor seems the only possible strategy. Nowadays, there is nothing more comical than demanding to be taken seriously: we'll grant you that favor, but only if you seem not to care or are too drunk and screwed up to notice. Canterbury does not have this fatal flaw. And even if we're guilty about our pleasures, Canterbury is the only Prog we've never had to feel guilty about. It's totally cool. Coming without most of Prog's baggage, it has never engendered in me that blend of acute embarrassment and pleasure that is such an integral part of the Prog Fancier's experience. I realize this is not typical and assure you that I know this experience only too well from my long-standing tenure in the Bee Gees fan club (I don't only like the cool bits) and the fact that all I have listened to this summer (and it's more or less the price for coming to dinner at my house) is Chicago.

And I wonder whether, living in America as I have these last twenty years, my impulse to Prog (regardless of all the other reasons to like it) came from the same place as my earlier urge to listen to traditional British folk music or that poster of Bob Dylan on my dormitory wall at Canterbury: homesickness, my own Achilles' Heel.

THE CANTERBURY SCENE WAS done by my schooldays, already a memory. I saw no sign of it, though I do remember the silly cartoon cover of Caravan's *Blind Dog at St. Dunstans*, and thinking: *What on earth is rock and roll about St. Dunstan's Gate on the High Street and why would anyone want to call an album after it?*

I'm not going to give a history of this scene—I recommend the excellent canterbury.free.fr or the Pete Frame family tree that accompanied *Triple Echo*—but basically, there was a band called The Wilde Flowers in the sixties, and that became Soft Machine, with Robert Wyatt and Kevin Ayers. After one album, Kevin Ayers went off and did his thing; and after four albums, Robert Wyatt left Soft Machine as they were going ever more jazz and needing less and less singing (which was still my favorite bit) to make his solo records.

There was also another band called Gong (whom I never quite liked so much)—and a band called Caravan (who were great)—with two Sinclairs, who left one by one and formed other bands, including the wonderful Hatfield and the North. And then there were others like Egg, Gilgamesh, and National Health—mostly instrumental, but if you think you're getting a well-researched history of Canterbury music out of me, you're quite wrong. It's all been highly influential music that's traveled around the world, and it all started in Canterbury. It's a bit jazzy, it's got lots of solos, and it's very Prog.

Or is it?

Canterbury is often written out of Prog history, at which, as a fan, I take slight affront, though not to the point of writing a letter about it (unless one considers this that letter). I read recently that Emerson, Lake & Palmer must be offended to be constantly represented, in every single documentary on the matter, as the poster boys for WHY PUNK HAD TO HAPPEN—to stand for, as if uniquely, the excess, stupidity, pseudo-intellectualism, and pretention of Progressive music that required Punk's new broom. Lazy stuff, for sure. But I'm certain that ELP are delighted to occupy this key position in musical history (quite apart from the fact that it's a distinct honor, and that, seemingly, nothing can diminish Keith Emerson's relentlessly high opinion of himself, a self-regard that has obviously been tested many times in the intervening years). Because when music flips round a bit and all that's bad is good, and the kids need something a little more serious, ELP will be right there in the catbird seat, still representing Progress and Pretention. Punk only did to Prog what Prog had attempted to do to the three-minute song; the difference is that Punk left destruction in its wake, while Prog merely offered a polite, somewhat nerdy, intellectual alternative to what had gone before: a Crushed Velvet Cape Revolution.

I now realize that *Rock Bottom* and *Triple Echo* are Prog; but at the time, I failed to notice. They didn't sound anything like *Yesshows* or, in fact, like anything I'd ever heard. Here I can open the window on the whole world of Canterbury: on Caravan's sensational string of albums, particularly *In the Land of Grey and Pink*; on Hatfield and the North's *The Rotter's Club*, so beautifully celebrated by Jonathan Coe in his novel of the same title; and National Health's amazing mostly-instrumental *Of Queues and Cures*; on other projects of

Robert Wyatt's, for example Matching Mole (you presumably know how they arrived at the name—from the French for Soft Machine: *machine molle*). I heard little of this music in Canterbury, however; I discovered it gradually, after years of immersing myself in the sad, lonely, epic, nonsensical world of *Rock Bottom* and the cracked, witty instrumentals and vocalese of *Ruth Is Stranger Than Richard* (which, because I'm still an idiot, I only recently realized, because I hadn't noticed it when I first bought the record, is *Truth Is Stranger Than Fiction*).

The music of Canterbury is intent on revealing the mechanism, letting you in on the joke, treating you as a democratic equal by allowing you to know what really goes on in a musician's mind; how mundane and dull it all is; and what fun making music can be. There is no self-mystification, no humblebraggery, no pretense: "If you call this sentimental crap / you'll make me mad," sings Wyatt on "O Caroline" from the first Matching Mole record. I'm thinking also of Richard Sinclair's beautiful delivery of the frankly bawdy lyrics to "Fitter Stokes Has a Bath" on *The Rotter's Club*; or Robert Wyatt's "Signed Curtain" (perhaps the most perfect lyric ever written: an extravagant claim, I realize), as sung on that same Matching Mole album:

This is the first verse
This is the first verse
This is the first verse
This is the first verse
This is the first verse, first verse
This is the first verse

And this is the chorus
Or perhaps it's a bridge
Or just another part
Of the song that we're singing

This is the second verse
Could be the last verse
This is the second verse
Probably the last verse

This is the second verse, second verse, second verse
Probably the last one

And this is the chorus
Or perhaps it's a bridge
Or just another key change

Never mind
It doesn't hurt
It only means that we've
Lost faith in this song
'Cos it won't help us reach you

On what level is that not beautiful, funny, humane, and moving? On what level are other Prog lyrics any of those things? "Signed Curtain" has often been performed at The Cabinet of Wonders, a variety show I "curate" (that's what you call it nowadays) in New York City; the show always ends with Kevin Ayers' "Religious Experience," of which the entire lyric is:

Singing a song in the morning
Singing it again at night
I don't even know what I'm singing about
But it makes me feel I feel all right, all right
It makes me feel I feel all right

And every performer gets to celebrate Canterbury, Kevin Ayers, and The Cabinet of Wonders by singing that one verse: one verse, by the way, that no one on the bill ever wonders whether they can remember or balks at singing. That means everyone from Rosanne Cash to A.C. Newman, from Steve Earle to Andrew VanWyngarden, from Andrew Bird to Tift Merritt. *Everyone* is happy to sing it. I can't even imagine another song that could fill those shoes, at least one that everybody doesn't already know.[1]

1   Between this essay's composition and its publication, Kevin Ayers died. Last night's Cabinet of Wonders (March 15th, 2013) was the first since his death: myself, Graham Parker, Dan Zanes, Fred Armisen, Hospitality, and a host of others sang "Religious Experience" once more and it made us feel we felt alright. Thank you, Kevin.

When Jonathan Coe read at the Cabinet, we also played, with that same writer on the keyboards, "Nigel Blows A Tune," the first movement of the suite "Nine Feet Underground" from Caravan's *In the Land of Grey and Pink*. The version we regularly play of The Monkees' "I'm A Believer" is in fact Robert Wyatt's cover from 1974. Sometimes it's like Canterbury is the only kind of music I know how to listen to or want to play. Apart from Bob Dylan, whose recent work and performances I am wildly unenthusiastic about, Canterbury has been the one constant on my soundtrack. I've flirted with this and that, but the Canterbury records are constant. I've bought them in every conceivable format and now once more listen to my original vinyl copies.

Clearly my way into the music was its lyrics, which makes Canterbury unique among Progressive music. One of the things about most Prog lyrics is that they're rubbish, which made it a difficult genre for someone like me who prized lyrics above all. As someone on television, perhaps a Hackett or a Rutherford, once explained: the idea behind Prog was that the music would be more serious than the poppy stuff in the charts. A thrillingly ambitious genre, Prog would have the weighty structure of classical music, movements comprising a suite or even a symphony, with preludes and leitmotifs, and would therefore gain the respect of serious-minded people everywhere; plus all those chops you'd had to learn in music lessons, while the cooler guys were jamming three chords to their hearts' content, could now be put to serious and loud use. Yet there still needed to be a singer, and he (let's be under no illusion about the sex of the singer and his audience) had to sing *something* and those lyrics were obviously not going to stoop to the level of Pop. They were going to be *heavy*. They were going to mean something. But though they could play like the Dickens, these public school-educated, emotionally repressed, young men (who went to places like The King's School, Canterbury, where they wore their own metaphorical wing collars) had no actual experience of life, could not write like the Dickens, and moreover had nothing to write about. However, they had all read *Lord of the Rings*, perhaps some H.P. Lovecraft, studied classical myth, had access to the odd Indian text, and they all owned a deck of tarot: *BINGO! Lyrics! Themes! Structure!*

I'm sure Ian Anderson's brutally smug observations about humanity (and I realize it's partly his delivery and my knowledge of his politics) have given Tull fans pause for thought, but I do my best to ignore them in favor of the music, in particular Martin Barre's guitar and Anderson's snorting, flutter-tongued flute. Ultimately, I prefer the purer, more classical flutings (and yodelings) of Thijs van Leer, leader of Focus, a band who never used an unnecessary word, and were devilishly effective when they used a necessary one. Here's the entire lyric of their eponymous, therefore self-explanatory, song "Focus":

> *Focus yourself on the love*
> *You all Mankind*
> *Come and make it show again*

Brilliant. Although, full disclosure, I don't know what the actual lyric is because the internet is uncertain. Apparently, it could also be:

> *Focus yourself on the love*
> *You own mankind*
> *Communication again*

Also brilliant. No one seems to know and no one apparently asks Thijs van Leer. It doesn't really matter. They're instrumentalists. They're Dutch. (The best flute of all, however, is Jimmy Hastings' on numerous Canterbury records. Prog loved the flute almost as much as it loved a demonic lead keyboard player.)

Yes's Jon Anderson, on the other hand, can espouse the benefits of Total Mass Retain (or warn of the danger? Who knows?), inform us of his Getting Up and Getting Down, but I am by no means sure that many people understand (or care) what he's Getting At. The grandeur of the surrounding music renders the meaning somewhat unnecessary, so the words operate as mere syllables of sound, like Sigur Ros' imaginary language or Meredith Monk's *Extended Techniques*. It's perhaps best to think of Yes lyrics that way. It saves having to ruminate upon them.

In Canterbury, no rumination is necessary: there are no goblins or Fountains of Salmacis. And though there is gibberish, it

proclaims its own gibberishness: these aren't portentous non sequi-
turs that hoped to coalesce into profundity. Self-awareness is all in
Canterbury. If you're singing a song on the radio, you might as well
sing about singing the song. Check out Hugh Hopper's lyrics for
"Thank You Pierrot Lunaire" from The Soft Machine's *Volume Two*:

> *In his organ solos*
> *He feels 'round the keyboards*
> *Knowing he must find the noisiest notes for you to hear*
> *And when I know that he's found them*
> *It feels so good...*
> *But I still can't see why people listen,*
> *Instead of doing it themselves*
> *But I'm grateful all the same*
> *You're very kind and I don't blame you*
> *I don't mind if you just watch*
> *In fact I'd welcome it, welcome it, welcome it...*

And in "Moon In June," an analogous thought:

> *Music-making still*
> *Performs a normal function*
> *Background noise for people*
> *Eating and talking and drinking and smoking*
> *That's all right by us*
> *Don't think that we're complaining*
> *After all it's only leisure time, isn't it?*

AND THESE THOUGHTS WERE, to a teenager, and even to this adult,
truly radical thoughts—truly democratic and truly progressive: *new*.
In short, they blew my mind. Perhaps they made me a musician.

This self-reflection often turned to whimsy—not perhaps the
dominant mode of Progressive music, but one amply exploited by
one of my favorite non-Cantuarian bands, Stackridge, with their
"Indifferent Hedgehog" and "Galloping Gaucho." Whimsy trumps
pomp. The Canterbury bands were never afraid to be childish; Caravan and Hatfield's Richard Sinclair performed a number of solos
by vibrating his finger between his lips as he hummed. Now *that's*

silly. Robert Wyatt sang a song from the point of view of a bowl of soup. Ivor Cutler intones a key role on *Rock Bottom*: "I fight with the handle of my little brown broom…" (I came across a line in Edward Lear's "The Daddy Long-legs And The Fly"; "And there they found a little boat / Whose sails were pink and gray." And *The Land of Grey and Pink* made sense to me all over again: it's all beautiful, beautiful nonsense.) Hatfield and the North recorded the song "Nan True's Hole" from Matching Mole's *Little Red Record* more than once (improving it by revealing the song's riff to be the heaviest in the history of rock) which versions were released under the names "Oh Len's Nature" and "Ethanol Nurse." It took me some time to work out that these were anagrams of the original title, though I suspect there to have been sound business reasons for this wordplay as well: presumably royalties increase if you're playing different songs rather than the same song over and over again.

And to digress, Prog Rock was nothing if not financially pragmatic. For example, business is the main reason why long pieces of Prog were broken up into numbered portions. *Close To The Edge* would only have earned Yes royalties on three songs ("Close to the Edge," "And You and I," and "Siberian Khatru"), since these are the only three songs on the album, had a publisher not had the idea—and Yes weren't the first to do this; I'm merely using them as an example—to subdivide the songs "Close to the Edge" and "And You and I" (note: it's rare to find a sense-making sentence where the word "and" can be written two times in four words) into sections, resulting in such uniquely familiar Prog formulations as:

1. Close to the Edge
   - I. The Solid Time of Change
   - II. Total Mass Retain
   - III. I Get Up, I Get Down
   - IV. Seasons of Man

2. And You and I
   - I. Cord of Life
   - II. Eclipse
   - III. The Preacher the Teacher
   - IV. Apocalypse

AND, THEREFORE, THROWING IN the unsubdivided "Siberian Khatru," Yes are paid for nine songs on *Close to the Edge* rather than three. *Of course!* You can understand the logic of all this financial sleight of hand: if you're handing over entire records of music, just like the Pop musicians, you shouldn't be financially penalized just because your ambitious classical-type songs are ten times as long. Progressive musicians were serious-minded, but they were business-minded, too. I wouldn't want you to think it was *only* about art. (It was a *lot* about art, of course.) My favorite instance of all is the entire second side of Caravan's *In the Land of Grey and Pink*:

1. Nine Feet Underground
   * I. Nigel Blows a Tune
   * II. Love's a Friend
   * III. Make It 76
   * IV. Dance of the Seven Paper Hankies
   * V. Hold Granddad by the Nose
   * VI. Honest I Did!
   * VII. Disassociation
   * VIII. 100% Proof

This looks like Canterbury poking fun at Prog. Though perhaps it was simply the band looking after its best interests *and* having a laugh.

Robert Wyatt's *Rock Bottom* does itself lapse into complete Lear-grade nonsense at more than one moment ("Burly bunch the water mole / Heli plop and finger hole / Not a-was it bundy, see? / For jangle and bojangle / Trip trip pipipipi tip-pit landerim"), though my favorite lyric is when the singer seems to be begging the listener to stop making him laugh in "Little Red Riding Hood Hits the Road":

> *Orlandon't tell me, oh no!*
> *Don't say, oh God don't tell me...*
> *Oh dear me*
> *Heavens above, oh no no*
> *Stop*
> *Please, oh deary me*

What in heaven's name?
Oh blimey!
Mercy me
Woe are we
Oh dear...
Oh stop it!
Stop it!

AND THEN THE WHOLE track flips backward while the vocal flips, too, so we hear what we've just heard in reverse, though the bass keeps surging forward—it's one of the craziest effects I've ever heard—until the singer comes to this jaw-droppingly intimate conclusion:

You've been so kind, I know I know
So why did I hurt you?
I didn't mean to hurt you
But I'll keep trying and I'm sure you will too

As though anything before it has signposted this.

Canterbury music, perhaps because of its jazzier influences, seems a lot more devil-may-care than other Prog: to make a dubious generalization (and I *never* make generalizations), women are more apt to like it. Prog might be unique in that its lyrical subject matter is not sex or relationships: that was Pop's province. Women are *around* in Prog lyrics, but they remain spiritual presences rather than actual girls with boobs and whatnot, floating ethereally like Poe women (who aren't very real either except in our nightmares). Not in Canterbury, of course: "Sea Song," the opener on *Rock Bottom*, is about mammary glands and menstruation; in "Hibou, Anemone and Bear" on Soft Machine's *Volume Two*, Wyatt opens with the frank: "In the spring, I think of sex and means to ends"; many of Caravan's lyrics are amusingly puerile in their sexuality; and Richard Sinclair was never scared to get right down to it with Hatfield ("Thank you, ladies, you had us all"), even amidst the instrumental mayhem. In fact, I'd say that most Prog, while short of being misogynistic, is generally afraid of women, hence its exclusion of them lyrically, its limited appeal to them musically, and—more generally—its not welcoming them into the band: it's a boy's world, the currency of which is traded among men—like the limerick, another notably male genre.

I once had an argument about whether Prog is essentially an emotional music, though I think my disputant who argued that it was emotional was being contrary. Though the music sometimes *concerns* emotion, and though the players might get their rocks off playing it live, Prog is not primarily emotional. Though of course great sweeps of musical movement, loud to soft and back again, can tug at the heartstrings: Prog offers a cerebral experience with little consideration of the needs of the body, other than the body's atavistic urge to play air guitar or nod its long hair up and down enthusiastically. Prog doesn't swing; Canterbury, on the other hand, swings like a pendulum do.

One more thing—I didn't realize it at the time, nor would have thought it important: another of the reasons Canterbury seems a little freer is, I think, Robert Wyatt's early love of the shortwave radio, through which he was exposed to the music of the world beyond Western Rock and its classical canon. On the early Soft Machine albums he's singing in Spanish. Even in a high lisp, it's sexy. Very little in Prog is sexy; unless you're moved by the sight of Chris Squire's spandex-bulging inner thigh.

IT'S GREAT THE WAY Canterbury slipped through my defenses. I knew all about Yes and Genesis, Tull, and ELP, but they were easy to keep at arm's length. Very few Prog singles made the charts (presumably because most of it was too generously epic to be restricted by the seven-inch format) so one never encountered the real Prog that way. Nothing was played on the radio (in the U.K. at least, and for much the same reasons). There was simply no need to pay any attention to these bands; they weren't in your face and the music press ignored them entirely. In fact, during the ice age of Punk and New Wave, they were licking their wounds, wondering what to do next; in some cases coming up with pretty unpalatable, if commercially successful, solutions (Yes and Genesis, particularly). Prog itself wasn't in the charts, but the bands that bore its brand, its avatars, were, singing "Owner of a Lonely Heart," or that song (or perhaps endless series of songs) where the three old blokes do line-dancing; not to mention other vaguely familiar faces in horrendous bands like Asia. So at that point, one didn't hate Prog so much as hate what those bands or singers or players who were supposedly its great exponents had become. (By comparison, Robert Wyatt was having bona fide aesthetically admired hit singles, noble ones, singing "Shipbuilding" by Elvis Costello. He was, in a way, better than ever. Even Stackridge had a New Wave hit under the name The Korgis.) For the old Prog, it was Marillion or nothing; and it was therefore nothing.

But the wonderful thing about a life spent listening to music is that all the music you haven't yet taken in is out there waiting for you when you're good and ready. I certainly didn't need the epic Prog when I was at school; nor at university; nor for many years. And I'm delighted that I waited. I like it for much better reasons now. I love and respect its ambition; I adore its pomp and circumstance; I admire its virtuosity; I ignore its terrible lyrics; I realize it was made in circumstances of time and place that can never be recreated, but that doesn't mean that I won't have a go myself at some point. Also, it makes me shake my head in wonder and laugh.

About ten years ago, a friend, in an attempt to persuade me about two of his favorite bands, gave me a cassette (possibly the last cassette I ever received) pairing Yes's *Going For The One* and *Katy Lied* by Steely Dan. I didn't previously care for either of these bands (and still don't love the latter). The only time I had considered Yes's potential was when beloved Philadelphia DJ Ed Sciaky told me that his all-time top two rock acts were Bruce Springsteen and Yes: this was patently ludicrous. And I listened to this cassette, often in the car. On *Going For The One*, I think (and you probably know far more about this than I do) you hear Yes trying to rock out a little more, be a little more modern—the way it starts with a count-in, and then sounds skanky for a little while, like Fleetwood Mac's *Tusk*. And it spoke to me—even, God help me, the lyrics of the title track which concern Jon Anderson's yearning for some spiritual whateverness. (Having said that, though I briefly considered it, I thought better of an acoustic cover of *Going For The One*—an acoustic cover is my default tribute to any music I love; all I can offer in exchange for the pleasure it's given me. It didn't happen: however much of an improvement those lyrics represented, they would still not stand the scrutiny of a solo performance. Or to put it another way: I'd be too embarrassed to sing them.) The whole album worked: Steve Howe's crazy guitar bending; that amazing choral ending, very Queen; Rick Wakeman tinkling away on *Awaken*; Anderson with the killer voice.

Because of that one album, the whole Yes catalogue—then the world of Prog—opened to me. And though I still don't adore Genesis (except *Seconds Out* and *Duke*), and secretly consider Phil Collins (whose solo work I have loathed with every bone in my body) a superior singer to Peter Gabriel (whose voice, at least by my reckoning, is too folky to hack it over a loud guitar and a great rhythm section), I now have infinite time for Mike Oldfield's records, notably *Hergest Ridge*, Steve Hackett's *Voyage of the Acolyte*, Gryphon's entire work (particularly *Pawn To Gryphon Four*), Gentle Giant (and I once signed for a record company purely because it was run by the lead singer of that band: terrible mistake), the amazing Strawbs (where a great singer-songwriter chooses to wrap his simple songs in maximum Prog Riffage), Nektar, Dave Bedford, and the whole wide world beyond Canterbury: almost all of it. And I have finally realized that the instrumental bits are often better. I guess because there are no lyrics.

Prog is such a distinctly British (or European) form of music. Look at that list above; only my own people. America has never done Prog very well (and there you have it) and has depended on various well-documented British invasions. The Prog invasion is simply one of the least well-documented (and I even attempted my own mini-invasion, which has only been modestly successful: historians differ on the matter.) So perhaps that's it. It's all because I miss home: Hastings, Canterbury.

Wesley Stace is a novelist (Misfortune; by George; Charles Jessold, Considered As A Murderer) who also records music under the name John Wesley Harding.

Defending The Indefensible
by Rick Moody

On Emerson, Lake & Palmer

Part One: In Which I Detail The Charges Against The Accused

1. They Are Twats

A FRIEND OF MINE calls them *twats*, and because the word cannot be used lightly, he is not using it lightly. Let us entertain for a moment the idea that this word is not entirely inappropriate under the circumstances. The members of Emerson, Lake & Palmer are, it is implied, rank egomaniacs; they are pretentious; they have inflated ideas about their importance, both personally or as a whole, and they held fast to these ideas throughout the period of their alleged relevance; they broke up because they could not agree about who was in control; everyone wanted to be in control, and, because no one could agree on who was in control, they broke up, and when they tried to get back together several times, they still could not agree about who was in control; they could not get out of their own way, and they believed the hype, even when there was no shortage of vituperative press that could have led them to think otherwise; Johnny Rotten made embittered remarks about them a great number of times (until he met Keith Emerson later in life, and, apparently, the two of them had a fine chat); even among people who are modest, or understated, who are given to reasonable opinions about music, Emerson, Lake & Palmer are considered worthy of scorn and belittlement; almost anyone will tell you they are *twats*, or they will look for words that are not dissimilar, if without the misogynistic brio.

2. They Liked Classical Music

WHAT THE FUCK IS *classical music*, preliminarily speaking? What the fuck is that? Isn't it just music that is made with orchestral instruments? No, wait, what about all those *classical* pieces for the nylon-stringed guitar or the lute? Is that classical music too? Is *classical music* just *old* music for *old* instruments? By that criterion, then a lot of African music is *classical*, because the drum is the oldest instrument of all, or so it is said. Or perhaps music for the Jew's Harp is classical, as that is also a very old instrument; or what about music for the didgeridoo, isn't music for the didgeridoo a kind of classical music? Is *classical music* music of any period for *old* instruments? Well, then John Adams couldn't be classical, because he has used a synthesizer, and Steve Reich has scored for electric guitar. Is *classical music* music with a lot of notes? Is it music that elderly music critics like? Is it music that conservatory students favor? Is *classical music* what they play in the showrooms of rug merchants? Is *classical music* the music of television advertisements for brokerage firms?

Evidently, Emerson, Lake & Palmer like *classical music*, because they once called an album *Works, Volume 1*, an album which scores high on the *twat-o-meter* for a number of reasons, but which also intends to prove their devotion to classical music. And: they recorded not one but two pieces by Aaron Copland (about as *classical* as Philip Glass), as well as an entire suite by Modest Mussorgsky, some Ginastera, a little Janacek, and so on. They borrowed from Ravel and J. S. Bach. I guess a lot of their output would be considered *classical music*, by people who are dead set on hating any ensemble that is or was preoccupied with *classical music*, but that doesn't mean that Emerson, Lake & Palmer weren't also interested in jazz (Dave Brubeck quotations on the first album, a Sonny Rollins quotation later on), in ragtime (Scott Joplin, on the dreaded *Works, Volume 2*), and, well, in rock and roll (plenty of Jerry Lee Lewis and Little Richard in those piano parts), even in psychedelia (as evident in the King Crimsonisms they fell into from time to time), and, transparently, in folk music—because of Greg Lake, who could be counted on to take his acoustic guitar down off the shelf in order to produce the occasional income generator.

3. They Toured With An Orchestra

No one should tour with an orchestra under any circumstances. Recently, there was an Antony and the Johnsons show at Radio City that had a grandiose orchestral accompaniment, and I am willing to bet that no one, at the time, seriously compared Antony to Emerson, Lake & Palmer, but still: it probably wasn't a good idea in this case either—Antony plus orchestra. You couldn't hear the orchestra, or, perhaps, you couldn't hear the band, or you couldn't hear Antony. Many of the bands from the seventies who might fall under the rubric of *Prog* have flirted with orchestra—viz., Yes, Jethro Tull, Pink Floyd, and Genesis. Nothing, in truth, is worse than a Genesis song as reinterpreted by an orchestra.

And the other part of it, the other part of the dreadfulness of touring with an orchestra is that it's *expensive*. If your goal is to try to make money on touring (this is all from *before* the time in which the principle revenue for the working musician became the t-shirt), then taking the orchestra out with you is lunacy. Nevertheless, Emerson, Lake & Palmer tried this in, I believe, 1978, and they managed a few shows before they, like others before them, realized that this was not such a fiscally prudent idea. They let the orchestra go, and, presumably, stopped playing "Piano Concerto #1" by Keith Emerson. By that time, the band was on its last legs.

4. There Was Robot Imagery

The lyrics of Emerson, Lake & Palmer, at least up until 1973, when Peter Sinfield, the lyricist for King Crimson, became a frequent collaborator, were without redeeming merit of any kind. "Lucky Man," written by Greg Lake when he was a *tween*, is the best they could manage. Apparently his lyrical skills did not improve with the advent of puberty. Sinfield made things better, but only marginally, at least when you consider the evidence: "Karn Evil 9, 3rd Impression," from *Brain Salad Surgery* features the dreaded *robot voice*, a robot voice that was really Keith Emerson fed through a ring modulator, and this robot voice was all about oppressing the humans, and prognosticating as to the grim future that we could expect upon intermarrying with our technological creations. Nothing could be more *quaint*, nor more perfectly calibrated to alert the attentions of the unlovable adolescent male than: robot voice! It wasn't like in Kraftwerk, where the robot chic involved some will-to-dehumanization. In this case, the robot voice was more like the lamer examples of the *science fiction* genre that were so popular in that day and age. There was a little bit of this futurism in *Tarkus*, too, which preceded *Brain Salad Surgery*, at least if you took the album art for some genuine representation of the contents. Lake's lyrics did not exactly feature an anthropomorphic *Tarkus* animal as pictured on the record sleeve. But there was a veneer of futurism on *Tarkus*, and there was the *robot voice* on *Brain Salad Surgery*, and this was enough to secure the reputation for futuristic credibility, just as the band called Yes, at the same time, was maintaining science fiction cred with the hippie-futurist illustrations of Roger Dean on their sleeves.

Oh, I forgot to mention the jacket art on *Brain Salad Surgery*, the unsettling image by H. R. Giger, the guy who later designed the alien for *Alien* (the 1979 Ridley Scott film). *Alien* was the first film I ever saw during which I had to *leave* the theater to calm down—during the sequence in which the shipmates are eating pasta (is it pasta? or is this in my imagination?), and a little alien fetus bursts forth from John Hurt's alimentary canal. Blood everywhere. After which: the *thing* grows large and menaces the ship. And displays its *jaws within its jaws*. Salivates with battery acid. H. R. Giger! Same guy! He made the woman/machine hybrid thing on the cover of *Brain Salad Surgery*. Which passes, in my book, for futurism of the kind that geeky, loveless kids like me so admired.

5. Up-To-Date Equipment!

KEITH EMERSON WANTED A synthesizer as soon as he heard *Switched-On Bach* in a record shop, and I don't know if that ennobles him or not. He purchased an early modular synthesizer thereafter, which included a massive patch bay that looked like the spaghetti dinner that John Hurt ate before the alien fetus burst from him, etc. Later on, in the mid-seventies Emerson was one of the first people to get a polyphonic synthesizer. I do not know if this is such a great approach, this approach which always fetishizes whatever the new piece of gear is, because music that is predicated on gear alone *dates the fastest*. This is partly why the later Emerson, Lake & Palmer recordings, such as *Black Moon*, are awful, because they sound as though the artists were honor-bound to remain up-to-date, and were therefore less interested in the compositional aspect of their job than they were interested in the new gear. Which is another way of saying: even though ELP believed themselves impervious to *trends* in rock and roll, they were in fact chasing the fads, even when this kind of thing is anathema to: *classical music*.

6. The Believed In Virtuosity

YES, THEY TOTALLY BELIEVED in virtuosity, and by this I mean the meatheaded notion that that musician is most successful who can play the fastest, which certainly is an idea from *classical music*, where that first violinist is best who can perform all the really fast runs, and that soprano is best who can climb up to high C and shatter wine glasses. It would be hard, if being thorough, to convict Greg Lake of this, though he was and is an extraordinary bass player. His bass lines were exceptionally melodic, maybe because they had to be in order to keep up with the density of keyboards. Lake's voice was also very good, it's true. And not good to a stupid degree. His voice was not fussy, nor prim, the way Kerry Minnear's (of Gentle Giant) was. Although toward the end, there were occasional Broadway belter moments. But upon excusing Lake from this portion of the discussion we are forced to conclude the entire remainder of the band (66.666%) was indeed preoccupied with the idea of virtuosity.

Let us consider Carl Palmer for a moment. I actually liked his drum sound, at least until he got the hideous drum *pads* of the eighties for *Black Moon*, etc. Early on, Palmer was more jazz oriented, sort of in the way that Bill Buford was a beautiful drummer, a jazz-inflected drummer. Later in his career Palmer started to have a Neil Peart-ish obsession with extremely large drum kits, with gongs (what is more objectionable than a gong?), and with fills where no fill should be. And there's a fine line between an unusual time signature that exists simply in order that the melody do something that it can't do in fours and a fancy time signature that is there to prove that the band can *play*. Palmer never met a rhythmically tricky passage that he didn't like, and on his "side" of *Works, Volume 1* (they each got one), he played some Bach, and some funk, and a little jazz, and in some ways managed to be *more* pompous than Emerson was on his Aaron Copland-obsessed piano concerto.

And what can we say about Keith Emerson's playing? We could go on and on. Really, no keyboard player in rock and roll (and there were a lot of extremely able keyboard players in the Prog era, like Kerry Minnear of Gentle Giant, and Tony Banks of Genesis, and John Evans of Jethro Tull, and Mike Ratledge of Soft Machine) played with quite as much haste, sometimes sounding a little bit like he was falling over himself, though with great clarity in the arpeggios (I learned what arpeggios were from listening to him), and with the octaves, where he sounds a little bit New Orleans and a little bit Jerry Lee Lewis. He was a show-off, even more than Rick Wakeman (his frequently mentioned opposite number in Yes), and he made the most of the showing off on the Hammond organ. On the piano, he played the piano like a blunt force instrument. You can count the *quiet* bits almost on one hand. He always seemed to be revving up for the pounding. To his credit: he did not to my knowledge put on a tux for a gig, and in the end the same is true of his playing. He was all over the place, and no wonder that he liked to tip the organ over unto himself (when he was in The Nice), and used a Nazi-era German knife given to him by Lemmy (from Motörhead) to hold down the keys sometimes, and would even do a solo where he and the organ were suspended from wires. Which is not that far from Rick Wakeman's one-time *spectacular* in which he performed on ice, surrounded by *skaters*.

7. *They Didn't Actually Put Out That Many Albums*

ON TOP OF EVERYTHING else they seemed to be a little bit disinclined to write. If you consider that *Pictures At An Exhibition* was merely an arranging task (and it had already been arranged for orchestra before Emerson got there), and *Works, Volume 2* was just leftover bits, then they had only a few major works: the eponymous first album; *Tarkus; Trilogy; Brain Salad Surgery;* and *Works, Volume 1,* and that was in eight or nine years. They must have come to hate each other rather early on. There's no other conclusion. But, considering how popular they were, could they not have chosen to sit in different sections of the plane? Why the hatred, if not from the desire to be *in control?* Emerson, perhaps, hated Lake, because all the hits were the Lake ballads, and because Lake got the producer credit on the early albums; Lake hated Emerson because Emerson was pyrotechnical and had no real interest in the lyrics, and because Lake wasn't a strong reader of music as Emerson was, and Lake was thus an unsophisticate by comparison, and Palmer hated everyone because they couldn't get along, and they were endangering his paycheck. (Which was why he joined Asia and secured a steady royalty for the rest of his natural life. By the way: is it possible to think about so-called Progressive music without considering that Asia is the death knell for the form? As soon as there is Asia and its earnest banality, its insipidness, the subordination of the playing to the mincing, girl-group love songs, the kind of thing that only a thirteen year old Japanese girl could love, and a band name that was tailored especially to secure the love of Japanese girls, there is the smell of a rotting subgenre. Carl Palmer played in that band, and still does occasionally, and that means he is hated by the other two, even as he hates them.) The enmities were such, I would imagine, as to prevent working together, and that is why they could not get their shit together to *write*. Eight years. Five albums. Two almost-albums. In a similar interval, the Beatles made twelve studio albums, and innumerable compilations. And the Beatles were perfectionists too. Gentle Giant made ten studio albums in the same span, give or take, and Genesis made eight, and Jethro Tull made something astounding like thirteen, all original material. These days, the ELP reissues, such as they are, never offer unreleased material, because they have none to offer. They must have spent a lot of time rehearsing.

8. And I Haven't Even Mentioned

LOVE BEACH. IT PREDICTS the aforementioned Asia, really, the last album (1979) by Emerson, Lake & Palmer (in their original incarnation). It summons up Asia in a variety of ways: incredibly trite songs somewhat about love. Disagreeable digital keyboard sounds that over-rely on string pre-sets. Working to fulfill contractual obligations. Suppressing everything challenging about the earlier work. A stupid album title (it is an *actual* beach in the Bahamas where the thing was recorded, but still). An album cover so surpassingly embarrassing that it is hard to imagine they agreed to do it: the three pretentious *twats*, the kinds of guys who stayed home to *practice* when other rock and roll stars were on the town downing fifths and stalking groupies, pictured on the beach, sporting various amounts of skin that no man, outside of a film about Italian discos, should be sporting, shirts unbuttoned or hiked up so that some belly is showing. It's a truly gay front cover, and that is fine with me, I like gay culture, and a really gay album cover like, say, *Diamond Dogs*, or *Macho Man*, this is great, and hilarious, and *transcendent*, but no one in The Village People was boasting about their classical music bona fides and the muscularity of their playing. Who could possibly have thought this was a good jacket for an album by Emerson, Lake & Palmer? Was the record company actually attempting to destroy what little was left of the band? Was the record company trying to make it impossible for them to record again? Have I mentioned the unmistakably lazy songwriting on *Love Beach* (with the possible exception of one suite of tunes by Emerson on side two) and the *first thought, best thought* arrangements. A total embarrassment, really, an embarrassment in every way. It was only nine years since the rather plucky, adventurous, and totally confident first album by the group. How had they come to this? And did this not ruin what was good about the band, the reputation they fashioned for themselves on the earlier albums?[1]

Part Two: So Why Do I Still Like Them Anyway?

1. The Argument From History

IS LIKE TOO STRONG a word? If I came on this work now, knowing nothing, the way I have come on, for example, Manheim Steamroller, which is not that far off when you think about it, I would not be able to last two minutes. Still: there is yet something about Emerson, Lake & Palmer that moves me, which moves me to paroxysms of loyalty the more people repeat *twat*, etc., and not because I think they are *not* arrogant pricks exactly, but because they were part of a brave journey in music in the early seventies and they have reaped what they sowed, both on the upside and the downside, and they never carped about it before or after the fact.

I like what their period meant to musical history. That period, let's say, which begins with *Sgt. Pepper's Lonely Hearts Club Band*, and the inventive and ambitious arrangements on that album. Now, personally, I like some of *Revolver* better, and I think that for

---

1   An amusing exercise for those with time on their hands is the refashioning of the title *Love Beach* into more accurate versions thereof: *Love Belch, Lame Breech, Last Blecch, Needs Bleach, Loved Bach, Lucky Break, Licks Balls, Long Bore, Life's a Bitch,* etc.

sheer imagination *Revolver* is the masterpiece. But *Sgt. Pepper* took the art of Pop arrangement to a new place, and this was the place of serious music. That is, the Beatles rose to a spot where it was clear that there was no particular form of music that could *not* be adapted to their melodic purpose, and that included serious music, which meant, at that moment, not necessarily "classical" music of the Romantic tradition, or Baroque music, but even dissonant and serial impulses (which are apparent on "A Day In the Life," and, more potently, later on "Revolution #9"). Once this *revolution* was effected, once the *djinn* was released from the bottle, there was serious ground that others could cover, and beginning in 1968, others did. I don't mean that other people could merely produce rather heady psychedelic music, because obviously a lot of people were doing that, both in England and the United States and throughout Europe, even in Latin America (tropicalia!), what I mean is that there was hybrid activity made possible by the Beatles, and a lot of people swept in to take advantage of it. Procol Harum, The Moody Blues, Yes, Pink Floyd, and so on. The Nice, Keith Emerson's first band, was one of the foremost agents of this hybrid activity. And if you could do it with so-called "classical" music, why not with "jazz," or with other musical dialects worldwide. Emerson, Lake & Palmer were diggers in this field, and so they were part of a movement in history that was fertile between 1968 and 1973 or 1974. What was great about this early Prog flourishing was that there was, as yet, no real name for the subgenre, and so when Jethro Tull made their early albums, there was no name for what they did, and when Emerson, Lake & Palmer made their first album, there was no real name for what they did either. As Derrida remarked, once a genre is *named*, the genre is over. That we can now call this work *Progressive* means that it no longer sounds progressive. But you couldn't hear that subgeneric exhaustion when ELP released their first album. Back then, it was just something *new* that you could do with a Pop song. You could make an organ the lead instrument, and you didn't need to have verses and choruses, and it was all right if the song wasn't in common time, and if the lyrics weren't about love and relationships. There was a new way of doing things between 1968 and 1974, and the new way was toward more *liberty*, liberty in form, arrangement, performance. This was the case for Prog, at least, until Johnny Rotten walked into Vivienne Westwood's shop on King's Row. Or, perhaps, until Asia had their first rehearsal.

2. The Argument With Respect To Mood

IT'S TRUE THAT VIRTUOSITY does not automatically result in a compelling listening experience and that rock and roll that is simply about how well people can play their instruments is dull, and who gives a shit if anyone can play their instrument. Mo Tucker cannot play the drums in the conventional way, and yet she was and is one of the best drummers in all of rock and roll. Modest ability does not impact the expressive power of a *song*. But: what of the argument that for the great player to play well is an expression of joy? It doesn't have to be the fleet fingers for the sake of the fleet fingers, but what if playing well is like that disagreeable runner in that disagreeable *Chariots of Fire* who says that when he runs he "feels God's pleasure?" What if Keith Emerson playing the way he played was feeling God's pleasure, after a fashion? What if this were an elucidation of the *joy of playing?* Because that was how I took it at the time. I took it that playing well was a joyful thing. It wasn't phallic power, it was the enthusiasm of being filled with *performative ability*. The only way to describe this is to say that there's something about Emerson, Lake & Palmer that I do not find austere and pretentious, but, rather, kind of funny. Funny, as in the band taking a particular delight in how many kinds of music they could funnel in, and how the song could be forced in so many directions at the same time. (I feel the same way about Frank Zappa, which is why I like Frank Zappa so much, despite the incredibly silly lyrics. I like the unpredictability of genre, and the way that anything, anywhere, can be used, at any time, for any reason.) No idea in Emerson, Lake & Palmer lasts very long, almost like in John Zorn's incredibly great band Naked City, where no genre lasts more than eight bars. The showing-off qualities of Emerson, Lake & Palmer are less evident to me, than they are in, e.g., The Allman Brothers Band, or The Grateful Dead, because the songs here are more about composition than they are about jamming. There are improvised *moments* in an Emerson, Lake & Palmer concert, but by and large the band are sticking to their own songbook, or to their well-traveled arrangements of the "classics." At the outset, the band was satisfied, even happy, about their incredibly disparate influences, which could range from Hard Bop to New Music to Romanticism to Jerry Lee Lewis. The difficulty only began when they stopped innovating in terms of their compositional interests. In their later work, the innovations are *only* technological. They aren't musical. For a while, Emerson, Lake & Palmer managed to do it, to innovate on every album, and perhaps we should be grateful that they fell apart quickly, because we are spared the grim beholding of decades of not terribly good studio recordings, which we have, e.g., in the case of Yes (last uniformly good album, *Going For the One*, in 1976), or in the case of Genesis (last good album, *Wind and Wuthering*, 1977), or in the case of Jethro Tull (last good album, *Heavy Horses*, 1978).

3. The Argument From Personal History

I GOT MY FIRST Emerson, Lake & Palmer album in 1975, at the suggestion of a good friend who said that if I liked Yes I might like this band. I bought the first album. Not long after, I became friends with a couple of guys in a dorm far away from mine (I was away at *boarding school*), who also liked this kind of thing. They had *all* the ELP albums and played them a lot. While this was not the only band we listened to back then, we listened to this band a lot. This band was a kind of a soundtrack for our small, homely group of misfits.

As I have mentioned elsewhere, at length, during these years we were also experimenting with drugs. It went with the times. For me, however, as someone with, I suppose, a lack of guile and a tendency to be defenseless against some of the harder hearts among my fellow men, the hallucinogens took a toll. The bad trips were too much for me. It could take me a long time to shake off the after-effects. I was the kind of person who should have fled in the opposite direction where LSD was concerned. One particularly bad night of florid hallucination nearly got me expelled, and for a long time after I couldn't listen to music that had anything *creepy* or *sinister* about it. If there had been death metal in those days, and I heard some, it would probably have set me back years.

I chose very carefully what I listened to, therefore, and one of those things was *Trilogy* by Emerson, Lake & Palmer. ELP hadn't yet given way entirely to the grandiosity and posturing, and they hadn't let go of the restlessness that characterized their first album. Moreover, a lot of *Trilogy* was instrumental, so it didn't really matter what the lyrics were like. I mostly listened for how the music *felt*, and how *Trilogy* felt to me was overpowered with joy. The melodies leaned in the direction of the major keys, and they were sort of fancy and old world, and resolved the way church music resolved (and we had to go to chapel four days a week at school, so we heard a lot of church music), but there was also some of the abandon of rock and roll. I would say that my favorite track was "Trilogy,"[2] the title track, which had this elegiac and beautiful melody by Emerson that was first stated on some kind of string synthesizer, and then was unpacked in a rather wonderful piano-and-voice section, the lyrics of which had an art-song quality. It all sounded like something sturdy and reliable to me, and I certainly *needed* to feel sturdier.

A few months passed in this way, and I had stopped taking the same liberal amount of drugs, and one day we all decided we were going down to Boston to see ELP play a stadium show. My friend's mom had a pilot's license, and she volunteered to fly us down (from New Hampshire). I had a really bad head cold at the time. We were all excited to be seeing our *idols* play, and it seemed *cool* to be taking the plane down, and I remember that we got just elevated enough (in a Piper Cub, or some such) that I could see the landscape below clearly, and what I saw was: nature trying to shake off a malignancy (the cities of humankind); what I saw was: a cancer that was rapidly depleting the natural organism. I couldn't stop thinking about it. The American cities as a cancer. It was a painful thing to have to think, and I couldn't shake it. And then Carol's mom was supposed to *land* the plane, and she got the runway wrong, and we were landing somewhere where we were not supposed to be landing, and she was almost purple with anxiety, and my eardrum imploded, because the plane went down so fast, and I couldn't hear anything

---

2   Though I also loved "Hoedown," Emerson's adaptation of Copland's piece of the same name, from the ballet score for *Rodeo*. "Hoedown" mixes some excellent organ work, at nearly impossible tempos, with some analogue synth work. The drumming is also lovely. Emerson manages to solo by quoting dozens of snippets of Americana, just as Copland does in the orchestral version. It's a happy piece of music, one that makes velocity and folk music themes sound totally at home together.

on the one side at all. We got a taxi into town. I was in some pain. And I wasn't doing any drugs then, and of course the moment the first note was played by ELP, everyone started lighting up. It was a concert to promote *Works, Volume 2*, which means that ELP were obligated to play a fair amount of *classical* crap, and they probably hated each other, and my friends were tired of all of my crazy remarks about the human cancer eating up the landscape.

I can remember little else from the show. I *ought* to remember more. Somehow we found a bus to take us back north to school. That's my recollection. It could have been Greyhound. I was distraught, exhausted, and farther away from the people who were supposed to be my friends.

You'd think this would be enough to cause me to turn away from the band associated with my comedy of errors. But it wasn't enough, because everything that came before, came from the life *before* this dark passage, I clung to as though it was a handhold on a rock face, including those songs from *Trilogy*, like the title track, and "Hoedown," and some of Greg Lake's ballads, and, believe it or not, the middle movement of Keith Emerson's piano concerto on *Works, Volume 1*, all of this stuff kept me feeling like I could remember when things didn't feel quite as menacing as they felt now, and after a while, I came down from the ledge.

It may have had nothing to do with Emerson, Lake & Palmer. Or it may have had everything to do with the spirit in which their compositions were made. Theirs was some of the music that was playing at the time I began to feel less unsturdy, and so it is music that had the powerful effect of stirring me back toward things human, gentle, kind. They coincided with relief, and in that way, too, I am grateful to them.

There's a lot of *Prog* going around now. The kids like stuff like The Mars Volta, that is totally informed by *Prog*. And then there's Dream Theater and Glass Hammer. And the present moment is nothing if not also the era of showoffy arrangements—Joanna Newsom and Grizzly Bear and Antony and the Johnsons all feature their fancy orchestral turns. I don't think this music is excessive. I like some of it a lot. But this music wasn't playing in my youth. I like ELP just because *it was there*, but also because history made it plausible, and because it was unapologetic. And now when I look back, the music looks moving to me, and cocky, and ambitious, and hilarious, no matter that most people dislike it.

4. The Argument About How To Appreciate What Is Lost

WHERE ARE THEY NOW? You sort of expect that some musicians from the seventies would go back to playing in the bars, or would get day jobs (John Evans of Jethro Tull, for example, left the band and started a construction firm), and there's a poignancy to these reduced circumstances that could turn the coldest heart. And: many of those musicians from the seventies are dead, of course, because of the high cost of that touring life. But an even sadder circumstance is to be found when all the members of a band are living, but they are unable to play together again in any substantial way.

At the time ELP broke up, they'd probably all made a lot of money and socked a lot of it away in high-yield financial instruments, and they were feeling pretty good about things, good enough that they didn't have to go through with playing with one another. Emerson and Lake had the publishing credits, and they probably got a good piece of change every time their recording of "Fanfare For the Common Man" was played during a sports broadcast. And Carl Palmer had Asia.

Well, Keith Emerson and Greg Lake did a mostly acoustic tour, recently, just the two of them. And Greg Lake tours sometimes, and sings his half of the ELP songbook, and Keith toured with a band a couple of years ago that was a lot more guitar heavy than his original band, with a sort of journeyman singer who did all of Lake's parts in a bluesier style. The Keith Emerson Band played lots and lots of ELP and Nice compositions. But that Emerson could launch this tour, at all, is sort of miraculous, because, physically, *he can't really play anymore.*

Like many pianists, Emerson was stricken with nerve damage in his right hand, as far back as the nineties, and he had surgery thereupon, unsuccessful surgery, and he has had trouble playing ever since. If you watch the Emerson, Lake & Palmer *Live at Royal Albert Hall (1992)* footage, e.g., you can see Emerson rubbing his wrist after the really challenging runs (and that was more than twenty years ago), and by the time of the recent tours of Eastern Europe with the Keith Emerson Band, it seems evident that the arrangements have been retrofitted for a diminished right hand. Emerson tries to compensate by making the left hand play a more important role, and he has a guitar player along to take up slack, but something is missing nonetheless. I have even found an account online of a fan who went to some of the Emerson/Lake shows who reports Emerson visibly choked up when talking during a Q&A about the surgeries he has had on his arm. No one, no one at all, can possibly think of Keith Emerson, the louche prince of keyboard excess being a guy who can't play at peak condition and who weeps about it, and it's from this cognitive dissonance that there is an inevitable surfeiting of poignancy—for even the cynics of the musical world.

It bears mentioning that Lake's voice is diminished, too, and that Lake is not the svelte and confident producer and songwriter he was then. He's a rather portly guy with glasses. Whatever this band was once it now has only one fully functioning member remaining, and he's the one who goes on a lot of tours with Asia. The aura of magisterial invincibility that some bands have (Led Zeppelin comes to mind) is just that, an aura, not much more, and it is probably the result of a lot of very effective hot air from publicists and record companies. Nothing good in music lasts except on the recordings. Even if you try to repeat yourself absolutely from record to record it doesn't last, whatever it is, and the period of effectiveness in the end is fleeting, and then after you are left with the memories, and the audience is left with the memories, too. And so I remember the Emerson, Lake & Palmer of old, before they were a punchline in a lot of jokes by Johnny Rotten and Steve Jones, and I feel the loss of a certain kind of uncompromising ambition, especially in times when musical pandering is often the coin of the realm. Sure, ELP were *de trop*, but they believed in what they did, and just because history ran afoul of them, there *is* something to admire there, and I am not willing to give up on them, nor on the time in my own life when this ambition was a kind of lifeline.

Rick Moody is the author of five novels, three collections of stories, a memoir, and most recently a volume of criticism, On Celestial Music. *He also sings and plays in* The Wingdale Community Singers.

The Cherokee Record Club

by Paul Myers

But maybe someday when they learn
Cherokee nation will return, will return, will return, will return
    —"Indian Reservation," Paul Revere & The Raiders

W

OODY ALLEN ONCE QUOTED Groucho Marx (whom he suspected was paraphrasing Sigmund Freud), when he said: "I would never want to belong to any club that would have someone like me for a member."

To some extent, this quote from *Annie Hall* best expresses the anxiety I felt as a lonely teenager, growing up in the wilds of suburban Toronto, in the seventies. Sure, I sometimes hung out at the mall with kids from my school. And, yes, my two brothers and I were close enough in age that we could pool our Led Zeppelin albums. But, by and large, these relationships were *inherited.* I had very little choice in the matter.

In fact, it wasn't until my older brother recommended me as a possible second guitarist for his friend Dave's basement band that I reluctantly allowed myself to be drafted into the first gang I ever joined.

Nighthawk was the hilariously gothic name of Dave's band, and we practiced every Sunday evening in the back room of The Advent Lutheran Church, mainly because Dave's dad was the Pastor there. For a time, the gang and I agreed on the basics: that rock and roll was cool, platform shoes and satin pants were worth saving up for, and—most importantly—it's always the *other* guitarist who needs to turn down his amp.

Being in a band made this a time of firsts. My first time getting completely shitfaced on alcohol—four Labatt's 50 Ale (Canadian domestic beer) and repeated shots of turgid Southern Comfort—followed by my subsequent first drunken bed spins, resulting in my first time puking my guts out. I also got my first taste of low potency high school grade marijuana and the truancy that it inspired. My first masturbatory porn crush was on *Playboy*'s Playmate of the Year 1977, Patti McGuire, consummated by the ritual beating back of the grim realization that my left hand would be my only girlfriend for many years to come. My first actual sex would be the tentative and decidedly humiliating blow job I'd receive while lying on a stack of coats in a bedroom at a friend's party.

All were firsts. None were bests. It was an ugly time but, to paraphrase Leonard Cohen, "we had the music."

As for the band, we generally agreed on the set list, which was drawn from the prevailing radio rock of our time. We tackled songs by Canadian heroes Bachman-Turner Overdrive, the gods of rock Led Zeppelin, and the flashy pawty rawk of KISS. Since the thinking man's power trio, Rush, came from our very own neighborhood, we also found room for a couple of that band's less athletic works, while our singer, Peter, who was a wiry extrovert with a big voice and a theatrical personality, insisted that we learn a few Alice Cooper and David Bowie tunes. At first, I was so dazzled by discovering that music was my calling, and grateful to be playing guitar outside my family room, that I ignored the feeling that something was missing. Even when I finally got the platforms and the satin pants, I couldn't ignore this sense that I was becoming a stranger in my own band. I fit in with *them*, but did they fit in with *me*? Whereas Dave's guitar solos leaned toward the flashy licks of Ace Frehley and Alex Lifeson, I was drawn to the soulful whole notes of Jeff Beck and the slow, *sinuous* string bends of George Harrison. My slow hand just wasn't sexy to the crew of suburban hangers-on who piled into the back room of the Advent Lutheran. I felt awkward and uncool, pretty much all the time. We drank a lot of beer in the ravine in those days, laying the foundation for years of alcoholism that would follow. But at the time, escapism was just fun. You didn't give it much thought. Thinking was why you drank in the first place.

Eventually, I was booted out of Nighthawk, like a teenage Brian Jones without the unfortunate swimming pool end. At first, I assumed that my dismissal had a lot to do with the aforementioned awkwardness, but in reality I had become increasingly mutinous toward the end. I had begun grumbling about breaking out of our three-chord universe and into the so-called *Progressive* bands like Yes, Genesis, and Pink Floyd. These were the bands our favorite bands were listening to, and I wanted to learn.

Thirty years later, I can now see that I wasn't so much interested in fitting in with a group as I was finding a pack of like-minded loners with whom we could all go our own way, together. And shortly before my exile from Nighthawk, I singled out two such loners among the kids who hung around at our band practices.

Michael, who was younger than me, would come early to set up the kit for our drummer, Steve. Each time he built the kit, I observed that Michael was actually a pretty good drummer himself, and as we chatted, it transpired that his influences were heavier cats like Deep Purple's Ian Paice, or Chicago's Danny Seraphine. We'd sneak in a little jam session before Steve got there, and Michael's playing was fluid, adventurous, and a little jazzy; frankly, I liked his style better.

Dan was Michael's friend, and among the first things I noticed about him was that, at age sixteen, he was already a big, burly, chain-smoking bear of a man. Dan didn't play an instrument, but he always knew a ton about records. He'd lived in Montreal, Toronto's French speaking rival, which always seemed more exotic and European to me, and he insisted that the Progressive FM radio in Quebec was "way cooler" than ours in Toronto. After practice, the three of us would end up over at The Counter, at Fairview Mall, where we'd share rock talk over endless refills of industrial strength coffee. These earliest conversations marked the first time I'd been introduced to bands like Frank Zappa & The Mothers of Invention, or Todd Rundgren's Utopia. Michael and Dan seemed to get me, I think I got them, and we all shared a desire to get somewhere, anywhere, else, and music was going to get us there.

They had both been the outsiders in their schools and were being raised by single mothers in apartment buildings. Dan's mom left him to his own devices in his spacious bedroom in a condominium just north of us, on Cherokee Boulevard, where he stayed up all night drinking coffee, listening to records and finding weird radio stations. What was not to like?

Curiously, we discovered that we all separately knew this radical kid from the neighborhood by the name of John Wallace. Standing just over four feet tall, John sported a full Afro that made his head seem larger than his entire body, like a cross between Gil Scott-Heron and the Great Gazoo. Besides being the first black guy

I'd known personally at this point, he was also one of the first true iconoclasts I'd ever met. He once balked at the mention of Pink Floyd's *Dark Side of The Moon*, sniffing that the band had sold out, and dismissing that ubiquitous suburban stoner album as "not as good as *The Piper At The Gates of Dawn* or *Ummagumma*." John Wallace didn't hang out with us. He didn't need a gang; he was a gang unto himself. He was more like our spirit animal, and as we delved deeper into Prog, the question—"What Would Wallace Think?"— would often cross my mind.

After Nighthawk, I had developed a weekend ritual of taking the subway downtown, with Michael and Dan, to Toronto's best record shops, and spending a lot of time talking to the guys behind the counters. These places had names like Records On Wheels, The Record Peddler, and the mother of all record stores, Sam The Record Man, Toronto's legendary three-story vinyl funhouse. Incidentally, all of these have vanished, and I sure hope that in your lifetime you got to visit a record palace of similar grandeur in your own hometown. These places define an era but, sadly, I suspect the one in your town is also gone.

For some reason, Dan always seemed able to buy at least two or three more albums than Michael or me. It didn't really matter all that much, however, because when we were done shopping, we'd take them all back to Dan's room on Cherokee Boulevard, our sort of clubhouse for what I now remember as The Cherokee Record Club. If the world gave out blue plaques to structures according to their personal significance to me, Dan's room would be designated as a historic site, with all of the repurposed plastic milk crates (stolen from behind supermarkets) preserved. The inscription on the plaque would read:

> *The Cherokee Record Club: on this spot in the mid-seventies,*
> *minds were blown, worlds discovered, and three young, lonely*
> *boys found salvation in vinyl.*

WE ALL HAD OPINIONS and reasons to be drawn to Prog that summer. Historically speaking, it was the peak time for Prog Rock, and at sixteen years old, male, and very single, we were smack in the middle of what marketers call the "target demographic."

We drank a heavy imported Quebec beer called Brador, and I puked again. And while we all smoked some pot, I could never do it without coughing until my lungs were on fire. None of us had girl-friends and, speaking for myself, I found the prospect of talking to girls terrifying. I think all three of us had an unspoken understanding that we could hide out in Dan's room and stall the inevitable by talking about records, music magazines, and bands. I assume the other two were masturbating as much as I was, but we never shared that ritual. Some things were better left unshared.

Being a young musician, still learning how to play, I was enamored of the technical wizardry of players like Chris Squire and Steve Howe of Yes, every member of Rush, Genesis, or Emerson, Lake & Palmer. I shared the core beliefs of most Prog fans: the fetishization of musical prowess, the near deification of flash instrumentalists who, in their heyday, were heralded like WWI flying aces and treated like princes. I remember Dan once said that to be truly Progressive, you had to be British; American bands, such as Kansas or Styx, just didn't cut it. Years later, when I became a professional music writer, I interviewed Bill Bruford of Yes and King Crimson and he told me that, at the time, he'd felt more in common with jazz guys than the previous generation of blues infused London rockers. Genesis and Gentle Giant would stymie the kids with their bizarre time signatures in weird fractions like 9/8 and 5/4, which lead inevitably to jazz but, sadly, it also steered us straight into unfortunate hybrids, such as the dreaded "fusion jazz." Despite some ambitious playing from greats like guitarist Allan Holdsworth, or space fiddler Jean-Luc Ponty, it never really took with me. Dan always championed the work of Frank Zappa, however, and his post-rock, quasi-social commentaries with extended instrumental jams seemed to transcend chops. On the other end of the scale, we delved into the synth tapestries of Wendy (then Walter) Carlos, whose *Switched-On Bach* and the soundtrack to *A Clockwork Orange* were big finds, with honorable mentions to Isao Tomita's *Snowflakes Are Dancing* and Jean-Michel Jarre's *Oxygene*.

Bruford also recalled that his fellow Prog rockers were always surprised at the wads of cash being thrown at them during Prog's heyday, without any seeming pressure to sell their souls for a three-minute Pop single. Of course, Yes's record label did perform bypass surgery on "Roundabout," removing five whole minutes from its middle section to make it fit on AM radio, but Prog snobs like us preferred the full 8:29 version from the *Fragile* album. I mean, what would John Wallace think? It was the era of the double gatefold sleeve and, while most of the kids used these cardboard sleeves to roll joints on, the three of us barely smoked weed and actually cared about the records inside those sleeves.

By the following summer, The Cherokee Record Club had reached a pinnacle. The end was in sight for both Prog and the club itself.

During one of his all-night radio binges, Dan had discovered a faint signal emanating from a renegade FM station in nearby Brampton, Ontario. That year, CFNY FM became a kind of ghost member of the club. They were a free-form station, with no formal playlist, and their DJs made music choices that challenged and inspired us. Soon, our weekend record safaris became missions to find stuff we'd heard, or heard about, on CFNY. Weaned on tales of Progressive radio from Montreal, Dan became particularly involved with the station, and took to engaging the all-night DJs in long, off-air conversations that lasted two or three whole album sides. This culminated in the three of us taking a little field trip, by Greyhound bus, up to the unlikely source of all of this mind-blowing music, the unassuming yellow house in Brampton that was CFNY's studio.

As a direct result of CFNY's open playlist, we were exposed to Prog's glammy brother, English Art Rock, like Brian Eno's *Another Green World* or Sparks' *Kimono My House*, and albums by Roxy Music, Steve Harley, and Chris Spedding. On the surface, this music wasn't as acrobatic as Prog, but its sophistication was all there in the arrangements. Significantly, Art Rock made it easier for Prog fans like me to accept it when, gradually, CFNY began playing the snotty new Punk and New Wave music emanating from far off London and New York City, or nearby downtown Toronto.

Unlike the music of our previous Prog Rock summers Punk cared less for, and in some ways, actively despised, precision, and technique. Yet, what it lacked in flash and athletic prowess, it made up for in pure energy, grit, and immediacy. Johnny Rotten's rebellious sneer made Jon Anderson's Tolkien-inspired reveries seem quaint. After months of listening to the Sex Pistols, Television,

Talking Heads' *Talking Heads: 77*, XTC's *Go2*, and The Clash's *London Calling*—plus albums by Magazine and the Ramones, the debuts by The Police and Gang of Four—Michael and I decided it was time to get in the game and start a band.

We called our new wave group, space Invaders (the lower case "s" was intentional) after the arcade video game that was the brand new craze of that year. I sang and played the guitar, Michael was on the drums, which left Dan, who played no instrument, out of the picture. More and more time was spent in the basement of The Happy Place, the beauty salon of Mike's hairstylist mother, and our visits to The Cherokee Record Club suffered. Mike and I had moved from being purely consumers to actual producers of music, recording and pressing our very own seven-inch vinyl single and playing downtown club gigs. The balance had been disturbed, and while Dan was supportive, there was no real role for him in this new club.

The moment had passed; The Cherokee Record Club never reconvened.

It had, however, done its job. It had insulated us during the storm times, the loneliest years of adolescence, and had built a sturdy bridge for us into young adulthood. We'd moved from passive fans to engaged musical explorers, and eventually, out of the suburban gloom to the stimulation of downtown life.

Over the next decade, the core members of The Cherokee Record Club pursued diverse musical directions. Michael became an award-winning record producer and engineer, and continues to be among my favorite drummers to play with. He has also evolved into one of the most sonically adventurous electronic composers I know. Despite being the only non-musician among us, Dan was actually the first to head out on the road with a touring rock band, initially as a lighting director, later as a tour manager, and he continues to produce live events. He remains a tireless vinyl collector and frequently spins his records on Toronto community radio.

I continued to be a songwriter and performer, and later added music journalist and broadcaster to my palette. I have written a few musicians' biographies, and one of these, *A Wizard A True Star: Todd Rundgren In The Studio*, enabled me to interview a great number of the musicians—Rundgren, Patti Smith, David Johansen, and members of Sparks—that I'd first heard in Dan's bedroom on Cherokee Boulevard, I dedicated that work to Dan and Michael.

Michael and I still get together to jam on those rare occasions where I find myself back in Toronto and, thanks to social networking, all three of us are still in touch and still talking about records, whether they're on vinyl or any other format. I've also noticed that certain music from the summer of Prog has returned to front of mind lately and I'm increasingly searching YouTube for Gentle Giant, Yes, and Genesis clips to post on the Facebook walls of my two fellow travelers.

It could be argued, then, that The Cherokee Record Club is alive and well, only the clubhouse is in cyberspace. We've come a long way, Michael, Dan, and I, but we're still just three music-loving loners going our separate ways, together.

*Paul Myers is the Berkeley-based, Toronto-born, author of the critically ac-
claimed,* A Wizard A True Star: Todd Rundgren In The Studio *and*
It Ain't Easy: Long John Baldry and the Birth of the British Blues.
*Additionally, Paul has written for a wide variety of periodicals, and earned
a Gemini Award (Canadian Emmy) nomination for writing the BBC4
documentary,* Long John Baldry: In The Shadow Of the Blues, *in
which he also appears. In 2013, his musical duo, The Paul & John, release
their debut recording,* Inner Sunset.

City In My Head
by Larry Karaszewski

Love rules without rules.
   —Sir Thomas More

I'VE SEEN TODD RUNDGREN in concert close to a hundred times. Easily more than any other artist. As a kid I even sneaked onto a soundstage at NBC and saw him host *The Midnight Special*. You can YouTube it. August 1978. I'm the guy dancing like an idiot in the front row to "You Cried Wolf." The floor director finally threatened to evict me unless I sat down.

I get very emotional when it comes to Rundgren. I've been obsessed with him. I've been disappointed with him. He has somehow worked his way into my DNA. The first time I saw Todd live was on the *Oops! Wrong Planet* tour in 1977. That concert was divided into two halves. The first was a stripped-down Power Pop performance with Todd and his group Utopia in t-shirts and jeans. The second half went Prog Rock batshit crazy. Using an elaborate set left over from the previous tour, Todd climbed atop a giant pyramid. He played guitar like a reincarnated Hendrix as his fellow band members battled massive windstorms, ocean swells, and a fire-breathing dragon. My sixteen year old mouth was agog. *Who the hell was this guy? The two sets were so different. How was one man responsible for both visions?* I set out to buy every record, see every show, read every interview. I wanted to know it all.

In the early seventies, no one was making better Pop music than Todd Rundgren. He put out three insanely catchy albums in a row that boasted simple, uncluttered songwriting. Emotional, yet funny. Human. And not only did he, amazingly, write and produce every cut, he also sang all the vocals and played every instrument. *Runt, The Ballad of Todd Rundgren*, and *Something/Anything* are still—to this day—Power Pop's most perfect trilogy. *Something/Anything* is a flat out masterpiece. Not a bum track on the record. The tunes feel effortless and really smart. To most critics, Todd appeared to be on the verge of becoming the American Beatles—but all in one man. And in a weird way, he did. Certainly not in record sales or influence (Todd had neither). But he is one of the few artists who followed the Beatles' path of radical change and growth. The way the sound of *Meet the Beatles!* in 1964 could morph into the sonic genius of *Sgt. Pepper* then into the force of 1968's "White Album" over just a short period of years. Todd's mid-seventies output took him on an ever-changing musical quest from pure Pop and beautiful melodies to Acid rock, Jazz Fusion, and a spiritual search for the Utopian ideal.

Something/Anything contains Todd's biggest hit single, "Hello It's Me." It was actually more of a late blooming success, and by the time the song had hit top ten on the charts in 1973, he had already recorded his follow up album, *A Wizard/A True Star*. Wizard was a radical departure from the music Todd had created up to that point. His record company must have been stunned. They had finally broken Todd to radio, sold the industry on this friendly Pop wunderkind, and now he had somehow devolved into a LSD-taking, Frank Zappa-inspired freak. (And I say that as a compliment.) Rundgren seems to want to destroy his cuddly image here. Gone is the likable studio nerd. Now he's wearing elaborate makeup and multicolored hair, peacock feathers for eyelashes, and wings on his back. The album cover for *Wizard* is also clearly influenced by psychedelics: a drawing of Todd's head with extra ears and mouths. The music is designed for headphones and mushrooms. Songs like "Dogfight Giggle," "You Need Your Head," and "Flamingo" sometimes have more sound effects than melodies. There isn't even a potential single. The loveliest tune is married to lyrics about a dog being run over by a car. Todd seems aware of the damage he was doing to his career, though. On "International Feel" he recognizes it might be "the start of the end." But he promises to keep at it. There'll be more: "Wait another year, Utopia is here."

This version of Utopia had a possessory credit. "Todd Rundgren's Utopia" wasn't a place—it was a group. Todd had flirted with bands before, but he had never really been a team player. Everything always seemed easier and quicker if he just did it all himself. There were so many ideas in his brain, it was simpler to just play them all out himself rather than explain to others and teach the parts. This even extended to touring. Todd would often enter the concert arena with only a keyboard and a reel-to-reel tape deck. He pushed buttons and sang with himself. It seemed radical at the time. This wasn't Ashley Simpson or Tiffany lip-syncing to back up tracks. It was cutting edge technology brought to the stage. It was also not very satisfying. Being on the cutting edge often means doing things before they really work. Todd messing around with tapes felt at times like being trapped with a preoccupied computer geek in his basement. The live set had no momentum. And Todd could never really show off what an amazing instrumentalist he truly was. So the band Utopia was born. And the concerts exploded.

IF AT FIRST HE had his Beatles phase, then his Frank Zappa phase, now we were entering Todd's fusion period. He was particularly awed by the Mahavishnu Orchestra. In the early seventies it had not yet been scientifically proven that Jazz Fusion was a horrible idea. (*It's not jazz, it's not rock...what is it?*) At the time it seemed like a natural progression for music. The most proficient players were embracing it. This wasn't three-chord rock—this was complicated don't-try-this-at-home musicianship. You had to know what you were doing. Rock was growing up. Mahuvishnu's John McLaughlin was not only a master guitarist; he also added stony metaphysical elements to the music. The long twenty-minute jams were exercises in finding your inner self. Todd completely embraced this sound and search for higher meaning with his Utopia bandmates. And strangely, by throwing himself into a collective unit, Todd wound up actually writing his most personal music. Here was a man seeking some sort of spiritual truth. Alternate religion and synthesizers oddly blended together quite nicely. If Utopia in literature and philosophy had come to symbolize an ideal—the perfect place—Todd turned it into a "city in my head."

But, unfortunately, the public didn't buy the records. Todd was moving so fast it was impossible to keep up. By the time you liked one flavor he had moved on to the next. But things were different out on the road. Ticket sales skyrocketed. Utopia became known as one of the best live acts in the country. Never-ending shows. Blistering guitar virtuosity. And three, count 'em (three), keyboard players. The band members were elite session players with names like Moogy and Frog. Simply put: They were far fucking out.

Rundgren would no longer bother to play commercial stuff like "Hello It's Me." Instead he sang of searching for "The Seven Rays" or dreaming of "Another Life" on "The Wheel" of Karma. His songs were complex compositions. "Freak Parade" alone changes chords, tempo, meter, and melody every few seconds. There was energy to these live shows and fans embraced them.

At the time, the synthesizer was relatively new on the scene. It was still something to be played with. *How far could this electronic miracle take rock and roll?* It seemed to open so many musical possibilities for Rundgren. This was the sound of the future. He found a fellow convert in keyboardist Roger Powell. The two searched for sounds and sequences. On his solo project, *Initiation*, Todd decided to devote an entire album side to a singular synthesizer composition. The only other folks doing stuff like that were a few Germans and Walter Carlos.

Todd's spiritual search led him to the writings of Alice Bailey. He used her book, *A Treatise on Comic Fire*, as an inspiration. Critics would call it pretentious and unlistenable. But Todd didn't care. *Treatise* seemed to release Todd artistically. He was literally doing whatever the fuck he wanted. There was no filter. Even the Pop songs on *Initiation* seem like personal statements. Several songs fight back against criticism and take issue with colleagues trying to keep Todd in a musical box. Particularly on a cut that foretells "The Death of Rock and Roll": "Just the other day I got a call from a friend / I heard what you've been playing and I think it's a sin / Why can't you make a living like the rest of the boys? / Instead of filling your head with all that synthesized noise?"

Throughout his career, Todd liked saving sides of albums for interconnected conceptual pieces. "Treatise..." on *Initiation*. The side of other artists' songs on *Faithful*. "Singring and the Glass Guitar" from *Ra*. The "Healing" side of *Healing*. Hell, even *Something/Anything* boasts a sidelong rock opera. Todd was nothing if not ambitious. He wanted to push the boundaries of what a rock album could be. And not only with his own compositions. Todd kept himself busy (and paid the bills) by producing albums for other artists: Badfinger, The Band, Patti Smith, XTC, New York Dolls, Steve Hillage, to name just a few. His productions were rarely subtle. More was better. Even his Hall & Oates record is apocalyptic metal. With his productions, Todd created some of the most bombastic rock and roll ever. Grand Funk Railroad's *We're An American Band* and Meatloaf's *Bat Out Of Hell* built sonic walls arguably even bigger than Phil Spector.

By the mid-seventies, Todd had chosen to simplify Utopia. The team went from having trumpet players and backup singers to a stripped-down four-piece band. A tight Beatlesesque quartet: Roger Powell on synthesizer, Kasim Sulton on bass, Willie Wilcox on drums, and Todd on guitar. Rundgren also wanted to make it an equal partnership. Everyone would write the songs. Everyone would sing leads. But being the master of sending out mixed messages, Todd partnered this simplification of the group dynamics with his most elaborate stage show ever—the *Ra* tour. This was Utopia at its best, and yet it was also Utopia at its most Spinal Tap-ian. The stage design was a massive pyramid with everyone wearing Egyptian garb. They played rock versions of Bernard Herman compositions and sang a tune about the atomic destruction of Hiroshima. The concert climax outdid everything until Cirque du Soleil came to town: A Tolkien-inspired "electrified fairy tale" called "Singring and the Glass Guitar." According to the tale, Singring lives happily in a town called Harmony until he is kidnapped by Evil Forces and trapped in a mystical glass guitar. He can only be freed if four keys can be found to unlock his prison. The keys have been scattered to the corners of the world and four brave men set out to retrieve them. Willie Wilcox goes to the deepest ocean. He plays an elaborate drum solo as fountains sprout up on stage spraying to the beat. Kasim Sulton plucks a bass solo while battling against hurricane winds. Roger Powell shoots laser beams out of his synthesizer while combating a fire-breathing dragon. And Todd brings it all home by climbing the highest mountain—the *pyramid*—and smashing a glass guitar. Even in the era of KISS and Pink Floyd's *Animals*, Utopia's show was wackadoodle. It's a testament to the enormous talent of each player that the concerts actually worked. While it may sound extremely silly on paper, it was actually very entertaining live. Perhaps the ultimate rock and roll "you had to be there." Audiences loved it.

The *Ra* tour was both a triumph and a dead end for Rundgren. The set and costumes were so expensive that profitability was out of the question. The Punk Rock movement was also rumbling forward, making such overblown production seem old-fashioned and foolish. Todd seemed to realize this, and for the next Utopia album he stripped it all down. Gone were the tunics. Utopia now wore t-shirts and jeans. They looked more like the Ramones.

This is where I came in. There were no long solos on *Oops! Wrong Planet*. Just short, bouncy, rock solid Pop songs. Up until this point, one could usually divide Todd's output into two categories: under the name Todd Rundgren one would find his more conventional Pop compositions; under the name Utopia you got indulgent, album-oriented Progressive Rock. But now those distinctions were gone. Utopia's subsequent release, *Adventures in Utopia*, would be Rundgren's most radio-friendly in years. And the solo effort, *Healing*, was Todd at his most navel-gazing new age. Once these lines were blurred, Utopia stopped having a reason to exist. In the early nineties, Todd became a permanent solo act. The "city in his head" was no more.

TODD AND UTOPIA NEVER sold a lot of records and they are sometimes best remembered for the crazy opulence of the stage show. One always has to figure out at what point in a new relationship can you reveal that you are a massive Todd Rundgren fan. Too soon and it can scare people away quicker than *Dungeons & Dragons* or herpes. But when you stumble across a fellow Todd fan, you know you have found a friend for life. It's like you fought in war together.

Through all these ups and downs, Todd somehow never seems to lose his loyal fan base. The people who love Todd, really, really love Todd. All the commercial missteps don't matter. If anything, they reinforce the admiration. He is your secret. You are the only one who understands how great Todd Rundgren is. The "phonies" don't get him. It makes sense that assassin Mark David Chapman's other obsessions beside John Lennon were J. D. Salinger and Todd Rundgren. All three artists inspire an intense personal devotion. Fans feel as if these artists speak directly to them and no one else. This "Todd is Godd" army has allowed Rundgren to carry on over the years. They keep coming to see him, buying his records, and following him wherever he chooses to go. Whether it's an album of Robert Johnson covers or lounge versions of Todd's own songs—a

Rundgren fan stays true. I know I have. This has allowed Todd to keep creating and take risks long after more successful acts have gone bye-bye. Because of his ever-changing style, Rundgren is sometimes called a musical chameleon. But that is a mistake. Todd has never blended into the background. He doesn't fade; he stands out with a rich individualism that is rare in the music industry. Written in hieroglyphics on the cover of *A Wizard/A True Star* is the phrase: "Be true to your work and your work will be true to you." Todd Rundgren has kept that promise.

Larry Karaszewski is writing, directing, and producing partners with Scott Alexander. The two won the Best Screenplay Golden Globe for The People vs Larry Flynt, *as well as Writer's Guild of America's Paul Selvin Award. They also received a Best Screenplay nomination from the WGA for the Tim Burton directed* Ed Wood. *Other credits include writing the Milos Forman film* Man On The Moon, *adapting the Stephen King story* 1408, *and producing Paul Schrader's* Auto Focus. *Larry's humorous commentaries on cult films can be seen on the website TrailersFromHell.com.*

Ode To The Giant Hogweeds

by Jim DeRogatis

No man is rich enough to buy back his past.
　　　　　　　　　　—Oscar Wilde

S HOW ME SOME HUMAN beings in their mid-sixties who are not in the least bit embarrassed by some of the things they did in their early twenties, and I'll show you some liars or the sort of people who never had an ounce of fun in their lives. The dalliances with a partner, perhaps even of one's own sex, who you'd never look at much less talk to in situations not involving furtive, lustful, and sticky grappling; the night you found out what jail was really like; the devotion to sacred and profound texts that would read more like bad comic books in the cold, hard light of a later day, and the regular attempts to pursue what Rimbaud called "the systematic derangement of the senses"—all are rights of passage. If we wince a bit when recollecting them from a vantage point further on in life, the wisest among us proceed to proudly own them, though never in the braggadocios manner of the high school athlete gone to seed and living in the past. Ultimately, we smile slyly when we're reminded of them, because they shaped who we are—and because they were a stone cold gas, to boot.

Sadly, the three remaining members of Genesis—despite their status as fabulously wealthy country squires able to rest on their bank accounts while indulging in arcane pursuits such as making classical albums no one listens to (Tony Banks), becoming the foremost collector in the world of militaria relating to the siege of the Alamo (Phil Collins), or pretending still to be a Pop star by touring with the wretched Mike + The Mechanics (Mike Rutherford)—seem not to have reached this healthy place. They groan when reminded of those years some four decades passed when perhaps they embarrassed themselves ever so slightly, in the process also making some brilliant music, and they quickly change the subject, doing their best to ignore and sometimes even disavow that stretch of their lives. Nor have their former band mates come to terms any better, with Peter Gabriel finding himself torn always between moving forward as the goofy purveyor of simple Pop pleasures (at this writing, he is preparing to celebrate the twenty-fifth anniversary of *So*, his most successful if least interesting solo album) and striking the pose of the *serious artiste* (witness his two recent discs of ponderous and joyless covers arranged for orchestra), while poor Steve Hackett... well, he's just forever waiting for that call about putting the band back together.

That never would work, we all know that: you can't go home again, change is the law of life, the living moment is everything—*yadda, yadda, yadda*, so on and so forth, etcetera, and good riddance. Nostalgia is the enemy of all great art, rock and roll most of all, since at its best it is a celebration of the *now*. But that now is in some sense eternal: there is no reason to stop celebrating the moment when the moment is over, not when listening again yields such enduring pleasures. And if the five musicians named above— the members of the best lineup of, for my money, the best band making the best albums in that chronically underappreciated and wrongly reviled heyday of Progressive Rock—cannot or will not do it, well, I certainly will. Because for four glorious studio albums and one live set issued between the productive years of 1971 to 1974, those bearded nerdy dweebs fucking ruled.

Yes, there were pleasures before those years and those discs, and to some extent, there were pleasures afterward, though never so consistent, delightful, laser-focused, and alternately supremely silly and super-serious. So it is to those years that we will pay homage here, but first, a brief look at how we arrived.

IN THE BEGINNING, AS at the start of many a slow-moving British art-house film about beautifully awkward teens coming of age, there were the polite, proper, upper middle class public school boys with just a little bit more courage, curiosity, and lust for life than their peers who'd become bankers, accountants, and government clerks. Banks and Gabriel met as newly arrived thirteen year olds at the Charterhouse School near Godalming, Surrey, an all-male bastion of the conservative establishment devoted to pretending that the sun had never set upon the empire, the blitz and postwar economic collapse be damned. They struck up a friendship based on playing songs by the Beatles, Otis Redding, and Nina Simone, all sweet and slightly forbidden fruits, and as their extracurricular sessions in the music room progressed from huddling around the phonograph the way some lads sneaked cigarettes by the trash cans to tentatively messing about with the borrowed orchestral instruments—Banks drawing on endless years of classical piano lessons, and Gabriel thinking he could play the drums—they eventually were joined by several Charterhouse classmates, including Rutherford and Anthony Phillips.

In late 1968 this loose-knit group recorded a demo, skipped school one afternoon, and slipped the tape to Charterhouse graduate Jonathan King, who had scored a sub-Donovan novelty hit in 1965 with "Everyone's Gone to the Moon." The would-be Pop impresario liked the band's gentle, wispy melodies, and he produced its first album, *From Genesis to Revelation*, released on the Decca label in March 1969. The record sold only six hundred copies, including those purchased by the boys' still generally disapproving mums and dads, and the band was dropped, but the now eighteen year old musicians weren't easily discouraged. They moved into an isolated cottage in Dorking, forswore earthly comfort such as food and fuel to ward off the omnipresent soggy chill, devoted their meager budget instead to pot, hash, and acid, and set up in a circle, jamming for hours every day for six months. And here they forged the flowing, pastoral, dramatic, and whimsical sound that would characterize their best early work.

As noted earlier, there would be hints of this on both *From Genesis to Revelation*—though the musicians later admitted to being entirely too influenced by the still paisley-pop Bee Gees and largely crafting the music in an attempt to give King what they thought he'd want—and *Trespass*, the album that arrived in 1970, after Tony Stratton-Smith, a manager about town during the swinging London of the psychedelic era, caught one of the group's rare gigs and signed it to his new label, Charisma Records. *Trespass* is in fact the birth of the uniquely Genesis take on the then-burgeoning Prog movement, especially with the lovely "Stagnation" and the epic, churning rocker, "The Knife," but it's sunk by a dreadfully murky production, Phillip's conventionally folkie acoustic twelve-string guitar, and John Mayhew's drumming, which neither is assertive enough during the more ferocious moments nor properly subtle during the many quiet interludes.

Enter Hackett and Collins. "Genesis was full of charm and weakness," Hackett said of the period before his arrival in *Genesis: I Know What I Like* (D.I.Y., 1980), the definitive chronicle of the band by its obsessive Italian biographer Armando Gallo. "Feminine, you know. Very pastel shades. 'Stagnation' is a very impressionist sort of thing, very evocative of branches and leaves. It conjures up feelings of scenery to me."

What Hackett would bring to the mix as a wildly inventive, effects-crazed player whose guitar only rarely sounded like a guitar was a measure of the controlled chaos necessary to make things *rock*, while the other new arrival, former West End child actor, model, and experienced rock drummer, Collins, would excel at the extremes of both soft and loud that frustrated Mayhew while adding a bit of theatrical flair and exuberant personality, encouraging Gabriel to amplify these nascent tendencies in his own stage persona, as well as chiming in with some very useful and very Gabriel-like high-register backing vocals.

To be fair, when Genesis returned to London's Trident Studios to once again inflict maximum abuse on the still new and relatively rare sixteen-track recorder, Hackett only recently had joined the group, and he hardly can be heard on the 1971 release *Nursery Cryme*; most of the guitar parts are played by Rutherford, though Phillips still lingers with some contributions. And the wicked rock-roll snickers and sneers that would so effectively complement and contrast with the ornate beauty of the next few records cannot be attributed solely to any one member, since they are in ample evidence in everything the band is doing, from the cover art—that young Victorian schoolgirl batting about severed heads with her croquet mallet—to the primarily Gabriel-penned lyrics, resonant as they are of the guilty-pleasure fantasy worlds of Renaissance Faires, Frodo and Gandalf, Isaac Asimov, and Robert A. Heinlein, the proto-goth and steampunk aesthetics, and even what today we'd call vampire erotica or naughty fan fiction.

Nursery Cryme opens with the striking tune "The Musical Box," Gabriel's attempt at a typically twisted fairy tale about a nine year old girl who removes her eight year old playmate's head with a croquet mallet, discovers the mystical musical box he left behind, then is overwhelmed by the sexual desires inflicted upon her during the attempted seduction by his ghost. The language may be typically Victorian, but let us remember that for all its prim and proper pomp and circumstance, that was one of the randiest periods in British history, and you can't mistake the desire Gabriel expresses as he lovingly lingers on the last word in the line, "Brush back your hair...and let me get to know your f-l-e-s-h." Oh, baby, talk about steam.

We also get the immortal and sublimely ridiculous "The Return of the Giant Hogweed," an apocalyptic tale about a killer plant brought back to the Royal Gardens at Kew by a Victorian explorer returning from Russia (think of Jules Verne or H. G. Wells rewriting *The Day of the Triffids*); a reworking of the Greek mythological tale of the nymph Salmacis attempting to rape Hermaphroditus (a horny lad our Peter was back then), aptly entitled "The Fountain of Salmacis," and "Harold the Barrel," which tells of an English restaurateur who jumps to his death, presumably after unspeakable acts, not unlike those of *Sweeney Todd*. "Father of three, it's disgusting / Such a horrible thing to do," Gabriel sings, relating part of the story in the voice of the man in the street, one of several different roles in the tune. "Harold the Barrel cut off his toes and he served them all for tea / Can't go far, he can't go far / Hasn't got a leg to stand on." (Ha! Get it? Horny *and* witty, our boy!)

Meanwhile, the music perfectly matches the gonzo spirit of the are-they-or-aren't-they-a-put-on words, contrasting moments of bombastic rock with sweet, timeless melodies that transcend genre and those classical flourishes so beloved of all Prog rockers in their rush to emphasize that what they were doing was Art with a capital "A." Yet unlike peers such as Yes and ELP, Genesis always was more interested in creating unique sounds, textures, and moods than in unleashing virtuosic solos, though virtuosos its members certainly were. At his nastiest, Banks pushes his Hohner electric piano through a fuzz box, a veritable Hendrix of the ivories on "The Musical Box" and "The Return of the Giant Hogweed," while in quiet mode, he makes just as strong an impression with the Mellotron, newly acquired as a piece of used gear from King Crimson, decorating "The Fountain of Salmacis" and "Seven Stones" with gorgeous filigree. For his part, Collins navigates complicated time signatures like a slalom course he's run a thousand times, injecting perfectly placed accents along the way like the master chef sprinkling just the right seasonings in the sauce. Though no one ever would accuse him of being a bassist of the booty-shaking variety, Rutherford provides the slinky, sensual lines that tie it all together. And things only get better from here as Hackett really settles in and makes his mark.

Released in October 1972, the band's fourth album *Foxtrot* is its first undeniable, beginning-to-end masterpiece. Banks' regal Mellotron intonations introduce the opening "Watcher of the Skies," and it's thought that the primitive tape-loop machine's "foxtrot" rhythm setting gave the album its title and fox-in-a-red-dress cover art. The sound itself would prove so popular and influential that the manufacturers of this precursor to the synthesizer, Streetly Electronics, eventually provided a "Watcher Mix" set of tape loops. As for the lyrics, while Gabriel delivers a bravura vocal over the absolutely frenetic rhythms, the ruminations of aliens surveying the remains of the planet we've ruined were written by Banks and Rutherford—the singer wasn't the only band member enamored of science fiction—apparently after the sound check for a gig at an old, deserted airfield in Naples, with Vesuvius and the even older and more deserted ruins of Pompeii standing hovering far in the distance.

From there, we shift gears and celebrate the return of the twelve-string for the lovely and dramatic modern madrigal "Time Table," which couches familiar Vietnam-era anti-war sentiments in an unfamiliar medieval setting. We see this new flourishing of social consciousness taken to an even higher level in "Get 'Em Out By Friday," which finds Gabriel playing several different roles in a deliriously rambunctious tune that satirizes greedy slumlords and real estate speculators. "Can-Utility and the Coastliners" boasts an ungainly title that actually refers to the lyrics drawing from the legend of King Canute—punning fellows, these Brits—and together with the short guitar instrumental "Horizons," it provides the album's slightest moment, though in context, both are a welcome chance to catch one's breath before one of the grandest finales in rock history, the sidelong, twenty-three minutes and six-seconds of "Supper's Ready."

This grandest of grand statements is, in essence, a song disguised as a musical play, or perhaps vice-versa, dealing with no less than the balance between good and evil and man's place in the universe, ending up with a reinterpretation of "The Book of Revelations," and sprinkling plenty more Greek mythology as well as some William Blake into the stew along the way. One might shudder from a whiff of Scientology weirdness to it all, if it wasn't such a sublime sensual pleasure—this, never forget, still is rock and roll—and if Gabriel didn't actually really believe in it all at the time, without proselytizing that we must, too. The mystical journey was inspired by an odd experience the singer had with his first wife, Jill, at her parents' house in Kensington. "We just stared at each other, and strange things began to happen," he told Gallo. "We saw other faces in each other, and I was very frightened. It was almost as if something had come into us and was using us as a meeting point. It was late at night, and we were tired and all the rest, so it was quite easy for us to hallucinate, [though] we hadn't been drinking or drugging."

Well, not at that moment, perhaps. Yet for all the protoplasmic mumbo-jumbo, there is plenty of clear-eyed humor and sheer, un-selfconscious absurdity en route to the majestic crescendo and its declaration of a New Jerusalem, including the section (one of seven movements) entitled "Apocalypse in 9/8 (Co-Starring the Delicious Talents of Gabble the Ratchet)" and the thoroughly Monty Python-like, oh-so-Briddish wordplay of the music hall-sounding "Willow Farm." ("There's Winston Churchill dressed in drag / He used to be a British flag / Plastic bag / What a drag!" Gabriel exclaims.) And because the melodies and arrangements are so damn strong, you don't have to give a fig about what it all means to enjoy it.

Foxtrot was the band's most successful release to date, peaking at number twelve in the U.K.'s top twenty, and charting in the top five in Belgium and Italy, though America remained blissfully oblivious, until the group crossed the ocean and began to perform live. Mention must be made, and this is the time to make it, of the full-on, theatrical, multimedia mind trip that Genesis had become in concert by this time. Early on, the group could have put to shame the later generation of British public schoolers in the movement that would be dubbed shoegazer or the sensitive, introspective beard rockers so beloved of *Pitchfork*-obsessed indie hipsters nowadays, as the members of Genesis sat down throughout their shows, just as they'd done during those long rehearsals as the cottage in Dorking, and they seemingly were too frightened or too shy even to look up from their instruments.

In the years that followed, as he performed the increasingly sweeping and colorful music the band crafted in the studio, Gabriel began to inhabit the characters he sang about, donning masks, robes, and giant bat wings as the light show grew ever more elaborate and the sound system increasingly intense. Perhaps the costumes allowed him to become what he couldn't be when he was just Peter. Yet despite what some have said, or what some artists were doing in the concurrent glam scene, the music remained the focus, not the showmanship. None of the frills would have mattered if the band could not replicate and even improve upon what it had done on record, and lest anyone think that an exaggeration, turn to *Genesis Live*, recorded in Leicester and Manchester during the 1973 tour supporting *Foxtrot*.

The hardcore fans were and are disappointed that "Supper's Ready" was left off the single vinyl album (the recording from this period eventually would surface on a box set), and that more of Gabriel's fanciful between-songs monologues didn't make the cut; at the time, he spun off these bizarre tales much as Robyn Hitchcock later would, but rather than entertaining, he just was trying to buy time for the musicians to change their ever-more complicated tunings. Still, the stuff that did make the record—"Watcher of the Skies," "Get 'Em Out By Friday," "The Return of the Giant Hogweed," and "The Musical Box"—adds an electric edginess to the studio versions, and Hackett and Collins finally have the opportunity to make "The Knife," the best song from the era predating them, not only their own, but all that it ever aspired to be.

Part contractual obligation and part a move to bide time before the next studio release, *Genesis Live* is followed in the chronology by *Selling England By The Pound*, which arrived a year later in October 1973. Like *Nursery Cryme*, this is less a stunning masterpiece than merely a very, very good album. By now, we know the familiar Genesis sounds and stories, and nothing comes as a revelation—though how could it, after "Supper's Ready"? Nevertheless, in addition to some overly elaborate, melody-shy arrangements and entirely too many of the bad puns that used to come as unexpected surprises, we have several worthy additions to the canon: "Firth of Fifth," the band's most rhythmically complex tune (stretches of 13/16 and 15/16 alternate with a waltz-like 2/4); the pretty and Spartan Pop song "More Fool Me," Phil Collins' second lead vocal with the group (after "For Absent Friends" on *Nursery Cryme*); "I Know What I Like (In Your Wardrobe)," the sweetly undulating tale of a groundskeeper who might have stepped out of *Lady Chatterley's Lover* but who's supremely happy with his modest station in life, a rare-in-the-Prog-era hit on the British singles chart, and "The Battle of Epping Forest," which points to the next step in the band's evolution and the pinnacle of its achievement by turning a news story about the territorial battle between two rival East London gangs into an ever-shifting musical and lyrical tour de force.

This, of course, brings us to *The Lamb*.

Released in November 1974, the ninety-four minute, twenty-two second double concept album *The Lamb Lies Down On Broadway* is, in the generally accepted Genesis fan/rock critic shorthand, the band's most ambitious and effective merger of theater and musical invention. But me, I prefer to think of it as one of the most wonderfully fucked-up recordings I've ever heard, and one that still holds a captivating power over the listener lo these many years later, leaving you scratching your head in wondrous stupefaction while grinning like a thoroughly satisfied idiot.

Recorded at a time when Gabriel was pulling away from the group, as well as being removed from the proceedings by the necessity of dealing with his wife's difficult pregnancy, complaints persist from most involved of occasionally unsuccessful combinations of lyrics, vocals and music. Gabriel wrote the vast majority of the book (and why not talk in musical theater terms here?) on his own as part of a tale even more epic and inscrutable than that of "Supper's Ready," while the musicians developed most of the backing tracks out of improvised jams when their singer was missing in action. But as we approach the end of this lineup and this era, the intensity of these years of nonstop playing and recording had made the band a more cohesive unit than it ever had been, and the alleged disconnections between singer and musicians never have been audible to me. Besides, Banks and Rutherford did write some of the lyrics, notably for "The Light Dies Down on Broadway"; Gabriel did contribute some of the melodies, chief among them the breathtakingly beautiful tune that powers "The Carpet Crawlers," and parts of tracks such as "Lilywhite Lilith" and "Anyway" actually dated back to songs that had been hanging around and evolving in rehearsal since 1969. *The Lamb Lies Down On Broadway* is in every way the culmination of all this band was—as well as its summing up and farewell.

As with "The Battle of Epping Forest," gangs and what we'd now call the thug life provide the unlikely spark of inspiration for a progressively more hallucinatory story of a Puerto Rican graffiti artist, a New York street kid named Rael (a play on Gabriel's surname), swept into a strange underworld of Lamia, Slippermen, and disturbing underground chambers with thirty-two doors. He apparently is trying to rescue his brother John, though no less a firsthand participant than Collins, in the 1991 documentary *Genesis: A History*, said there's really an element of split personality to all of this, with Rael in fact looking for a missing part of himself, a not surprising topic for a singer so flamboyant under the spotlights and so retiring in his private life. And, as usual, we also get musings on other topics far and wide, including that old faithful Greek mythology, the sexual revolution, and rampant consumerism. In some ways, it's a confused and confusing Progressive Rock answer to *West Side Story*. Yet, again, as with "Supper's Ready," you don't need to understand, follow, or even enjoy any of the story in order to blissfully loose yourself in the sounds and songs.

The live edginess the band brought to *Genesis Live* but which previously eluded it on albums finally is realized in the studio, with Gabriel delivering an at-times positively furious vocal performance and Banks's exotic synthesizer textures and Hackett's unconventional guitar lines evoking the world of sampling to come, where almost any sound could become a musical instrument. The simplified histories of popular music hold that the punks who'd soon burst onto the scene and give rock some much-needed CPR vilified, hated, and pushed back against bands like Genesis and all that they had become: big, bloated, distant, and pompous dinosaurs. Yet if we willingly accept the invention of the early solo albums by Brian Eno as harbingers of the no rules/no limits ethos and unbridled experimentation of certain strains of Punk, shouldn't we also consider *The Lamb Lies Down On Broadway* in the same light? Heck, Eno himself deigned to add his "enossification" or sonic treatments to some tracks, while Collins returned the favor by playing for him in the studio. Yet only rarely have the many art-punks who've followed admitted any debt to Genesis; in fact, I only can think of one: Ronald Jones of The Flaming Lips, who had an enduring fascination with Hackett's guitar sounds. Maybe they were turned off by the beards, or maybe it was what the group would become post-Gabriel. But we're getting ahead of things.

In any event, and this never is said often enough, the magic of *The Lamb Lies Down On Broadway* is that amid all of the musical strangeness and conceptual pretension, the melodies never are lacking. It's a goddamn catchy album, pure and simple, from the way the title track nicks from and reimagines the Drifters' classic "On Broadway," to the aforementioned and absolutely unforgettable seduction of "The Carpet Crawlers"; from the anti-Capitalist anthem "The Grand Parade of Lifeless Packaging" to "Counting Out Time," the funniest song the band ever recorded, and one that finds Gabriel as the protagonist fumbling with the advice in a well-meaning but sometimes befuddling sex manual (one thinks of *The Joy of Sex*, then recently published, with those awful illustrations of hirsute hippies contorting their bodies in impossible ways), and from the endearing and unceasingly hummable "Lillywhite Lilith," to the positively jaunty and rollicking closer "*it*," which ends the day and deflates any unfair charges of joyless self-importance with a chant appropriated from The Rolling Stones: "It's only rock and roll, but I like it."

Needless to say, the album inspired the band's most elaborate stage show yet, with more lights, more visuals, and more costume changes than ever before, and the group performed it in its entirety more than one hundred times. But much of the press attention focused on Gabriel, and the resentments that caused ultimately contributed to the end of the group's most remarkable lineup. When Gabriel announced that he would be leaving the band at the end of the tour, the musicians didn't try to dissuade him. "They didn't like what I was becoming," he told Gallo. "I felt that my hands were beginning to feel tied within the group because the publicity thing was getting worse rather than better; the jealousy."

The singer launched his solo career in 1976 with the first of three self-titled albums. Produced by Bob Ezrin, the high point of the debut is the celebratory single "Solsbury Hill," a messianic fantasy with an indelible melody that some saw as his comment about leaving Genesis, as well as the sequel to "Supper's Ready." The 1978 follow-up was produced by Robert Fripp, and it's a darker, sparer effort that pays tribute (not uncharacteristic, as noted earlier) to the Punk aesthetic on the tune "D.I.Y." But the singer's best post-Genesis album is the third *Peter Gabriel*, produced by Steve Lillywhite and released in 1980. Working with Kate Bush, XTC's Dave Gregory, Robert Fripp, and bassist Tony Levin, among others, Gabriel focused on the rhythms (he was, after all, a former drummer) and his vocals, using the other instruments to add color, texture, or the odd instrumental hook. Over tribal, cymbal-less, pseudo-African grooves, he delivers ten vignettes that explore the minds of a presidential assassin ("Family Snapshot"), a burglar/home invader ("Intruder"), and an imprisoned mental patient ("Lead A Normal Life"); clearly, role-playing was something he didn't leave behind with Genesis, even if science fiction was.

Gabriel's subsequent efforts offer increasingly less satisfying variations on these formulas, incorporating ethnic instruments and more elaborate beats, or streamlining the production for MTV-friendly dance tunes. Late-eighties and early-nineties hits such as "Sledgehammer" and "Steam" changed his status from Art rocker to Pop celebrity, but he continued to experiment with more ethereal sounds on soundtracks such as *Birdy* and *The Last Temptation of Christ*. He championed worthy artists from around the world, his live shows consistently set new standards for what was possible in the enormodomes, and he made a welcome return to form after a ten year wait with 2002's *Up*, even if he's pretty much calcified since.

The artist doesn't talk much about the songs he wrote with Genesis, and it's unlikely that "Harold the Barrel" ever will turn up on his set list again. But he is often pressed on the issue of reuniting with his old mates, and he generally dodges the question, much as they do. "In a way, you want to hang on to a moment that has come and gone," he told *Rolling Stone* in the fall of 2011. "And you may be able to bring back a lot of memories of that moment, but you are no longer in that moment—and nor are the other ones."

As for the other ones, after Collins famously came out from behind the drums to lead the band as vocalist, they crafted two strong but much more predictable albums, their purest if least inspired examples of Progressive Rock: the raucous A *Trick of the Tail* in 1976, and the more pastoral *Wind & Wuthering* in 1977. From there, Genesis followed a slow but steady decline into ever more stultifying mediocrity. Hackett left the group after *Wind & Wuthering*, and it slowly but surely became a vehicle for platinum-selling easy-listening hits such as "Misunderstanding," "Mama," "Invisible Touch," and "Land of Confusion." And let's not even venture near most of Collins' solo output, nor that of any of the others. (GTR? Really, Steve?)

Still, the magic of the band in the early seventies endures for many of us, and we make no apologies about saying that, even if we grimace at the mere mention of anything post-1981. In 1991, the year Punk broke (again) courtesy of Nirvana, I jumped at the opportunity to interview Banks, Rutherford, and Collins upon the occasion of what was then their first album in five years, the almost overwhelmingly dreadful *We Can't Dance*, for the late and lamented *Request* magazine. This was in the midst of my honeymoon, no less—the marriage, needless to say, did not last—yet such was my burning desire, not to meet the heroes of my own teen years (even twenty-one years ago, I was much too cynical and too professional to be susceptible to that sort of thing), but to probe the mystery of how they became what they'd become, if they at all regretted straying so far from what I and many others considered their ideal, and if they offered any glimmer of passion still for what they'd accomplished before they turned into what the first-wave punks wrongly derided them as: a soulless, corporate music machine.

Sitting in the presidential suite at New York's haughty Peninsula Hotel, the boys spewed a lot of the sorts of things that famous rich rock stars of their generation always say when interviewed on the downward slope of their careers. They maintained that no, they were not chagrined to still be making rock music as middle-aged men (they were forty and forty-one at the time), and that they saw no reason not to continue doing so indefinitely. They insisted that the many solo albums they'd each churned out had in fact been good for the band, with all of them bringing fresh perspectives back to the group after those detours. They asserted that they were happier than they'd ever been when they reconvened to add another hopefully lucrative entry to their long discography, and that they were eager to play these great new songs on the inevitable and hopefully even more lucrative tour to follow.

I could not bring myself to ask them how they'd felt when doing those pathetic dance moves for the video of the title track. But frustrated by the banality of our chat, I did near the end of our allotted time work up the courage to pose my big question, the only one I really wanted answered: did they ever wish they could record under a different name, lock themselves in a studio, get really stoned, and cut loose to make another album as willfully weird, wonderfully fucked-up, and purely brilliant as *The Lamb Lies Down On Broadway?*

"I suppose if one was doing that, one would probably try to be more off the wall," Banks said wistfully, transformed for a moment into the teenage geek jamming in the cottage in Dorking. "I think the sheer reason for doing it would surely be to try to do a few things that might be disastrous."

"At the same time, it might be nice to do something like we've just done and call it a different name and see how it's received," Collins added with more than a touch of bristling agitation. "By saying that, you're playing into—what's your name?—Jim's hands, because you're admitting that, because we're going in and calling it a different band, we actually have confines within Genesis that we want to stick to!"

"Well that's a fair enough comment to make," Banks said, scowling at his partner. "Because there's probably some truth in it."

Show me the man in his mid-sixties who won't admit that, in many ways, those slightly embarrassing years in his early twenties also were perhaps the best of his life, and I'll show you a liar, or someone delusional enough to think "Sussudio" is as good a song as "The Return of the Giant Hogweed."

Jim DeRogatis teaches "Reviewing the Arts" and "Journalism as Literature" at Columbia College Chicago. He has written nine books about music, continues to critique new sounds on his blog at WBEZ.org, and co-hosts Sound Opinions, "the world's only rock 'n' roll talk show," which can be heard nationally on Public Radio or podcast at soundopinions.org.

The Grand Parade Of Lifeless Packaging
by James Greer

A few items of interest about the album by Genesis called The Lamb Lies Down On Broadway *as it relates or does not relate to the music of Dayton, Ohio indie rock luminaries Guided By Voices*

1.

SOMEBODY WROTE A WHOLE book about one album (*Genesis and The Lamb Lies Down On Broadway* by Kevin Holm-Hudson; Ashgate, 2008).

2. The book retails for $31.50.

3. You can buy the remastered version of the original album on two CDs for $11.99 online.

4. There exists on the internet a fan-sourced *Annotated Lamb Lies Down On Broadway*. I will be cribbing heavily from this.

5. It's not a particularly well-kept secret that Robert Pollard, the songwriter/gang leader of Guided By Voices (of which I was once a member), is a Prog Rock fan. He's said as much in any number of interviews, back when he used to give interviews. When pressed to compile a top-ten-albums-of-all-time listicle, as indie rock luminaries are often asked to do, an album by Genesis inevitably makes the cut alongside more expected works by Wire, the Beatles, The Who, Cheap Trick, and Alice Cooper. Prog Rock is one of the four pillars of Pollard's core aesthetic: Pop, Prog, Punk, and Psych, not necessarily in that order, but always those four; and those four are always in evidence in his songwriting.

The Genesis album that usually makes his cut is *Selling England By The Pound*, but that's not the one, in my opinion, that left its deepest mark on Pollard's psyche.

The Lamb Lies Down On Broadway was released on Virgin Records in 1974 when Bob was twenty years old. Though by no means the first concept album, it has over time become one of the better known examples of that benighted genre, and fittingly so: it's also one of the best. Despite the fact that it was Peter Gabriel's swan song with the band he started seven years earlier in 1967 (though which had really only found its footing in 1971 with *Nursery Cryme*) it represents an almost perfect blend of the band's complex but melodic song structures with Gabriel's out-there lyrical constructs and his even more out-there visual/theatrical/conceptual mojo.

6. From the actual 1974 *Lamb Lies Down On Broadway* Tour Program: "Back in the late sixties Progressive music seemed all but dead, barely kept alive by the faint spark of a lingering Mellotron. Rock audiences had overdosed on loud psychedelic riffs and gentle acoustic flower-power tunes, wondering all the time if there was anything more to Progressive music than strobe lights, incense, and the odd synthesizer. Just when adventurous rock seemed forever moving backward, Genesis began flirting with multimedia concepts. The sixties had taken rock music through a natural evolution where technical equipment and musical proficiency had been developed to its sophisticated best. The obvious goal for forward moving seventies rock bands then, was to fuse the two together in a working relationship where music, words, lights, and visuals would ideally come together forming a unified whole."

Note the use of the word "multimedia" in 1974. Also the use of the phrase "back in the late sixties" in 1974. Note also that this frank promotional copy defines Progressive Rock by what it is not, or at least not anymore, than by what it is. "Technical equipment and musical proficiency" don't really help narrow the gap between the Beatles and Yes.

7. "The first Genesis record I got was *Genesis Live*, actually. I was rummaging through the cut-out bins and what attracted me was the cover. Peter Gabriel's costumes. Just the weird imagery, and the strange titles. When I first listened to it I didn't understand it. The songs were too long, the structure's too complicated. But the important thing was that they were melodic. They had great melodies. As long as the melodies are there, you can allow yourself time for them to grow on you."

–Robert Pollard, August 2012

8. Pollard has a nearly eidetic memory for lyrics, melodies, song titles, band members, cover art, release dates...in essence, anything

and everything to do with rock and its ephemera. If you hear an old Pop song on the radio—say from the sixties, and you can't remember who wrote and/or performed it or maybe you never even heard it before, because it's that obscure—call up Bob Pollard and sing two bars of any portion of the song and he'll identify the performer and the song immediately. This has never failed. It's uncanny, really.

9. From the *Annotated Lamb Lies Down On Broadway* by Jason Finegan, Scott McMahan, and other members of Paperlate (a Genesis discussion group):

> "One of the most frequently asked questions by any Genesis fan is 'What is the *Lamb* about?' Most people are baffled by the subject-matter of the *Lamb*, since it is one of the most dense and obfuscated works of art ever created.
>
> "I think it is a mistake to think the *Lamb* is 'about' something, especially about one particular thing, and to think there is some correct answer to the question that starts 'the *Lamb* is about...' and goes on with a single 'true' answer. (I would also advise you to be wary of people who claim to have a one true answer to the question, because they are probably missing a lot.) *The Lamb Lies Down On Broadway* is something that every listener must decide a personal meaning that satisfies as an explanation.
>
> "But, it is not enough to just listen to the *Lamb* and try to puzzle it out. This is an "annotation," not an end in itself. It does not give you an explanation of what the *Lamb* is about. It does, however, arm you with the tools you need to form your own ideas. The *Lamb* is packed solid with some of the most obscure literary and cultural references, things that all of which even a well-read and well-educated person would probably not have encountered."

10. Some of the obscure literary and cultural references unpacked in the *Annotated Lamb*: Shakespeare's *King Lear*, Leonard Cohen's "Suzanne," Andy Warhol, Lenny Bruce, Marshall McLuhan, Ho-

mer's *Odyssey*, Howard Hughes, "Runaway" by Del Shannon, John Lennon, Superman, Lilith, John Keats' *The Lamia*, William Wordsworth.

11. "You didn't get turned on in Dayton, you had to turn yourself on. It was musical masturbation. I was fifteen when I first listened to Genesis, and I think that's the age when your musical taste kind of gets set. Maybe if I'd encountered Genesis at a different age, I wouldn't have been into them as much.

In the lo-fi period, we were the anti-Genesis. We were Prog but we separated it into fragments. They just practiced a lot harder than we did. [The 1992 Guided By Voices record] *Propeller* was originally supposed to be one long song on the first side, but we practiced it and after about ten minutes it would fall apart, so I said fuck it, let's just break it up into separate songs."

—Robert Pollard, August 2012

12. You could make the argument that every Guided By Voices album is a concept album. However fractured the production/ arrangement, or however variously recorded or however ineptly/ expertly played, the songs are always the result of a fairly brief and intense period of songwriting, and so reflects a particular and particularly consistent frame of mind, if not an actual framing concept.

In 1995 we tried to make an actual concept album, called *The Power of Suck*, which was meant to be a semi-autobiographical double album, for which I wrote a story (borrowing more from *Quadrophenia* than from *The Lamb Lies Down On Broadway*, but that's because I was more influenced by/familiar with *Quadrophenia*). Pollard recorded an initial batch of twelve demos, which swelled pretty quickly to twenty-two, then thirty, and we had gotten to the stage of regularly practicing the songs and uncharacteristically working on the arrangements, no evidence of which remains. Bob had even printed out the lyrics and the song sequence that fit the concept (in essence: band from nowhere, despised in their hometown, suddenly hits the big time, is tempted but refuses to compromise, returns home sadder but wiser, etc.). But then one night he smoked a bunch of pot and decided that the lyrics "made too much sense" (I still remember those exact words), and thus rewrote all the lyrics so that they didn't make sense, and cut a bunch of the songs that were too direct and personal, replacing them with songs/lyrics that were no less engaging but featured much less accessible imagery.

The Power Of Suck never did get made, although it exists in freely circulated fan bootlegs which are problematic not just for their dub-of-a-dub-of-a-dub sound quality but because there never was one definitive Power Of Suck track listing, so any re-creation is proximal at best. It also shrunk from a double to a single album, which was released eventually as Under The Bushes, Under The Stars, and is still one of the band's finest albums, according to people who are me.

Shards of Power Of Suck remain on UTBUTS, and these are, I think, particularly reflective of Bob's Prog leanings. "The Official Ironmen Rally Song," "Cocksoldiers and Their Postwar Stubble," "Here Comes the Supernatural Anaesthetist," "Burning Flag Birthday Suit," "The Colony of Slippermen." Two of those titles were from Lamb Lies Down On Broadway, but that's my point, in part.

> "I was heavily influenced by [Gabriel's] titles and his imagery and his word play," says Pollard. "It's pure escapism, and I love escapism. Really, for me it's just an extension of the Beatles' stuff that I liked best, the surrealism of 'Happiness Is A Warm Gun.' That's a Prog song. 'I Am The Walrus' is Prog. I understand why when Punk came along the Punk bands hated Prog Rock. You have a tendency to like what you're able to do. For me, I like good songs. I don't care about genre. Genesis was a Pop band, they were actually very poppy."

13. Peter Gabriel: "There's an art to [writing Pop songs]. I always thought the melody of 'Carpet Crawlers' [from Lamb] was one of the choicest things I'd written. To me, that was a Pop song."

14. I use the example of The Power Of Suck/Under The Bushes, Under The Stars because I have direct firsthand experience with the process by which it fell apart/came about. But parallels to Gabriel-era Genesis' titles, imagery, and wordplay are not difficult to find in the work of a band whose Greatest Hits collection is called Human Amusements At Hourly Rates. One listen to the shape-shifting "Over

the Neptune/Mesh Gear Fox" from the aforementioned *Propeller* (1992) will convince anyone of Pollard's Prog bona fides, but really, in a recorded output now numbering into the thousands of songs over thirty years, it's hard to find titles/imagery/lyrics that aren't at least partially and indirectly related to the Genesis wellspring, but see entry eight and you'll realize that it's not just Genesis, it's more or less everything Pollard has stored in his nigh-infallible rock memory, all mashed together and stitched up any which way, performed off-handedly, recorded indifferently, released unendingly in a torrent (pre-internet sense) that nearly defies belief.

The reunited Guided By Voices released three albums in 2012 alone, and Pollard wrote and recorded two solo albums while putting together a double-disc retrospective of one of his higher profile post-GBV projects, Boston Spaceships.

In an output that vast, that all-encompassing, you can pretty much find anything you want to find, including traces of sixties British freakbeat, eighties American indie and post-Punk (especially Homestead/SST mainstays like Dinosaur Jr., Sonic Youth, Hüsker Dü, etc.) alt-touchstones R.E.M. and The Replacements, early Bee Gees, The Turtles, this new band called Flight—now I'm basically just listing the records he played the last time I was at his house, but you get the idea.

15. Peter Gabriel quit Genesis somewhere during the *Lamb* tour, but stuck it out until the end. He then put out a press release entitled "Out, Angels Out—An Investigation," wherein he explained that: "The vehicle we had built as a co-op to serve our songwriting became our master and had cooped us up inside the success we had wanted. It affected the attitudes and the spirit of the whole band. The music had not dried up and I still respect the other musicians, but our roles had set in hard." As most people probably know, Genesis carried on without him, drummer Phil Collins subbing as lead vocalist for the next record, *A Trick of the Tail*.

16. "I didn't even know Peter Gabriel had quit," says Pollard. "It sounded exactly the same. I think that tends to happen when people are in a band together for a long time. [Guitarist and frequent songwriting contributor] Toby [Sprout] and I sometimes sound alike. It's inevitable."

17. I'm not sure that's true.

18. When Pollard broke up Guided By Voices in 2004, he asked me to write the press release announcing the move. It was not called "Out, Angels Out," although if I had been aware of that title at the time I would have been tempted to recycle it. Instead, I wrote (in part):

> "Here is the last Guided By Voices album. If it's true in movies where the voice-over says 'You never really appreciate something until it's gone,' and the credits roll, and you leave the theater with little bits of popcorn stuck to your shoes, then you will soon appreciate Guided By Voices. Because following this album and its ensuing tour, the band will be gone. After twenty-odd years, twenty-odd lineups, and twenty-odd albums, EPs, singles, triples, stolen bases, misdemeanor convictions, and broken hearts, Dayton, OH's fortunate sons are taking leave of your senses."

I then quoted Pollard as saying: "I need to get back to a lack of professionalism where there's a certain degree of awkwardness."

19. Peter Gabriel, "Out, Angels Out" press release: "For any band, transferring the heart from idealistic enthusiasm to professionalism is a difficult operation."

20. The first song on the current Guided By Voices record is called "King Arthur the Red."

James Greer is the author of the novels Artificial Light *(Akashic, 2006) and* The Failure *(Akashic, 2010), and the nonfiction book* Guided By Voices: A Brief History *(Grove, 2005), a biography of a band for which he played bass guitar. His new band is called* Détective.

The Satori Underground

by John Albert

Anything that can be done chemically can be done by other means.
—William S. Burroughs

I F THE PROGRESSIVE ROCK band King Crimson conveyed a sense of epic grandeur and complexity, on that November morning in 1981 my friend Dwight and I were at the opposite end of the universe. We were both sixteen years old, standing in a fenced patch of cracked dirt and tumbleweeds in the backyard of his mom's home on the edge of the Southern California desert. He was tall and black and I was white and blond. The sun was burning bright and we were each wearing tattered thrift store suits.

The neighborhood was a cheap approximation of the suburban dream—a cheaply constructed stucco slum for the working poor fleeing nearby Los Angeles. An area towards the back was unofficially designated for blacks and so that's where Dwight and his single mother Rosa were living. It was also where I was temporarily staying, having run away from my parent's tree-shaded and book-filled home. Like so many restless middle-class teenagers, I had rejected a world of comfort for hard drugs and a thrilling sense of downward mobility. Dwight and I had met our first year of high school, bonding over Punk music, drugs, and vandalism.

We were looking across a barren field towards a small bar attached to a bowling alley. There were several choppers parked outside, one draped with a leather jacket adorned with a patch reading "Devils Disciples MC, Southern Cal."

"You can get it," Dee told me. "You're fast. I have complete confidence."

"Those Vikings would lasso me with a chain before I got halfway back," I replied.

"That jacket's worth a few hundred at some shop on Melrose."

"Then you fucking do it."

"Always trying to get the black man to do your dirty work," he said with a laugh, taking a hit off a joint and passing it to me.

DWIGHT REACHED DOWN AND pressed play on his battered ghetto blaster. The futuristic sound of the David Bowie song "Heroes" filled the little yard. "Heroes" is the title song from Bowie's 1977 album of the same name. Recorded in Berlin it features a stark and atmospheric sound created by Bowie and co-writer Brian Eno. The sonic centerpiece of the song is a dissonant guitar played by Robert Fripp, a founding member of the aforementioned King Crimson.

Neither Dwight nor I were fans of King Crimson nor any other Progressive Rock bands. When Punk came along, my pot smoking skateboarding friends and I, like a cadre of rock Maoists, had obliterated the past in order to rewrite our musical landscape. Taking a cue from Sex Pistols singer Johnny Rotten, who had marched through London in a homemade "I hate Pink Floyd" shirt, we rejected previously cherished bands like Led Zeppelin as irrelevant dinosaurs while Prog Rock practitioners like Yes became objects of outright derision.

Yet we continued to revere David Bowie. While his signature glitter albums predated and influenced Punk, his subsequent Berlin-era records *Low*, *Heroes*, and *Lodger* helped usher in the post-Punk movement that more perfectly mirrored our personal descents into teenage nihilism. This was relevant because Fripp and Adrian Belew, another guitarist who played on Bowie's album *Lodger* and with Bowie's band during the *Stage* tour of 1978, were scheduled to perform that November night in 1981 with a reformed version of King Crimson. Dwight and I planned to go.

The closest I had come to seeing a Prog Rock show before that had been when a bunch of my prepubescent friends had stolen some wine and gone to see a screening of the Yes concert film *Yessongs*. After consuming a bottle concealed in my jacket, I had loudly addressed the theater full of hippies, accusing the band's cape-adorned keyboardist Rick Wakeman of being a warlock. Why I thought that was news to anyone can only be attributed to the pilfered Zinfandel. After another outburst regarding Yes singer Jon Anderson being a eunuch, we were thrown out as the surrounding long hairs applauded. But at the advanced age of sixteen, we were doing everything possible to distance ourselves from any such youthful exuberance. For some inexplicable reason we wanted desperately to be old and jaded. Instead of skateboarding we had started injecting heroin and dressing like middle-aged criminals from some nonexistent European city.

As we drove to the city in his mom's Chevy Camero, Dwight slipped in a cassette of Brian Eno's album *Here Come The Warm Jets*. The mix of theatrical Glitter Rock and dissonant futurism merged perfectly with the scenes outside as the desert turned to suburbia and then the lights and chaos of Hollywood. Back then the intersection of Hollywood and Western was a bustling outdoor market of drugs and prostitution. We slowed to survey the scene. The song playing was "Baby's On Fire," a tension filled track where Eno sings in a mocking sneer accompanied by a beautifully violent guitar solo from Robert Fripp.

"That's my dad," Dwight said, looking out the window.

I spotted a tall forty-something African American man standing on the corner wearing a white captain's hat.

"Are you serious?" I asked.

"Yeah."

Years later I would find out that Dwight's mom had lived in constant fear that her son would some day reconnect with his career criminal father, anticipating the pull his presence might have on her gifted but troubled son. We parked and walked to where his dad was standing. The two greeted one another with smiles. Dwight introduced us.

"So what you young men doing out here in Hollywood?" His father asked.

"Going to Pasadena and seeing a band—was looking to go downtown first," Dwight answered, using an old term for heroin.

"Ain't none around here," his dad answered. "Maybe over on the Eastside—I'll take a ride with you if you want, but I can't guarantee we'll find anything."

"You got anything else?" Dwight asked.

"Got some loads—doors and fours."

"They're pills, right?" Dwight asked, disappointed.

"Put your head in your chest better than the strongest her-ron," his father said, putting a hand on Dwight's shoulder. "I wouldn't steer you wrong, son."

A HALF AN HOUR later, Dwight and I were in a park across the street from Perkin's Palace in Pasadena. The old theater's marquee read

"King Crimson" with the band member's names—Adrian Belew, Bill Bruford, Robert Fripp, Tony Levin—spelled out below. We washed down the pills with a can of Pepsi and watched the crowd. The people filing in were worlds apart from the jaded black clad Hollywood scene we were used to. They appeared to be a mix of serious musicians and aging hippies. Having neither tickets nor money, we walked around to the back door of the theater and asked for Dennis. Dennis was a part-time bouncer I knew from my parent's neighborhood. A long-haired giant with a bushy beard, Dennis had a metal plate in his head from a botched suicide attempt. That night he smiled and let us in, teasing that we were finally going to hear some "real" music. A year later he would promise to kill me, thinking incorrectly that I had burglarized his house—but Dennis would overdose before he could make good on that promise.

Dwight and I stood in front of the stage and waited for both the band and the pills to take effect. The band arrived first. The houselights dimmed and four musicians strolled out looking like New Wave college professors. They took their places and began the song "Frippertronics." Accustomed to the bombast of Hard Rock and the aggression of Punk, the complex Math rock was foreign to me. While the rest of the audience appeared to marvel at the musicianship on display, Dwight and I were lost. It felt more like an academic presentation than a performance.

But like the pills we had recently swallowed, the effect of King Crimson took a while to kick in. As the synthetic warmth of the drugs began to spread throughout our teenage bodies, the group launched into a song called "Satori In Tangier." They were suddenly playing with a newfound urgency, drums and bass propelling the song with a jagged tension. After a minute or so, Robert Fripp let loose with a solo unlike any guitar I had ever heard. It was a frantic and beautifully evocative wall of noise that conveyed both an otherworldly exoticism and profound sense of yearning over the band's energetic rhythms. I looked over and saw Dwight doing a herky-jerky New Wave-like dance resembling one of the twisting suit and tie characters from artist Robert Longo's "Men in the Cities" series. I remember laughing and then closing my eyes.

When I eventually woke up, Dwight was driving the car back into the desert as the sun rose. I remember thinking that he looked old in his suit, staring out at the road with heavy-lidded eyes. I faded out again and when I regained consciousness it was the afternoon and I was in Dwight's mom's house. I wandered into the backyard. Dwight was sitting in a lawn chair holding a guitar. His six year old brother Selino was next to him listening as his big brother played the David Bowie song "Heroes," singing the words in a raspy whisper: "We can beat them—for ever and ever, we can be heroes—just for one day."

Dwight died just a few years later. As his mother had feared, he returned to Hollywood and reconnected with his father. The two had lived with a roving band of thieves, dealers, and prostitutes in the motels around Hollywood while his dad schooled him in the criminal life. The afternoon of his death, Dwight was sharing a jail cell with his dad. Both of them were facing separate life sentences for different drug-related murders. At twenty-one years old, Dwight took a rope he had constructed out of bed sheets and climbed out an eleventh story window. He lost his grip and slipped away.

Decades after that, I was riding through Los Angeles in the back of a sleek Mercedes with a famous and rich rock star I was interviewing. As we drove into the Hollywood hills, he put on the King Crimson album *In the Court of the Crimson King*. The epic music played loudly and I began to think about the band and then my friend. In the silence between songs, the rock star had looked at the lights below and asked if I had grown up in Los Angeles. I told him I had.

John Albert grew up in Los Angeles. He has written for the Los Angeles Times, LA Weekly, Fader, Black Book *and others, winning several journalism awards. His essays have appeared in numerous national literary anthologies. The film rights to his book* Wrecking Crew *(Scribner) have been optioned four times, most recently by the esteemed actor Philip Seymour Hoffman. As a teenager he co-founded the seminal "Death Rock" band Christian Death and then played drums for a stint in Bad Religion.*

A Clockwork Wall

by Rodrigo Fresán

Translated from the Spanish by Mara Lethem

Pink, Alex, and The Show Must Go On

1

IN HIS LATEST BOOK—AN anthology of his essays titled *Otherwise Known As The Human Condition*—the always ingenious and often genius Geoff Dyer discusses his experience seeing and hearing the rock group Def Leppard live.

In the essay, Dyer says something very intelligent that you always think but never write down: rock concerts are pure anticipation, and once the band or soloist comes on stage with an electric burst "nothing that happens subsequently can live up to those opening moments when all the power suddenly erupts, and you are, emphatically, no longer waiting for something to begin. Pretty soon, though, you are waiting for it to end."

Dyer's right: it happened to me recently with Arcade Fire. I went to the Canadian band's tour for *The Suburbs* in Barcelona and, by the third song, I was only thinking about getting out of there and getting back home as fast as I could, perhaps to put on *The Suburbs* by Arcade Fire. I held out a little longer, but I left by the fifth song, happy to have gone and happy to be leaving. As if it were one of those parties or meetings or presentations that you attend as part of an obligation to your present or your past and, please, let the future, the exit, come quickly.[1] Arcade Fire isn't Def Leppard. But, obviously, Arcade Fire isn't Pink Floyd either.

And Arcade Fire is not, and will never be, Roger Waters performing *The Wall*, in a concert in Barcelona for which, happy with anticipation, I bought tickets so many months ago. The very first song makes an allusion to that feeling Dyer describes: "To feel the warm thrill of confusion / That space cadet glow." It's what we feel when the lights go out and the music comes up those few brief seconds that aspire to immortality. Or something close to orgasm.

1   The true social/psychological utility of every rock concert (and of its glorified, epic mega-mutation that is the rock festival) is, during puberty and adolescence, getting out of your parents' house. Once you've moved out, it loses a lot of its charm and usefulness, in my opinion.

But, of course, Pink Floyd and *The Wall* are something else. They are the idealized memory of an orgasm. They are important twists and turns and spirals in my musical DNA. They are defining and definitive bricks holding up the structure of a wall whose construction began so long ago.

2

AROUND THE TIME OF the Barcelona Arcade Fire concert, I was asked to write something about the anniversary (yet another anniversary) of the Argentine coup d'état and I remembered *I Remember* by Joe Brainard. And, since then, I can't stop adding to the things "I remember..." about those years. One on top of another. Once again: like bricks in a wall.

I remember—as I read *A Clockwork Orange* by Anthony Burgess—the first time I heard "Another Brick in the Wall, Part 2," in Viedma, in the province of Río Negro, Argentina, where the end of the world began, in late 1979, on the loudspeakers of a record store whose sound ascended to the bed of my Patagonian siesta, rising like a rare, exotic fever, and I remember thinking, "What is that? Disco music? And those guys shouting, 'We don't need no education'? Where did they come from? Where are they going? What time is it?"

Whatever *it* was, *it* was soon number one all over the world including Argentina, where the censors of the time must have been hypnotized by ABBA's "Chiquitita" (the wall of involuntary military Pop hits was completed by "Give a Little Bit" and "The Logical Song" by Supertramp and "Last Train to London" by Electric Light Orchestra and "Don't Stop" by Fleetwood Mac and that ridiculous track by Genesis with its ominous, paranoid title, "Follow You, Follow Me.") And, it seems, they didn't catch what was being proclaimed there, in the voice of an anarchist kid who had already breakfasted on clockwork orange juice. Because, clearly, Young Pink in *The Wall* heralds Alex in *A Clockwork Orange*, even as he is his chronological descendant.

Alex the droog of Burgess's novel and Stanley Kubrick's film presages the führer Pink of the album. With one noteworthy difference: Alex goes out on the streets, while Pink stays in his hotel room. But both end up "cured" by a necessary "education."

A *Clockwork Orange* is the most "rocker" book and the novel that
has most influenced the Pop universe, although in its film version
there is no trace of feedback or distortion (but rather synthesized
Beethoven and Gene Kelly steps for stomping on old folks). Burgess's book—sketched out in 1960 when its author was erroneously
informed that he had a brain tumor and had begun a very short
countdown to the other side—was one of the six novels the British
author completed at breakneck speed in order to leave something
to his wife, who in 1944 had been attacked in the street by a band
of AWOL American soldiers, causing her to miscarry. The first version was contemporary, suffused with the teenage slang of the moment, and Burgess knew that it would age quickly.

Then he decided to move everything into the future: he in-
vented a language/dialect called Nadsat using parts of Russian and
Cockney, in order to be modern and "ultraviolent." It didn't fare
well with critics when published in 1962 (it is also Burgess's least
favorite of his novels, and he would later disdain the film adaptation while never denying his gratitude for the international fame
and material comfort that it brought him). But young readers took
to *A Clockwork Orange*. The then newly formed band The Rolling
Stones considered filming it (can you imagine a better droog than
a young Keith Richards?), but it never went anywhere. Over time,
Stanley Kubrick sensed that the book offered him his only possible
next step. After having destroyed the world in *Dr. Strangelove* and
having chronicled the beginning and the end of history in *2001: A
Space Odyssey*, *A Clockwork Orange* was a defense of the modern and
a death knell for the hippie dream.

Kubrick's cancerous film debuted in 1971, almost like a coda to
the end of the Age of Aquarius, or as an effective and dramatic pro-
logue to an infamous decade: in its shadow, the politically correct
of the time argued, murders, rapes and various crimes were commit-
ted. The kids were not alright and they left movie theaters dressed
up as droogs and did what kids will do. The negative coverage led
to death threats for Kubrick and his family until he himself decided
to take the monster out of theaters, ban it, lock himself away. So
A Clockwork Orange became some sort of final original gesture by
a man who, from then on, made cleverly encrypted self-remakes:
the historical drama *Barry Lyndon* as a revisiting of *Spartacus*; the

hotel claustrophobia of *The Shining* as a distant reflection of the lockdown in the control room of *Dr. Strangelove*; the imbecilic war of *Full Metal Jacket* marching to supplant the other imbecilic war of *Paths of Glory*; and the nocturnal comings and goings of *Eyes Wide Shut* as a sexualized, decadent, and post Humbert-Humbertian echo of Alex's sleepwalking wanderings in *A Clockwork Orange*.

But perhaps most important is that *A Clockwork Orange* begins to narrate what 1979's *The Wall* completes in song.[2] Pure teenage wasteland. Tribal, criminal Alex, whose violence ends up being assimilated by society through brain and pupil washing—the Ludovico technique—as a symbol of the guerrilla and disco-Watergate seventies that would culminate in lonely, solipsistic Pink of *The Wall* as the perfect portent to the soulless eighties, where there are no longer social battles to be waged and just watching television long enough can justify throwing the damn set out the window of your hotel suite.

Sex, droogs, and rock and roll.[3]

2   And for all those for whom a Pink Floyd/Stanley Kubrick axis looks and sounds a bit gratuitous and far-fetched, it's worth mentioning a little-known fact found in Mark Blake's biography of the band, *Pigs Might Fly: The Inside Story of Pink Floyd* (2007). Stanley Kubrick got in touch with Pink Floyd about using their *Atom Heart Mother* (1970)—that totemic cow on the cover, those milk bars that Alex frequents—as part of the soundtrack for *A Clockwork Orange*. Which would make Pink Floyd's music the mutant sound inside Alex's head. The band initially agreed but withdrew their authorization when they learned that Kubrick would cut and edit their music at whim. The film director took his revenge when, years later, Waters contacted him to use dialogue from *2001: A Space Odyssey* in his *Amused to Death* (1992). Kubrick said no and Waters sent him a barely audible cryptic message in "Perfect Sense, Part 1."

3   A paradox: the one who suffers most in *A Clockwork Orange* is Alex. He has some fun at the beginning, but he is soon enthusiastically beaten by Mr. Alexander's bodyguard (played by a tall, muscular actor who later would find anonymous fame beneath Darth Vader's costume [which Pink would so envy as he waits for the worms] in the first three *Star Wars* films) and subjected to a readaptation process that I certainly wouldn't volunteer for. The actor Malcolm McDowell still has nightmares remembering Kubrick's compulsion to shoot each scene a hundred times (which, for him, meant damaged corneas, broken ribs, and getting his young, resigned face spit at hundreds of times so Stanley could get the gob in the perfect spot and angle on the hero's upper lip). As for the subject of ultraviolence, McDowell maintains that his work was a service to society, since: "If they [juvenile delinquents] did do that, if they dressed like Alex, the police would know where to find them. I mean, in a codpiece and a bowler?" The central moment and most terrible point in the story is Alex's re-encounter with his gang and the discovery that they have switched their white coveralls,

3

I REMEMBER THE FIRST time I saw the video for "Another Brick in the Wall, Part 2": on the ATC channel, which was still broadcast in black and white, as part of the program *Música Total*, the Argentine version of MTV.

Chaplinesque hats, and fake noses for police uniforms. Roger Waters—indisputable creative force behind Pink Floyd after the disputable Syd Barrett fried his brain in LSD oil—must have felt something similar when the collapse of the Big Wall translated into the collapse of Pink Floyd as a group entity. From that point on, Pink Floyd became merely the backup band to Waters' most intimate obsessions, which would continue in that lovely, almost unplugged coda that was *The Final Cut*, where the war over a few little islands in the South Atlantic was the backdrop on which to again project and cry over the death of a father in World War II. It could be argued that Waters was partly right; *The Wall*—chosen by the band instead of another project that would become *The Pros and Cons of Hitchhiking* (1984) with Waters already solo—is one of the bestselling albums in history and more than paid off for the quartet.

Looking beyond the years, the scandals and the fights, *A Clockwork Orange* and *The Wall* continue functioning with the timeliness of powerful, influential creations. Kubrick's film not only stuck in rocker consciousness (from the birth of technopop by Cabaret Voltaire and The Human League anticipated by the music of then Walter and now Wendy Carlos to the attitude of the Sex Pistols, who also considered re-filming it; from Blur's video for the song "The Universal" to the name Heaven 17, a band mentioned by Burgess in his book; not to mention the quite Floydian musical adaptation done by Bono and The Edge for the theater, that virtual *The Dark Side of the Wall* that is OK Computer by Radiohead and all those little bands that still today are writing songs in Nadsat slang) but spawned an entire aesthetic of ultraviolent cinema: the gang rage in *The Warriors*, the amphetamine-fueled desperation of *Quadrophenia*, the violence as leisure activity of *Natural Born Killers*, the idea that one can dance and cut off an ear at the same time in *Reservoir Dogs*, the way *Trainspotting* is set to music and the bored angst of *Fight Club* come—with much more desire to shock and much less elegance—from the segments of an orange that may never stop peeling and from a constantly growing wall. British violence today has far exceeded the anticipatory rage of *A Clockwork Orange*, for the simple fact that Kubrick's film was, even then, fake futurism in order to talk about, unhindered, what was going to happen the next weekend. As for the Pink Floyd album—a moral fable on the dangers and privileges of messianic rock—it came to life in idols who rose and fell or decided to check out: Prince, Kurt Cobain, Mick Jagger, Michael Jackson, Peter Gabriel, Bruce Springsteen, Sting, Billy Corgan, Bono, the heroin-addicted and paranoid-delusional alternative John Lennon as depicted by Albert Goldman, and, of course, the list continues to grow. They were all a little bit like Pink when they erected the bricks of a public and private religion that sooner or later came down—or will come down—around them. It doesn't much matter that some of them end up "cured" like Alex and Pink: outside the wall where "the bleeding hearts and artist make their stand."

I remember going to buy *The Wall*—that sonic compendium with a place for everything, from paranoid folk and politically incorrect protest songs to symphonic Punk—and thinking: "This is another 'White Album' (white cover with grid and that label handwritten by *The Wall's* cover artist Gerald Scarfe) with a unifying concept, polymorphous and perverse." But, unlike the album by the Beatles, who were at that point concerned with not being or no longer being the Beatles, *The Wall* is a "White Album" where all genres are filtered through the sieve of what is known as the "Pink Floyd Sound." Something that begins and ends in itself because...what genre does Pink Floyd belong to? Answer: the Pink Floyd genre. Pink Floyd is the only dinosaur that Punk couldn't exterminate because, in its way, Pink Floyd—see the incendiary and anti-establishment *Animals*—was much more Punk than any Punk. *No Future*, for sure. But also *No Present* and *No Past*.

4

THE WALL IS THE definitive expression of enlightened existentialist rock. There the great howler Waters (that air of sophisticated caveman would make him the perfect Mr. Hyde if Richard Gere would ever decide to play Dr. Jekyll) imagined a concept and a Wall.

That which separates the artist from his followers.

Roger Waters tells—in the sixty-four-page book that accompanies *Is There Anybody Out There?/The Wall Live 1980-1981*, a recording of the original tour of *The Wall* released in 2000—that his sudden enlightenment and impulse to build this wall came to him after he spit on a fan during the *Animals* tour. He was feeling the desperation of having reached a dead end, in his life and in his career. As a band, Pink Floyd was much greater than any of its members and had recorded three conceptual works that presaged the themes of *The Wall*: the universal classic *The Dark Side of the Moon*, the cult classic *Wish You Were Here*, and the widely popular but for many misbegotten, *Animals*.

By 1979, Pink Floyd was bankrupt due to one bad decision: trusting their considerable royalties to the investment management group Norton Warburg of the London Stock Exchange. From there came the idea of hiding, of playing behind a wall, of setting up one of the most successful and turbulent projects in the history of Pop music. Think of *The Wall* as the art of recouping your millions by publicly discussing your midlife crisis and, at the same time, creating the most lavish and enduringly blasphemous Punk manifesto, something artists like Sid Vicious and Marilyn Manson couldn't even imagine.

From a sociological standpoint, how can one *not* admire how *The Wall* remains standing following the earthquake that wiped the symphonic dinosaurs off the face of the earth, and achieving such a feat by using the strongest features of the new reigning species? Pink Floyd is to Genesis and Yes what Steely Dan is to The Eagles and The Doobie Brothers, just as *The Wall* still today punctures better than all the safety pins through cheeks back then. However: just as the moral fiction that is *A Clockwork Orange* (novel and film) is so easily misinterpreted and attributed quasi-Satanic properties, *The Wall* can be understood (or, better put, misunderstood) as an almost pornographic gesture of pained sincerity or as some sort of vacuous talk show specially designed for a teenage audience in need of mantras and war chants to reject learning like a facile Dickensian vignette where the teachers are always harridans: "We don't need no education..."–and all that.

Hence Waters' alter ego, Pink, who was already mentioned, as a stupid mistake from the mouth of the typical record executive, in a song from *Wish You Were Here* (my favorite of their albums, completely off all radar screens, as if it came to us from another dimension) called "Have A Cigar." A track where, at the end, the volume suddenly lowered and, for months, I thought that the sound system had broken or wasn't modern enough to register such an alien frequency. And then the monster quickly turned into Pop cliché: Pink as messianic rocker, Nazified and alienated, would reappear nameless but in spirit in the final track of 1983's *The Final Cut*, the end of the journey and disbanding and appendix and footnote and ingrown nail of *The Wall*. Both records are, for many, some sort of out of control ego trip by Waters. But for me, they are like Philip Roth set to music. The rock equivalent of Nathan Zuckerman for Holden Caulfield wannabes because, come on, raise your hand if you've never felt like Pink, never felt like trashing hotel rooms and throwing televisions out the window and killing all the phonies and calling that phone number that no one will answer.

The gesture in question—a paradigm of the rocker mystique—had already been introduced by fat Elvis (who liked to shoot guns at television screens) and the hermit tycoon Howard Hughes (who took the Do Not Disturb sign found on the doorknobs of hotel suites as his personal credo and religion), but finds in Pink Floyd's double album (and its unfortunate film version directed by the mediocre Alan Parker[4] and starring the faux-punkie Bob Geldof, who would soon canonize himself as the Pop Mother Teresa of Live Aid) its finest hour. The Wall is the cathartic and self-indulgent vomit of Roger Waters—one of the most unfairly ignored singers and lyricists in the history of the genre—and the continuation of those exorcisms and therapies that answer to the name John Lennon/Plastic Ono Band and Berlin and Blood on the Tracks and Time Out of Mind. The strange thing was to come upon such rage framed within the context of Pink Floyd, paradigm of sophisticated Arena rock that, in 1979, ran a certain risk of being devoured by the Punk and New Wave savagery waiting in the wings.

After all that, as we all know, Pink Floyd ceased being what we had previously known as Pink Floyd (if we leave out the brief but decisive and fundamental trajectory of Syd Barrett) and became something else,[5] and The Wall mutated into a vehicle for denunciation

4   A direct ancestor of Danny Boyle.
5   "I don't think they should be called Pink Floyd... Are Paul McCartney and Ringo Starr the Beatles?" declared an ultraviolent Waters at the time, referring to the fat guys who were once his droogs and who without him, he maintained, bought songs from prestigious rock ghost writers for the albums A Momentary Lapse of Reason (1987) and The Division Bell (1994) and then went on multi-million dollar tours with mini-skirted backup singers. He still has a point. The notable difference is that Roger Waters, David Gilmour, Nick Mason, and Richard Wright never had the archetypal power of John, Paul, George, and Ringo. Which brings us to another paradox: the Beatles without Ringo would never be the Beatles, while Pink Floyd without Waters could always keep on being Pink Floyd, whose main subject has always been Pink Floyd. And—earning Waters' rage and mockery—accept without blushing an award from America's National Association of Brick Distributors in recognition of their services to the building material. But all this had already been anticipated/satirized by Waters himself on the song titled "In the Flesh?"—track 1 of The Wall—which was played on the original record by Pink Floyd but in the live on-stage presentation was presented by a fake Pink Floyd. Four musicians with masks of Roger Waters, David Gilmour, Nick Mason, and Richard Wright—the same masks that illustrate the limited edition of Is There Anybody Out There? The Wall Live 1980-1981—clearly proving that it was no longer the individual that mattered, but only the product and the label.

where solipsism gave way to political demagoguery.[6] But all that was eclipsed for a few minutes as night fell on that sunny Saturday in London, July 2005, for the *Live 8* benefit, when the four members all got together on a stage in Hyde Park for a little while to play four songs (one of which was "Comfortably Numb") and stole the show handily with their intrinsic genius.

Then, a few days later, near the site of the concert, on the tube and on buses, some bombs went off.

And they weren't Pink Floydian special effects.

And soon after, the police killed a Brazilian man by mistake. Now his face, projected live, appears on the screens of *The Wall* performed on tour by Waters.

5

PRIOR TO *THE WALL*, the construction of walls for me had meant "The Door in the Wall" by H. G. Wells and "The Black Cat" and "The Cask of Amontillado" by Edgar Allan Poe.

A question: can you tell I am writing all this under the inescapable and viral influence of Kurt Vonnegut? Surely you can! Because I am rereading *Hocus Pocus* and there, on page 131, Vonnegut remembers that Adolf Hitler was a music lover. And that, every time a concert hall was bombed, Hitler ordered its immediate reconstruction. Priority number one. Why? Why does music calm the savage beasts or is it that it makes them feel, for a little while, less beastly? In any case, in *The Wall*, Pink ends up in an SS-style uniform, with a shield and crossed hammers, haranguing the masses, arm lifted in a Führer stance, disdaining fans, spitting at them as they applaud him. And here we go.

6

THE BIG ADVANTAGE TO a Roger Waters concert today—it happened to me a few years ago when he was touring *The Dark Side of The Moon*—is that they have a fixed script and follow the circular plot

6   Waters himself took *The Wall* to the site where months earlier the Berlin Wall had stood, with a supporting cast best described as polymorphous and perverse that included the irreconcilable differences of Van Morrison, Bryan Adams, Sinead O'Connor, Joni Mitchell, and Scorpions, and was recorded as the double album *The Wall–Live in Berlin* (1990).

of a record. As if you were watching a movie again or re-reading a novel or returning to a favorite painting. In this case, it would be watching and rereading and looking at *The Wall* so many years later. Knowing exactly what to expect, faithfully in tune with the waves of my memories. Waiting for that magical part to come—side three of the album—that is among the most inspired sequences of songs in the entire history of rock. Namely: "Hey You"; "Is There Anybody Out There?"; "Nobody Home";[7] "Vera"; "Bring The Boys Back Home"; and what perhaps is the high point in the entire Pink Floyd catalogue, the song in which Roger Waters and David Gilmour reach the dizzying heights of John Lennon and Paul McCartney in "A Day in the Life."

You already know what I'm referring to: "Comfortably Numb." In what is perhaps the most beautiful song ever created by Pink Floyd, they talk to us and sing to us with precise words and a supernatural guitar solo about the fever of a locked-up man remembering the fever of the boy he once was and the pressure of the outside world because, yes, the show must go on.[8]

7

RETURNING—BECAUSE, YOU'LL REMEMBER, the last thing heard on *The Wall* is the beginning of *The Wall*—to the beginning, going back to what Geoff Dyer wrote: I can't wait for it to begin, yes. But I also never want it to end. And I want to stay to the very end, till they collapse and the wall falls down and—"*There is no pain, you are receding...*"—I am reunited with what I was and still am. With that kid in 1979 first hearing *The Wall* who—something began, something that hasn't ended—keeps listening ever since then, from beginning to end. And—as I already mentioned earlier, don't forget that the final track, "Outside the Wall," closes the album's circuit, connecting

7   The screamer/whisperer Roger Waters never sang better than in this torch song put out by the ashes of his own disenchantment.

8   Minutes later, before "Run Like Hell" and off the script, Roger Waters asks: "Are there any paranoids in the audience tonight? This is for all the weak people in the audience! Is there anyone here who's weak?" And all together they respond, as if with a single remastered voice, with the orange clockwork discipline of a droog: "YEAH!"

with the opening of "In the Flesh?"—and begins again with Pink shouting out the question: "*So ya, thought ya, might like to go to the show.*"
Definitely.

Rodrigo Fresán was born in Buenos Aires, Argentina, in 1963 and has lived in Barcelona, Spain, since 1999. He's the author of the books Historia argentina, Vidas de santos, Trabajos manuales, Esperanto, La velocidad de las cosas, Mantra, Kensington Gardens *(FSG),* El fondo del cielo *and, coming soon,* La parte inventada. *His essays and journalism have been published in many places, including* Granta, The Believer, *and* Vanity Fair *(Spain).*

Do Gay Guys Listen To Yes?

by Andrew Mellen

At least one does.

PROGRESSIVE ROCK IS THE chess club or debate team of rock and roll. It's where smart, somewhat geeky guys (and even some gals) hang out. Imagine *Glee* with an actual edge rather than snark and sarcasm. And less coupling.

The province of subtlety and nuance, bombast and conceit, lyricism and fantasy, Prog Rock allows intelligence, passion, and talent to show off without feeling self-conscious—a genre where it's cool to be a virtuoso, regardless of what professional or amateur critics might say.

Which is why it's always been so surprising to me when gay men turn up their noses at Prog Rock, while extolling the virtues in various performances by Maria Callas, Montserrat Caballe, Renata Tebaldi, or Jessye Norman. A diva's a diva, whether that diva's singing or kicking over his Hammond B3.

I'm sure many of my gay friends know the names Pink Floyd, Yes, King Crimson, and Genesis. They may even be able to name a few tracks. But they're missing out if they've never had the joy of listening to Yes's almost nineteen-minute opus, "Close to the Edge," and its four exquisite movements.

Jon Anderson may not be Placido Domingo or Luciano Pavarotti, but his soaring tenor never falters in the repeated refrain of the fourth movement, even as Rick Wakeman's organ arpeggios pull us farther and farther north. There is something magical and grand in both the composition and performance of "Close to the Edge," and its relentless journey through self-doubt and alienation towards redemption and integration.

Together with "And You and I," it may or may not be a universal coming-of-age story, but it is definitely a gay coming-of-age story. Perhaps, like opera, Progressive Rock is an acquired taste.

Unless you take to it instantly.

MY FOLKS DIVORCED WHEN I was twelve years old. At thirteen, I went to live with my dad in Somerset, a sprawling apartment complex in Troy, Michigan. Even before my folks split up I was a bright, curious kid who often felt out of place. Neither their divorce nor my awakening sexuality did anything to help ease that sense of "other."

A Jewish boy who moved to a mostly WASP neighborhood, a gay boy surrounded by intense heterosexist messaging, and a kid whose folks were divorced in a community where most of my friends' parents were still married—these distinctions only amplified my isolation.

So when I met Rob, the manager of a record shop in the strip mall just south of Somerset, I found a friend and mentor at a crucial time in an unlikely place. For some reason, Rob took a shine to me and introduced me to a world of music that shaped not only my adolescence and young adulthood, but continues to inform my artistic sensibility to this day.

Music was the one place where feeling different didn't matter.

In fact, feeling different was often celebrated in song—Jethro Tull's "Thick as a Brick" comes to mind immediately. So even if most places beyond my front door felt dangerous and unpredictable, in my room with headphones on, I was safe.

As a young boy, I played the piano. And like many other young boys, I didn't want to practice. Baseball, riding my bike, and swimming were all more fun. They also involved being outdoors, not chained to a sound box in the living room.

And then I heard Elton John.

Racing to my piano lesson one day with a recording of "Crocodile Rock," I was certain that my teacher Mrs. Stasson would be as enthusiastic as I was and we'd start working on something I really enjoyed. Not surprisingly, her adamance was deeply disappointing.

I was not deterred.

I played that forty-five so much that it eventually wore out. So I went looking to buy Elton's album *Don't Shoot Me, I'm Only The Piano Player*, figuring I'd spring the five bucks to get not only a replacement for "Crocodile Rock," but also "Elderberry Wine," "Daniel," and "Have Mercy on the Criminal." I may not have been a math wiz, but cost per track wasn't hard to compute.

Rob was happy to oblige but with a twinkle in his eye, he pulled out a copy of *Madman Across The Water*, put it on the turntable and said, "If you like *Don't Shoot Me*, why don't you check this out, my friend," and he proceeded to, in the vernacular of the day, blow my mind.

This became a trope in our relationship. I'd hear something on the radio or at a friend's house and race to the store to get a copy. Then Rob, with that wry smile, would say: "Cool. Have you heard this yet?" And off we'd go on some musical adventure.

Did I have a crush on Rob, who happened to be an attractive, attentive "older" man? Probably.

Let's be clear, he was probably twenty-four or twenty-five and I was fourteen or fifteen. One thing's for sure, I loved the attention.

I'm pretty sure Rob was straight. But something about me must have amused him or seemed worthy, because he was always kind and surprisingly generous with his time.

And we genuinely connected around our appreciation of the history of Pop music—everything from the diversity of players to the formation, dissolution and reconstitution of many groups' lineups. A new song or album would become the catalyst for a lesson in an artist's previous work, or a session player's other tracks. And long before there was an internet, the incestuous web of rock musicians was laid out before me.

He taught me the various incarnations of Steely Dan, The Doobie Brothers, and The Allman Brothers. Starved for connection, I spent hours in that store soaking up both Rob's affection and knowledge. He lit a spark under my hungry curious heart that felt so alone, which was longing for creative expression and companionship.

Just as we were warned in school that marijuana often leads to LSD, mushrooms, or cocaine, so Classic Rock became my gateway to Prog Rock.

Sidebar: I grew up around a queer subculture at my family's bar in downtown Detroit. The Gold Dollar Show Bar featured female impersonators and burlesque comics and was home to a wide assortment of gay men and women, transgendered folks, and drag queens. It's the basis of my play, *My Life As Kim Novak*, but that's a story for another day.

The point is, even at fourteen, I knew what gay was, what I was, and what was expected of me. Sheltered, I wasn't.

And while I appreciated a certain amount of Glam Rock artifice, it was Bowie's alien Ziggy Stardust persona and Elton John's suits and platform shoes that caught my eye more than feathers, makeup, and chiffon. I appreciated a good bend on gender but liked my men to look like me, or how I felt—somewhat attractive, struggling for authenticity, and possibly from another planet.

Meanwhile, my friends were listening to CSNY, James Taylor, Jackson Browne, and Joni Mitchell, with occasional forays into Aerosmith, Led Zeppelin, and The Doors.

So when I went into the shop after hearing "Roundabout" for the first time, it's no surprise that Rob pulled out *The Yes Album*. I had never heard "I've Seen All Good People," or "Yours Is No Disgrace," or "Starship Trooper," and I was floored.

This was music that soared far beyond the catchy hooks and lyrics that had spoken to my angry, alienated soul in "Doctor My Eyes" or "Lady Stardust."

The musical virtuosity of groups such as Yes, King Crimson, and Emerson, Lake & Palmer was operatic and theatrical, and matched the scale of my youthful angst. Here were artists walking a razor's edge between rock and roll, classical music, and performance art in a way that spoke to me.

Prog Rock not only gave voice to my longings but also literally transported me beyond the pain that was so constant in adolescence. It was a late twentieth century version of the land "over the rainbow" that Judy Garland had sung so wistfully about thirty years earlier—beauty married to the gear-grinding sound and energy of rock.

In space, they may not be able to hear you scream but they can't hear you sob, either.

And as obscure (some might say pretentious) as those lyrics and their literary references may have been, they sounded enough like poetry to keep me searching for their meaning, which was certainly a welcome distraction from sorting out my own feelings at the time.

Well past Stonewall, there's a degree of gay visibility that brings with it increased attention of all kinds. More chances for queer youth to find role models creates more opportunities for bigots to zero in on their targets.

When I was a teenager, calling someone a fag was more about a perceived deficiency in masculinity than actual sexual behavior. Even so, as someone who was a faggot, it was a label I preferred to avoid.

Which is another reason why Prog Rock fit so well. It offered a relatively non-sexual focus as an antidote to the hyped up ambiguity and hormonal heat of Glam Rock, where sexual aggression was part of the show if not the scene.

As a gay man, I've always bristled at straight men that cross a line, flirting and strutting as if they might actually be gay. It's the ultimate hetero privilege—alluding to something, then distancing yourself from it with a smirk. When done from the stage, the offence is compounded. It's difficult not to view these mixed signals as arrogant acts of betrayal and shame, executed so cunningly with the clear knowledge that, at least on the perp's part, nothing was ever going to happen.

Prog Rock, on the other hand, sidestepped any controversy by focusing on the playing rather than the player. As a genre, it was chock full of bromances and erudite, slightly effete—yet clearly hetero—men. Instead of makeup and costumes, musicianship was the star attraction on stage.

Bowie's sexuality, Elton John's affairs—these gathered interest because of the murky vagueness surrounding their stage personas. Wakeman had some funky Mylar get-ups, but they were so ill-fitting you would never think him gay. And Robert Fripp was often sitting down while the rest of the band played onstage? Something you'd never see from Eno or Freddie Mercury.

Meanwhile, things weren't good at home. My dad and I often fought like two caged bears on short chains. And as my sexual urges became more insistent, I found myself checking out my male friends at the bus stop, in the locker room, and everywhere in between. I had a horrible sense that this was so far from cool as to be dangerous.

Prog Rock became an even greater refuge. The operatic journey that was *Close to the Edge* guaranteed me a few hours far away from domestic conflict or the burden of puberty.

I didn't have to be anywhere else but flying through outer space, eventually landing in some lush, damp rain forest with Jon

Anderson as my otherworldly, ethereal guide. Here was a man with long hair who was draped in gauzy, flowing costumes—as non-threatening and asexual a male presence as one could hope for. He was practically an elf with a powerful tenor voice.

And yet not an elf. Or an orc or a dragon or a wizard. And I was grateful for that.

Cisgendered and identified, I was keenly aware of what was required to pass and fit in. Prog Rock may have been a bit effete, but Carl Palmer was as muscular and masculine as any jock. And all that testosterone was tempered by Bill Bruford's meditative precision—no less aggressive a player, he never broke a sweat.

Capes and tights and codpieces may have been okay for Ian Anderson onstage, but they were otherwise too blatantly uncool or fey. The whole point was to sidestep sexuality, not draw attention to it. Inside the music, the journeys we embarked on were either interior and wrapped in some form of spiritual quest or exterior struggles between good and evil where systems of oppression focused more on economic power and access than sexual minorities or racism. Identity politics didn't really come up in Prog Rock—we were too focused on global inequities, madness, and evolution.

Years later, I still get weepy when I hear certain tracks. I feel lucky that this happens when listening to both Wilhelmina Wiggins singing "La Wally" and "Catherine of Aragon" from Wakeman's *Six Wives of Henry VIII*.

I can still access the existential sorrow of conceived mortality. I don't worry so much about whom I'm attracted to or what others may think of my choices. But I still seek communion with another's spirit, I crave connection on this plane with or without clothes. I desire to know my highest purpose and to achieve it, or something close.

In short, I get up, I get down...and I wouldn't have it any other way.

Andrew J. Mellen is an expert organizer, public speaker, and the best-selling author of Unstuff Your Life! *Andrew's often called "The Most Organized Man in America," and has addressed audiences from TEDx and Time, Inc. to the U.S. Dept. of Education. He's written for* O, The Oprah Magazine, Tricycle, Together, *and* Project You. *Previously, Andrew was an award-winning playwright, actor, producer, and director, and the former Artistic Director of Alice B. Theater, D.C. Arts Center, and Shuttle Theater Company. His first professional gig as a drummer was with the Punk blues band, Musical Dystrophy. Please visit andrewmellen.com.*

The Fool Explorers
by Margaret Wappler

Though lovers be lost love shall not.
                    —Dylan Thomas

IN OUR MARLBORO-CLOUDED LIVING room, my roommate Julie and I pinched locks of our oily hair between our fingers and pulled them out in front of our faces for inspection. We were waging the latest battle in our ongoing war of who was the grungier bohemian girl.

"Seven days," she said.

"Five," I answered back. I always lost. Julie had thick curly hair that could withstand weeks of neglect. My fine brown hair, however, looked a shade darker within forty-eight hours of not washing. After a week, I always lost my resolve and found myself scrubbing my scalp vigorously with Finesse. Somewhere in there, the former Margaret, the high school girl who had showered every day and carefully matched her Gap pants with her Limited Express sweater, was screaming, *What the fuck? Take a shower already!*

It was 1995, our first year in college, and Julie and I were in love with our own filth. The same obsession ruled our entire group of friends. Ratty flannels and army pants were our uniforms that signified we had loftier pursuits than scrubbing our bodies into pillars of lame-o normalcy. We were scumbag soldiers lock-stepping with the *grunge de corps* of the times.

Julie and I were living in Chicago's Wicker Park, a neighborhood just warming to the idea that it could be a thriving hipster enclave instead of a dumpy collection of Polish dives. Our apartment, a yellow-brick fortress on Crystal Avenue, was crawling with roaches. One skimmed across my naked stomach once in the middle of the night, disappearing into the whorl of sheets. It never did reveal its hiding spot, even when I popped up and repeatedly shook out the blankets.

Most of our decoration, if it could be called that, celebrated trash. For Christmas, Julie and I decorated our tree with playing cards, beer caps, and cigarette butts. Every piece of furniture we had was either an ancient hand-me-down or a product of our frequent dumpster dives. We laughed at the opulence of our street name when compared to our cruddy residence, which we'd sarcastically dubbed the Crystal Palace. Yep, a real mansion alright, if you could just ignore the stench of the mouse who once died in the pocket of Julie's leather jacket.

The other unofficial occupant of the Crystal Palace was my boyfriend, Adam, still finishing his last year of high school. At a certain point, Julie got annoyed that he wasn't paying rent so we started spending more time at his parents' house in the suburbs. As much as I loved the feral quarters of my very first apartment (my share of the rent was a whopping $260), it was a relief to be somewhere clean and orderly. Adam's parents were New York City Jewish hippies who let us do whatever we wanted, who never knocked on his bedroom door unless they were offering cooked food. His mother kept the house so clean, you'd put down your empty glass and within three minutes it'd be neatly stowed in the dishwasher, the counter wiped of condensation.

I wasn't a total newbie to sex before Adam, but my other sporadic encounters were isolated and meaningless. Adam was different. We were building something. I'd first fallen for him when I saw him wearing jeans that he'd doctored by stapling stripes of electrical tape down the sides. He made pencil drawings of strange men in big hats and wrote poems everyday in a black hardbound sketch book. When he lost it at one point, his mother helped him look for it. He had big brown eyes that sparkled playfully like some sort of madcap prank was always about to take place. He laughed by pushing air through his nose and then tittering loudly. Within a few months of him hanging around my particular band of misfits in high school, we were inseparable.

We rooted through all sorts of music together, him introducing me to a few bands like the Dead Kennedys and Ministry. I remember hearing Sonic Youth's "100%" with him, the serrated guitar sawing deep into our thrilled bones. The line, "I stick a knife in my head, but thinking 'bout your eyes," accurately captured our violently dizzy love.

We made out for hours and hours in his bed, outfitted in black sheets. They were cotton, matte black, and probably from Sears, but

I thought they were very cool and forbidden. Sometimes we'd have sex with lambskin condoms stolen from his parents' stash; other times he'd come outside of me, maybe on my stomach. Despite his parents' open attitudes towards sex—Adam told me they'd taught him about masturbation when he was thirteen; in my family, I had to consult Judy Blume for such information—we were still careful to cover up our noises in the bedroom. We played music constantly, some from our own CDs, but most of it was from his parents' record collection, with LP corners frayed and cover art worn down. His parents had good taste but we also figured if we were going to blast anything, it had better be something they liked, too. Somewhere in their stacks of Bob Dylan, Carole King, and David Bowie, we found King Crimson's first record, *In the Court of the Crimson King*. We knew about guitarist Robert Fripp, the only constant member through all the various permutations of King Crimson, through our love for Brian Eno.

Adam, Julie, and I—along with Julie's boyfriend Calvin—were all obsessed with Eno's solo debut, *Here Come the Warm Jets*. Calvin's older brother had passed it on like a torch that would safely light our entry into Better Music. There was one night at Crystal Palace where we did nothing but listen to *Warm Jets* while smoking weed and wrapping each other in Saran Wrap and aluminum foil. We wanted to unlock the fascinating mysteries of these seemingly ordinary kitchen supplies so we kept shearing off sheet after sheet, crunching them around our arms like armor. In the background were Eno's adenoidal vocals and the manic, ticking percussion of "Baby's On Fire." The song is framed around Fripp's guitar solo, which pours in like burning magnesium, scalding out a path with several switchbacks, pursued by little more than the song's rhythmic skeleton, the heavy footsteps of a stalker bass.

If Eno presented as some sort of hysterically gifted glam-dandy on *Warm Jets*, then Fripp was his mysterious shadow self. Lurking on a few of the album's tracks, Fripp's sound was distinctive, both exaggerated and subtle in its grand sense of focus and control. There was something simultaneously meditative and blistering about his playing. We were curious to know what a band anchored by this charismatic musician would sound like.

The King Crimson record quickly became a staple of our make-out sessions, at first because it was loud and it was long. With all five of the multi-part songs clocking in at longer than seven minutes, there was no sound our teenage lust could muster that was capable of piercing the shrieking haze of King Crimson. The first song, "21st Century Schizoid Man" (notably sampled by Kanye West in 2010), starts with a molten blast of guitar and saxophone and forges ahead like some kind of possessed lawnmower, making endless zigzagging cuts for a labyrinthine maze. The over-the-top music easily intertwined with our excessive exploits. We wanted to get lost in our bodies, following every sensation till it blinkered out or yielded something blinding. The point was to feel continuously rapturous, to revel in a suspension of thought. On the surface, it might sound anti-conscious but it was more like the best of both worlds: sex with Adam was a cerebral activity blissfully cleared of any self-conscious tracking of my body. If I wasn't feeling active pleasure, then I hovered in a content state and that's when my mind focused on the music, attaching temporarily to a crash of cymbals or the part in "Moonchild" that makes good on its hippie name with several minutes of free-form plunking around on the Mellotron.

I still don't think of that album as songs but as an atmosphere that's visited by musical events that function like weather. The atmosphere receives electrical charges and reacts. Many of the songs, such as "Epitaph," open at the moment when a brewing storm finally breaks into clattering rain. Fripp seemed to think something similar. He once famously said, "King Crimson lives in different bodies at different times and the particular form which the group takes changes. When music appears, which only King Crimson can play, then sooner or later King Crimson appears to play the music."

The joy of excess is one of the hallmarks of Prog Rock, along with a kind of push-and-pull between the physical and the cerebral, which are often viewed, whether erroneously or not, as opposing forces in music. On "In the Court of the Crimson King," there's rarely a musical idea that can't be expounded on in at least a few different ways. It's a process that requires the musicians to constantly reposition themselves in the map of the song, while still embracing a sense of heedless venturing with no key in sight. This is both the joke and the beauty of Prog: the tireless exploration that can be self-indulgent at its worst but always brave, always chasing after the profound. Why have a melodic line exist in one context when you could build seven different sonic environments for it? Why have one intro to a song when you could have roughly fifteen that eventually crisscross and maybe blow up? Why just play a piano sitting upright when you could whirl around upside down, strapped to the bench like Keith Emerson did in the seventies when Emerson, Lake & Palmer were Progging in stadiums across the U.S.?

It might seem strange that two kids fully steeped in the nineties, who felt little shivers of generational pride when watching the video for Nirvana's "Heart-Shaped Box," would be attracted to a psychedelic Prog record released in 1969 but there were parallels to our world at the time. Adam and I weren't afraid to be fools. We were teenagers, the fool explorers of the world. We weren't interested in music that just pinned itself to two minutes of Pop signifiers, made for easy swallowing. We wanted to court something big, or at least get lost in trying to find it.

Adam and I were both attracted to mazes, complex systems that might value obfuscation more than clarity. We liked wild goose chases. For my birthday that year, he wrote a bunch of "clues" on little pieces of paper and gave them to all of our friends. At a party at the Crystal Palace, the floor sticky with spilled beer, I had to go up to various friends and ask weird questions like, "Is Lionel's mouth filled with rocks?" But I couldn't ask it right away. I had to embed it in a seemingly casual conversation. If our conversation continued in a suitably random but inspired way, then I'd get the next piece of info sending me on to the next person.

I don't remember anymore what gift was waiting at the end of this game but I remember the excitement of crawling over drunk people on a couch, only to ask them some Dadaist question. The answers could be absurd and seemingly meaningless, yet they unlocked the next step.

When we weren't having sex, Adam and I tangled our legs together and talked about what we thought of life and art, death and religion. Those conversations were some beautiful teenage shit. We agreed that we were both artists. I was a writer, scratching my way through a creative writing program after ditching journalism school. He was a visual artist who once made a painting with a neon orange gun against a murky background. He was fascinated with violence, but he wanted to transcribe it in abstract terms that mitigated its association with horror and power.

Adam and I kept our relationship going for a long time—eleven years to be exact. But it wasn't long before different music was playing in our lives. The romantic fuzz of Yo La Tengo. The beats of A Tribe Called Quest that evoke the sway of a subway car. The lone siren call of Portishead that still makes me feel like winter is descending. But we still had those long conversations in our bed or driving around in his car that would only play music if a kitchen knife was jammed into the tape deck.

It's impossible to pinpoint when but at some point, we lost the conversation. I could hear his words, but they increasingly alienated or angered me. We didn't know how to revel in the excess anymore, of our bodies or our minds or any combination thereof. After being together for all those years, five of them married, we severed the connection.

While preparing for this essay, I went back to *In the Court of the Crimson King*. I'd heard the occasional song over the years, but never the complete album in the way that Adam and I listened to it. Admittedly, I probably didn't revisit it in the "right way." I didn't get high. I didn't lie down and try to have sex with anyone or myself. I listened on headphones, upright at my computer, the sober afternoon sun lighting up cobwebs in a nearby window frame.

Maybe I can blame too much time working as a professional music critic or the cold-eyed logic of being older, but it just didn't move me in the same way. Whatever footpath I had once taken into the music as an adolescent, using it to underscore sexual discovery and intellectual tomfoolery, seemed closed to me now. If my fiancé put this on tonight as mood music for the boudoir, I would laugh and be instantly paralyzed. What am I, a background handmaiden in a Hieronymus Bosch painting? Am I supposed to slither on the ground with a vine around my neck?

Instead, the music flowed into new channels of my brain, where so much music goes now: memory and nostalgia. It made me remember the days when Adam and I camped in rural South Dakota. We were having sex in our tent when a flashlight shined in on us. The owner of the light said nothing and didn't move.

Oddly, I felt completely safe the whole time. We paused in the act and then the light went away. Later, we talked about how we didn't hear footsteps when it left. Did we hallucinate it after weeks of barely seeing any people? Was it a ghost? Was it the spirit of my dead father? Those were the kinds of conversations that could sustain us for hours.

The greatest gift Prog Rock can bestow upon us is the gift of permission. To embrace ideas and their subtexts. To think of songs not as finite constructs, but as one undulating mutation. To just let loose and play fractal fantasies on the keyboard for ten minutes. King Crimson is particularly generous in all these ways—but I don't need it anymore to help me spin off into a million philosophical directions. This time I used it for something else: reconnection.

Adam and I haven't talked in a while, but listening to King Crimson made me feel like the thread of our conversation just fell below the pitch of my ears for a spell and now I'm hearing it again. In reality, I'm hearing long-gone spirits, those people we were.

I know if I saw Adam tomorrow, we'd trade small talk, practical conversation about jobs and apartments and such. But I wish we could have a conversation that would be absurd and endless. It would follow every lovely or silly turn, the kind of roaming chatter you can have only when every path is still open.

Margaret Wappler wrote about arts and culture for the Los Angeles Times *for seven years, and has also been published in* Rolling Stone, The Believer, LA Weekly, Nylon *and* JANE Magazine. *Her fiction has appeared in* Black Clock, Facsimile, Public Fiction, *and was recently anthologized in* Joyland Retro. *In 2011, she read from her novel-in-progress as part of the New American Writing series at the Hammer Museum. Visit her virtual abode at margaretwappler.com.*

The Angular Wheel
by Nathan Larson

My life as a professional musician is a joyless exercise in futility.

—Robert Fripp

I N 1993, I LOOKED like Dave Navarro. I'm not saying that's awesome, I'm just saying that was the deal. So envision a blurry Dave Navarro (picture, as well, the nipple rings and leather pants, if you must; yes, picture me shirtless and ripped, too) hurling a *Village Voice* into the narrow ventilation shaft of an East Village apartment house. Envision blue-black hair rendering and a general hissy fit, and you'll have a suitably accurate mental picture to kick this bitch off.

Cos here's what I had just read back in 1993, this from the quill of a very influential rock journalist, and mind you, this was when people still cared about this nonsense:

> Forget crap like King's X and Shudder To Think, if you're look-
> ing for real Progressive Rock look no further than the Jon Spencer
> Blues Explosion...

King's fucking X?? Progressive Rock?? What was this heresy? Spencer, that hunky no-talent from Pussy Galore? What the fuck was happening to my cool life?

THIS FORGOTTEN JOURNALIST HAD hit a nerve, roots exposed like my Samhain dye job. For the band he spoke of, Shudder To Think, was my band, was my *art*, and at twenty-three years old, having just inked a fat record deal with Epic, was my raison d'être and my single source of income. I had no real hankering to return to my shitty bartending job, so I was hoping against hope that things panned out. But much more than this, I was convinced I had the equation to re-frame rock and roll music.

Was it possible that this was how we—*my band*—were perceived? Like King's X? Overplaying music school jokers in Zildjian t-shirts?

It was unthinkable. From our standpoint we were sexy swashbucklers, confounding and captivating the public with our Dada

Rock, Anti-Rock, just-try-to-dance-to-this un-rock/rock, trying to kill that heartbeat in the manner of Captain Beefheart. Our fans loved it like they loved a hot, sexy Rubik's Cube. If you hated it, fuck you—we ate your ill energy, consumed it as further fuel for our metal machine.

Dammit, we aligned ourselves with Duchamp, Varese, John Cage, Ornette Coleman. We would sit in the van and meditate on Coleman's album *Free Jazz* at ridiculous volumes.

Introducing mathematical trickery to a traditional four-piece rock band may have been a formula that worked for Rush, ELP, Genesis, King Crimson, etc., but we considered these saggy-ass acts beneath contempt. We were emphatically not of that school. Our band was up to far more than those clowns of old. Cos let's face it: there was nothing sexy about those acts. Nothing. Our band was *sexy*, and had no precedence amongst those dinosaurs. Certainly not. *Right?* And our peers were assuredly not, as certain rock critics would frequently have it, the likes of Marillion and—yes, King's X—whom we viewed as the contemporary equivalent of the above mentioned prehistoric acts. No, we were most definitely *not* in that camp. We were an island, an outpost, and we operated in a vacuum, beyond history and tradition.

And yet, a secret area of our brains craved pure Def Lep, Journey, and Billy Idol. We dug huge, cheap, cheese-laden hooks. We lusted after *fame* on the basest level. We desired mega-stardom. We wanted to pour some sugar on ya, though we would have been loathe to admit it. No, this was an impulse we would tamp down—*silence*—keep forever stowed away.

And yet, and yet...in the repression of this aspect of our character, we ignored our heritage. We disregarded the raw facts. Cos as white boys all, we were *raised* on the dum-dum FM radio tit—Rush, Van Halen, Yes, Queen, Zeppelin, Sabbath, et al. Not a few of these bands were known for the kind of musical flights of fancy that might warrant the Progressive Rock label. This was and is the reality of the FM dial.

The perpetual (ancient, unwinnable) art versus commerce knock-em-sock-em underway at large waged its own internal campaign in our pants. We wanted to fuck with people, to repel them...and yet, and yet. We wanted to be motherfucking superstars, lavished with *fame and fortune and everything that goes with it (I thank you all).*

NOW THAT RIGHT THERE is an awful lot, actually far too much, to ask of the universe. And it just wasn't going to happen, not for us at least.

I didn't consider myself a muso. Hell, I had buds who attended Berklee, with their double bass drum clinics and climate-controlled gig bags, transporting that precious Chapman Stick through the hardcore Boston winters. Though I honestly respected their dedication, my primary reaction was sniggery. No sir, the School of Music was not my path.

Me, I came straight outta Punk. Which is like the flip of anything identifiably Prog. Being a fundamentalist when interpreting the Punk Rock dogma required a rejection of all musical bloat, abuse of technique, and anything most folks might find pleasant, or had heard of. Hence my desire to defy, to reject, to spurn, to fetishize all things deviant and outside. And hence my unease as I found myself becoming an ever more proficient guitarist, ever more inclined to compose the lopsided brainteaser of a riff. And yet I did so, in the spirit of Punk, to thumb my nose at those who would imagine that music could not be dangerous, a struggle.

Despite all these intellectual conceits, when the time came, my band did not hesitate to bail on a tiny, principled indie label in order to shift our operation to glitzy Epic records in that bizarre grunge-era window of time when these gigantor corporations were snorting any band with half a guitar (and in the process shooting themselves in the throat...this was the last golden shower of big label cash, and pairing this gross miscalculation with a new-fangled beast called internet spelled the end of the record industry as it had been known since the War). And it wasn't just 'cos everybody else was doing it; it was a power-move born of a molecular level *desire* to thrive and be adored.

Perhaps the term wasn't exactly in the public lexicon yet, but we were unquestionably a Math Rock band. Furthermore, we were a band's band. Rock stars of the day *felt* our fractal jams, lavished us with love and praise and bade us to join them on the road so we might strut our herky-jerky stuff in the enormodomes of the world. There we were met, as is the lot of most opening acts, with a hard rain of abuse and the occasional (unopened) beer bottle to the mouth. We elicited perhaps more anger than most openers, not helped by our refusal to keep a linear beat for more than thirty seconds, and perhaps because of our foppish/sexually ambiguous (read: faggy) presentation.

Though this disconnect with a larger audience broke our hearts in the moment, we could loiter in the confines of the backstage area and be smugly satisfied with the knowledge that we were executing far more sophisticated moves than the average Pearl Jam fan could process. This is how we interpreted these confrontations. But there was a tension there that went beyond the heckling: we observed the adoration heaped on our far more famous friends, and, uncomfortably, *we wanted it, too.*

As far as our own crowd went, well...the indigenous Math Rock consumer is invariably a dude, and not necessarily the most attractive type of dude to boot. I can't begin to describe what a soft-on it is to look out into the crowd and clock a clutch of mouth breathers air-drumming along to your "impossible" beats, along with the double bummer that these yo-yos have not only cracked your painstakingly crafted anti-code, but are not in the least bit hot and are most certainly not girls. Picture some yahoo parked directly in front of your stage—that space in the crowd reserved strictly for chicks—eyes on his hands, *taking notes on cleft paper.* That's the general vibe.

But to develop contempt for your core audience is deeply wrong. Besides being obviously ungracious and unfair, it is not a spiritually healthy thing, and can only lead to negative energy and an unsustainable dynamic. This (among many other factors) would fester, until I was unable to continue making this particular music in this particular context.

Mea culpas aside, our partial solution to being a band admired by sweaty-palmed males was to affect a glammy presentation with an emphasis on high style and stage dramatics, all of which worked to our advantage when on home turf. Neither were we hurt by the fact that we were relatively easy on the eyes. I say this with humility, hand to heart. As a result we pulled enough girls to offset the guys, this being a major component to our delusion that we could extend our vision as far as we chose and enjoy complete chart/world domination. This, of course, was not the case, but we clung to it despite all of our increasing experience to the contrary when exposed to the wider world.

Needless to say, it ended as most things do. And like most love affairs, the breakup was painful and Byronic. But we're all still friends, and I can look on it with nothing to protect, and a kinder perspective.

As an indie rocker of a certain age (cough-forty-something-cough-cough) given to self-reflection, it now seems absurd to deny the entrenchment of Prog Rock in our vocabulary. This is akin to the denial of our kidneys or some other internal organ. A denial that we were once growing boys, absorbing our musical environment during an era when Progressive Rock broadly defined the sonic landscape. Rock and roll radio thought nothing (and this is true today and will be true tomorrow forever ad infinitum) of rock-blocking eight-minute concertos like "Bohemian Rhapsody," "Stairway to Heaven," or "Roundabout." The average eleven year old's musical understanding has yet to fossilize into total snobbery, and we can only absorb that which irradiates us, then accept it. Classic Rock therefore takes up position in the spine, an inoperable yet benign tumor.

Moving past things musical, while the gals of our tweens had the early forms of YA lit (that behemoth that has come to completely dominate our culture)—Judy Blume, *Flowers In The Attic*, etc., I would argue that us dudes were saddled with Tolkien, *Star Wars* mythology, and *Dungeons & Dragons*. I suppose we could've done a lot worse, but this material doesn't do much for emotional development, or help a kid out with thorny bits like emerging sexuality.

But when Robert Plant moans from the "...darkest depths of Mordor," a light goes on somewhere. And in case you just tuned in and missed the first verse of "Ramble On," in verse two the Golden God deems it awesome to yodel on the subject of "Gollum, the evil one..."—at which point you would have to be a total luddite to not know my man is, indeed, talking about the motherfucking *Hobbit*. And in 1980, this is a deep-cut ref that would likely sail over the feathered coif of a Camaro-captaining jock, past the cool unknowable black kids, beyond the groupings of alien females, sailing to lodge like Cupid's arrow in the thorax of thickly bespectacled geeks—those of us in the "wrong jeans," fearfully ducking through hostile space with double-strapped Jansports.

This would be a fine development. Cos if the giants of rock can confidently drop Middle-Earth-y names in this context, maybe it's okay to have that worn ten-sided dice in your front pocket, and maybe it's okay that at that point your dream girl is an elf-princess named Elixir—herself an invention of your buddy Miles, whose Frazetta-style illustration of Elixir, on graph paper made grubby by your caress, is your first brush with anything resembling erotica.

I COULD GO ON. I now embrace the beauty of the Prog, and enjoy a good Renaissance Fair. I now find that in a group of my contemporaries, a tasty Rush reference is always on the tip of the tongue. And this feels good, it feels right. One of the truly great things about not being twenty-three is the fact that you no longer have *changing the fucking world* at the numero uno position on your to-do list.

As for the Math Rock, caution is advised. Innovation is one thing, but here's something to bear in mind when trying to reinvent the wheel: there's a pretty logical reason to account for its natural shape. If you make that wheel all sharp angles, sure it may rock a bit, but it will not likely roll you home.

Nathan Larson is best known as an award-winning film music composer, having created the scores for over thirty-five movies, including Boys Don't Cry, Dirty Pretty Things, *and* Margin Call. *In the 1990s, he was lead guitarist for the influential Prog-Punk outfit Shudder to Think. His debut novel,* The Dewey Decimal System, *was published in 2011, and its follow-up,* The Nervous System, *was released summer 2012. Larson lives in Harlem, New York City, with his wife and son.*

Catch The Mist

by Beth Lisick

Since their music derived as much from the new free jazz and African chant rhythms as from Delta blues, the songs tended to be rattly and wayward, clattering along on weirdly jabbering high-pitched guitars and sprung rhythms.

—Lester Bangs on Captain Beefheart's *Trout Mask Replica*

I WAS JUST LIKE ALL the other girls in my neighborhood that summer, getting tan and drinking Tab with a slice of lemon out of a mayonnaise jar, calling up KOME repeatedly to request they play "Tom Sawyer" over and over. KOME in San Jose, where the deejays bragged/threatened at every station break: *Don't touch your dial. It has KOME on it.* I imagined them doing something blurry in a dark booth with a fat microphone at their lips. I used to wonder more about them, the disembodied voices playing the songs, the ones who talked about the Classic Car Wash on Almaden Expressway or the Olde Spaghetti Factory downtown, than I did the bands. One KOME deejay was called Dennis Erectus. He was funny and had lady troubles. We liked him the best. There was something about "Tom Sawyer" that summer though. It was like the aliens I'd been promised in *Close Encounters of the Third Kind* were finally landing, which was somehow erasing the drummer's brain and making him play from a different energy grid. It was as creepy and confusing as being twelve was, and it made me want to sprint across Kerri Rosenblum's back lawn and jack knife into her swimming pool every time it came on. Eventually I went to Musicland at the mall and spent my allowance money on the whole album. I didn't like it. The songs were too long and that guy's voice freaked me out after awhile. I also didn't think they were very cute.

Soon I drifted onto some ska and mod stuff because of a friend's older sister, went to college and fell in love with the boy downstairs who never removed Jimmy Cliff's *The Harder They Come* from his turntable, had a professor who was into straight-ahead jazz, and lived with a gothy 4AD boyfriend who collected rare vinyl and wore clothes that required dry cleaning. Everyone around me, it seemed, lovers and roommates and co-workers and college radio deejays, had something they were into that was new to me. I'd seen Ella Fitzgerald,

Camper Van Beethoven, Sonic Youth, and Johnny Cash. What else was there? Punk shows at Gilman, the symphony with my parents, this local dude Charlie Hunter who could play bass notes, rhythm, and solos simultaneously on his custom guitars. Yes, Mom, I have heard of Ladysmith Black Mambazo. Like many twenty-four year olds, I knew everything there was to know about music.

While working at the *Bay Guardian*, one of San Francisco's weekly papers, I met this slightly older guy named John who'd worked there "forever." He ordered office supplies and sorted the mail. He told me he was never going to quit because it allowed him a lot of free time during the day to practice his guitar. It was pretty disappointing not to recognize the name of his band, and when he said they hardly ever played in San Francisco, it seemed sad. Oakland? That's were they played? What kind of band that's together for ten years mostly just plays in Oakland? I tried not to imagine a blues cover band on a wharf at happy hour.

Courting with the office guy included mix tapes, as it should, but they were the frustrating kind of mix tapes. Full of songs I didn't recognize with no written indication of who these bands were. I felt stupid when I listened to them. Weird, majestic, dramatic, heavy, odd. What were all these songs blaring out of the speakers of my 1989 Toyota pick-up as I crossed the Bay Bridge to finally see him play for the first time? It was true that he was sweet, and he brought me fried artichoke hearts and flowers and wrote haiku on Post-Its, but I was still hedging a little, stalling on committing. Embarrassing as it was, I was waiting to see what happened when he got onstage.

I showed up to a place called the Stork Club in downtown Oakland. It was a ghost town down there, with only a few cars parked on the street out front, but when I walked in, it was a full blown scene. The door guy was a skinny dude with an angel face I recognized from the counter at Amoeba Records, the bartender was an exhausted lady with a beehive who smoked long, skinny Mores and looked about sixty years old. At the bar sat black cowboys, Vietnam vets, a developmentally disabled girl, some West Oakland warehouse freaks. The club was decorated in a year-round Christmas style with tinsel hanging from the ceiling, colored lights, animatronic dolls, and a decorated tree on the low stage in back. It smelled like hot dog water.

And then John's band went on. Not his main band, Eskimo, but this offshoot band he had just started called Ebola Soup. *I know.* They took the stage, these four nerdy guys, and nearly cleared the room. The songs stopped, started up again, never went where I expected them to. Some lasted a little over a minute, a few went on for a very, very long time. John sang in a monster voice, alternating occasionally with a falsetto, while playing his guitar like he was wrestling with it, though his fingering was spot-on. The drummer was beating the shit out of his kit, interspersing that with tourettic flourishes, and was also, I had heard, a manicurist. The bass player had his bass strapped high in what seemed like an extremely uncool fashion, plus he was wearing sandals, but he could play better than most bassists I'd ever seen. Athletic, sinewy, complex, and profoundly musical. Approximately twenty people were delighted. So I fell in love, not exactly with the music, but with the energy, the vibe, the commitment to making something strange and original. And when someone told me that John had been the top of his class in biochemistry at UC Berkeley and had turned down full ride scholarships to grad school at Harvard and MIT in order to pursue his music, I fell in love with him. A misfit genius. To this day, I find no archetype more appealing.

I abandoned San Francisco with its cool kids and pricey $4 pints, and moved in with John in Oakland. We spent nearly every weekend at the Stork. One of his bands would play one night and the other nights we'd be seeing Thinking Fellers Union Local 282, Idiot Flesh, Charming Hostess, Deerhoof, Fibulator, Ubzub, Monopause, The Molecules, Ninewood. All Oakland bands pushing the boundaries of what I'd previously thought rock music could be, including the occasional use of puppets and costumes. I saw John Zorn's Masada there, and Melt Banana and Quasi. On Sundays we would go to Beanbender's, an improv night in an old bank where I got to see Nels Cline, Eugene Chadbourne, Otomo Yoshohide, Fred Frith, ROVA Saxophone Quartet, Evan Parker, Buckethead, and the Sun Ra Arkestra. Back at home, the complete discographies of Ornette Coleman, Captain Beefheart, Stockhausen, and Stravinsky were at my fingertips, and I discovered the best way to fall asleep was to put on a Morton Feldman record. And John really did practice his guitar. For hours each day, rehearsing and composing.

I definitely didn't love all the music. There was a relentless quality that I found exhausting sometimes. All those time changes and polyrhythms, it felt too cerebral. Just as I was getting into one part of the song, they would change it on me, like it was some kind of trick. See how smart we are? We could play the heaviest of metal or the swingingest of bebop or reproduce a Balkan folk song note for note, but we're choosing to do this, which incorporates theory from all three. And perhaps we shall wear capes while we do it.

During those shows when I needed a break, my version of "lie back and think of England" was "space out and imagine starting a band." I wasn't as smart as all these people, didn't play an instrument, and yet something in their approach to music had inspired me to think I could do it. I suppose there were just so many bands doing their own thing that it didn't seem scary to add another one to the mix. I recruited some of my favorite musicians from the scene: George Cremaschi, a curmudgeonly, monstrous contrabass player who had played with Cecil Taylor; and two guys from John's band Eskimo; Andrew Borger, a Cal music grad who later went on to play with Tom Waits and Norah Jones; and a vibraphonist named David Cooper who had a MIDI setup and a precision in playing that was somewhere on the autism spectrum.

Used to being sidemen, the guys in my band were stoked to bring in their own compositions. There were ballads in 7/4, power metal lurches, bowed bass, extended vibraphone solos, and then I was at the mic talking about riding the bus or car wrecks or Siegfried and Roy. To make matters worse, we were often joined by a crack trombonist. Our name was The Beth Lisick Ordeal, and to many we certainly were.

We made one record and a demo with Eric Drew Feldman, formerly of Snakefinger and Beefheart's band, but I kept being told, mostly from men at record labels, that what I needed to do was ditch those guys and front a rock band. A real rock band. I took this to mean they wanted something "more normal" and I wondered what steps we could take to make ourselves less weird. At the time it felt like we'd have to go backwards, against whatever instincts and circumstances had led us to become the band we were.

It's disingenuous to believe that no band ever contrives to be kooky or non-conformist or avant garde—*we'll show them!*—but if you think about humans (not to mention human musicians) those are very natural impulses. We want to grow and change, act out and explore, surprise and stun. And perhaps wire up an electric flute or write a song about Ayn Rand.

I think that's why hearing "Tom Sawyer" on the radio hit me as hard as it did. It didn't feel like a put-on. Even as a kid, I sensed that the band's weirdness was true. And that's what was so creepy and exciting.

Beth Lisick is a writer, performer, and author of four books. Her latest, Yokohama Threeway and Other Small Shames, will be out in fall 2013 from City Lights/Sister Spit. She lives in Brooklyn, New York.

HUNG UP ON THESE SILVER STRINGS

by Nick Coleman

Oh yeah, that was the thing to do at the time. This was before the new wave of bebop started.

—Martin Denny

B E-BOP DELUXE CAME IN through the out door. And, this being England, they brought some weather in with them. The scene was this. To some English provincial fifteen year olds in 1975, Progressive Rock was tired. It was airless, stuffy, bored. The opposite of progressive. The windows had jammed shut. The chimney was full of soot and birds' nests. Nothing in the Prog bunker seemed lively or new anymore; and when something did somehow contrive to seem new, then the newness felt effortful and self-regarding rather than imaginative and uncontainable. Prog Rock in 1975 had become a formalist art. Worse, it was commercially successful.

I had been nursing priggish worries about the ongoing viability of the Prog project since "The Gates of Delirium" on Yes's *Relayer*. The album had come out towards the end of the previous year and had, in my small world, soundtracked two weeks' bed-bound misery while I tried to outlast a kidney infection. I'd played "The Gates" both in a state of delirium and while perfectly *compos*. I'd tossed. I'd turned. The bedsheets had grown rank. I had failed to connect. It had been hard to tell which was crueler: the pain in my lower abdomen or the sheer emptiness of Yes's technical display.

The year 1975 was also the year in which Prog went mainstream, as far as it ever went mainstream. Only second- and third-division bands played our local fenland Corn Exchange now. The first-division ones did "shows" in arenas and football grounds at central locations miles away, and at crippling expense. Boys of my age could no more afford to attend Yes at Queen's Park Rangers' stadium in London than we could manage Led Zeppelin's week at Earl's Court—and Zep had *Physical Graffiti* out, which was getting a whole lot more attention in my bedroom than *Relayer*.

Here was an authentic tipping point. Progressive Rock had outgrown its original constituency and unbalanced the relationship be-

tween the two. At one end of the see-saw, Prog's increasing commercial bulk, its artistic blubber plus its vastly extended demographic
reach, ensured that its end of the plank stayed anchored firmly to
the ground, while at the other end, legs a-dangle and unsure of
where to look, Prog's natural fanbase of smartass freaks and ami-
able layabouts trailed their bellbottoms in thin air and wondered
how the hell they were going to get down from up here. Prog was
ballast, a dead weight way over yonder. It no longer came to you;
you had to slide over to *it*, like supplicants, and pay over the odds
for the privilege. Furthermore, you were now obliged to do it in the
company of straights and casuals. And, in some cases, their parents.

Fifteen year olds are incontinent in their desire for new things,
and so I took the wedged-open Prog door as an invitation. But I was
nervous about what might be coming in through the crack. What
was out there? What might take Prog's place?

In 1975, the ultimate middle-class white hipster must-have was
Bob Marley and the Wailers: music with gaps in it—an excellent
thing, no doubt, but what did Jamaican reggae have to say to the
dank and etiolated world of the fen freak? Possibly not that much.
There was also, unavoidably, the boiling hullabaloo surrounding
Bruce Springsteen, an all-American polysyllabic spree with a new
brand—a new *dimension*—of marketing muscle strapped across his
engines. *Born To Run* hadn't yet arrived, but everyone knew it was
coming. You could feel the blast of hot air coming down the tunnel.

And in the musty English corner? Welcome to the stark neo-ret-
ro fundamentalism of Dr. Feelgood...

The choice on offer seemed to require the exercise of bad faith,
whichever way you went.

I plumped for Dr. Feelgood.

Nevertheless, I still sloped down to the Corn Exchange in my
navy greatcoat every now and then to see those second-division
bands which still bothered to skulk through town, but Camel and
Barclay James Harvest and Greenslade were not doing it for me—
not like *Physical Graffiti* and *It's Only Rock And Roll* and *Down By
The Jetty* were at home (it is difficult now to convey just how stark
the Feelgoods' debut looked and sounded in the context of the prevailing rock *mores* of the time—like *puritanical*, man). And though I
still had the artfulness of Can and Robert Wyatt and Roxy and Eno

and Steve Hillage and the Sensational Alex Harvey Band and King Crimson and Genesis and the Floyd and Hatfield and the North to make me feel interesting, it was unshakably the case that my attachment to those institutions had more to do with habit, loyalty, and intellectual narcissism than naked excitement. Perhaps for the first time in my three-year career as a juvenile rocker, I began to feel feckless.

Then...

"Repent, Harlequin!" said the Ticktock Man.

BE-BOP DELUXE BROUGHT NEW weather through the crack in the door. It came in not with a hinge-rattling gust but as a thin spiral of cooler air—northern, melancholy, romantic, low in temperature, histrionic but composed and somehow landscape-y, wild with the scent of wet stone. That's what I thought anyway. They also appeared to rock. Sort of.

The great tastemaker of British radio John Peel had played Be-Bop's first album *Axe Victim* with some persistence throughout the previous winter and I had nodded along over my homework and, later at night, in bed, enjoying Be-Bop's parts: the licky fluency of Bill Nelson's guitar more than the flubbing of the rhythm section or the mannerisms of his singing (he had evidently gone to the same sort of art school as Bryan Ferry and David Bowie). "Adventures in a Yorkshire Landscape" took the premise of "My Favorite Things," inverted it, northerned it, and then sent it out into the world trailing a long, spongey guitar solo behind it, like a tail. We also learned about the existence of Nelson's homemade album, *Northern Dream*, a self-released, limited-edition super-rarity. It was virtually unheard-of, then, to release your own damn record, and *Northern Dream* was unheard as a recording by most people, which only added to its mystique.

Then *Futurama* came out in July. Peel played "Sister Seagull" and that was that: I was lost. The album took up my entire summer. I then took it to school, firstly, to introduce my school friend Thompson to its shiny chambers and then, much more dangerously, to propose that *Futurama* should be honored with a premiere at the first meeting of the school's Contemporary Music Society in October. To widespread consternation, the CMS responded positively to my suit (applying to get a record played at one of their monthly meetings felt every bit as onerous as asking your girlfriend's father for her hand in marriage) and the members-only audition of *Futurama* was duly announced in Assembly by a palpably suspicious headmaster, who was traditionally more at ease with Rory Gallagher. "On Wednesday at one-fifteen," he said with barely concealed distaste, "the Contemporary Music Society will be listening to and then discussing...er, ah...*Future* M.A. by Bee-Bore Deluce," before sitting down again with a bump.

I have no memory of how *Futurama* was received that Wednesday lunchtime in the Senior Mummery, nor how the formal debate on the album's merits proceeded after the playback. No memory at all. It's as if the experience has been effaced on grounds of inadequacy. Perhaps that's it: perhaps nothing much happened. Perhaps four greasy boys showed up to the CMS convocation, decided on first contact that Bee-Bore Deluce were indeed some sort of bore from outer space and then talked and larked insultingly for the rest of the lunch hour while the record played. Perhaps I fumed silently. Perhaps I raged. I have no recollection, and nor does Thompson (I checked: he can't remember either; he's not even sure that he showed up himself). Nothing remains. Although one thing's sure: *Futurama* did not secure for me the widespread admiration that I thought should be mine: for my taste, for my hipness and for my unerring insight into "what comes next" in rock's unfolding odyssey.

So what *did* I hear in *Futurama*? What did I feel, experience, imagine? What was the basis of my seething conviction?

Only one way to begin to find out: listen to it again, for the first time in thirty-five years.

BE-BOP WERE A TRIO that summer. The flubby, chubby *Axe Victim* rhythm section had been ditched in favor of a spindly drummer with an aesthetically cleft chin, Simon Fox, and a Maori bass player with massive hair, hot off the plane from New Zealand, Charlie Tumahai. Bill Nelson, *l'auteur* himself, had taken to wearing double-breasted suits with enormous lapels and saucers for buttons, teamed with the pointier kind of shirt collar, either flattened along the line of his shoulders or with a tie, sometimes a dickie-bow. His

cantilevered helmet of hair was sprayed into position like a suburban matriarch's.

To English teens, the iconography was not hard to read: Be-
Bop *not* Prog, the group's look said. Be-Bop possibly Glam. Be-Bop
certainly Art Rock, kind of like Bowie and Roxy, but only in the
vaguest "school-of" sense; and definitely not gay; and, judging by
the artwork of *Futurama* (a futurist black swan jets around a techno
cityscape), extremely keen that one should identify them not with
the giants of contemporary rock but with the giants of early European Modernist art: Cocteau, Picasso, Artaud, the *fin-de-siècle* Symbolist poets—Baudelaire, Rimbaud, Mallarmé...shimmering names,
all of them, whoever they were.

So, a sort of Euro-intellectual Art Rock power trio, then. Ta-
dah!

Futurama begins with a fanfare. A fanfare of guitars. Fanfares
go all the way back of course: they predate Bob & Earl and Nelson Riddle and Richard Strauss and Mussorgsky and Monteverdi
and Gabrieli and Scheidt; they go back to popes and emperors and
kings and beyond. Their primary function is to warn. "Alarums!"
as Shakespeare would say. "Important people in the area! Death
imminent!" Alexander probably whacked Darius II at Issus to the
sound of alarums. And we all know what brought down the walls
of Jericho.

But the fanfare which shouts at the top of "Stage Whispers"
isn't like that sort of historical fanfare at all. It doesn't intimidate or
proclaim. It could hardly be said to constitute a warning either—it's
far too questioning and wriggly for that, being in structure an extended cadence which never actually resolves completely. It doesn't
properly prefigure what's coming next either. Instead it implies a
conjunction between two things, the first of which has been lost to
time leaving only the second thing, which, if you stick around for
the next twenty seconds or so, you will surely dig—please be patient
while we sort out this harmonic knot... In essence, it's a peacocking
fanfare of display which has no real identity of its own because it
merely conjoins both the invisible place it has sprung from, off-
stage as it were, and the place it is leading to: an extempore moment
of *playing for time*, stylish, accomplished, pregnant with promise but
offering no guarantees at all that, after the fanfare ends, anything

of substance will be delivered. Are important things in the offing? Is death imminent?

It's a metaphor, folks.

Then...

"Stage Whispers" is one of only two or three songs on the whole of *Futurama* that owe much at all to the values of Progressive Rock, and these are manifest almost in a campy manner. Theatrical imagery, technical trickiness, and a preoccupation with musical form expressing Prog's debt to classical music: it's got the lot. The entire song is a rhetorical flourish predicated on the idea that—yep—all the world's a stage, especially my bit of it, oh lover of my soul ("baby" does not figure in the lexicon of Be-Bop), and "I'm waiting in the wings with all the strings and things that help me make the music." Be aware that it's your job, by the way, to ensure that, when I finally step away from the spotlight that compels this darkling fool, your kiss will teach me simpler truths...

This is what we English like to call "wank."

Furthermore, the damn thing does not sit still. It fidgets as it wanks. The primary Prog allusion expressed by "Stage Whispers" is its rejection of regulation 4/4: the song changes time, tempo, and key with greater frequency than "The Gates of Delirium," which in mid-1975 stood as the unofficial world record-holder for time, tempo, and key changes. "Stage Whispers" even has a funky bit, echoing the Floyd's funky bit in "Echoes." That it jitters to a close a little over three minutes after the closure of that opening fanfare one must take as a mercy—much as I took it to be in 1975. It's a set up and a knock down. "Stage Whispers" positions the narcissist art-rock hero-poet in a Prog hall of mirrors and wipes the slate clean for the arrival of "Love With The Madman," "Maid In Heaven," and "Sister Seagull," which, between the three of them, constitute the far-from-boiling core of a rather one-sided album.

Temperature was always an issue with Be-Bop Deluxe.

How can a band be both cool in temperature yet aspire to rock like the blazes? The answer lies in the way those three songs are put together, as songs. (And possibly in the technical approach of the producer Roy Thomas Baker, who, as studio guru for Queen, had discovered a thing or two about what you can do in small spaces with compressed guitars...)

Some bands just play. They get together in the studio or rehearsal space, plug in, face each other down, and discover their collective mojo. The upshot? If they're any good and they do aspire to rock, then heat is the traditional upshot. Heat is the consequence of friction when independent objects bump against each other in their natural pursuit of motion and rub and fight for space and *bore in*. You really don't need me to explain the science, do you?

But not in Be-Bop. Be-Bop were less a collective ensemble than an authored project, built from the top down with tweezers. The job of the rhythm section was not to set an agenda or drive tempo or instigate a vibe but to fill in space where required. They merely underpinned the tweezer work.

Upshot? Histrionic coolth.

"Love With The Madman" is a beautiful introductory guitar motif with a sweet Symbolist love song attached, all clouds of Gibson sustain and glinting harmonic suspension: "You'll go crazy with the wonder of it all." It doesn't actually go anywhere; it just sort of *hangs*. But it stirs as it hangs. I used to find this song strangely moving as a fifteen year old and I still do, possibly because it's the nearest thing in the Be-Bop canon to an Anglican hymn. It verges on the stately.

"Maid In Heaven," on the other hand, is where Nelson attempts to generate some good old-fashioned rockin' heat. The song is fun, all right, and bright, and it turns over at a fair rate of knots. But it stays resolutely chilled in temperature throughout, like a schematic for a rocking Pop song rather than the thing itself.

"Maid" was the single off the album, and it was the song the group performed on *The Old Grey Whistle Test* on BBC TV (which, for those readers not familiar with the format, usually required the group to pre-record the backing track in the television studio, then mime it back for the benefit of the cameras, but with live vocals. The studio being tiny, the cameras were hardly ever more than a couple of feet distant from the band—real up-nose photography, this—and rockin' heat seldom ensued, even when the New York Dolls were in town). "Maid" is classy, sophisticated even, in its willingness to show its girders. It works well as a song and as a structure, even though it barely disturbs the mercury. But what everyone *remembers* about "Maid In Heaven" is the wakka-wakka wakka-wakka bit at the end of the opening line, strummed fast by Nelson on heavily damped guitar strings against the void of a sudden musical caesura. "She's a ma-id in hea-ven / Wakka-wakka wakka-wakka" is how you'd write down the lyric, and people remember it for that. It is a marvelous hook and a pure one, a hook which serves as a reinforcing metaphor for Nelson's über-controlling approach to composition. *Hand-damping* is the wonder of it all really; tight, meticulous control of the tiniest compositional spaces is what's desired (almost more than sex), artistic hands working fiercely, tirelessly, while in the background somewhere, out of shot, two dedicated accountants keep quiet time in bowler hats.

Ensemble friction? *Qu'est-ce que c'est?*

You can hear in "Maid In Heaven" precisely how compositional Nelson's creative instinct is, and how compositionally precise, even when notionally abandoned to the rocking moment. It goes with the double-breasted suits and cantilevered hair; with the dickie-bow, for heaven's sake. Prog methodology brought to bear on Art Rock style.

Still, you can't argue with "Sister Seagull," which is the tour de force on *Futurama* and remains, to this writer's withering ears, the Be-Bop song for the ages. Be-Bop Deluxe *deluxe*.

It's a ripple song. A ripple and surge song. You can hear, just by listening, that it arose simply and chastely from a chord sequence that conveys a mood, rather than from a series of smartass technical ideas conveying poetic strategies that might reflect like German Expressionist lighting on its composer. The "Sister Seagull" lyrics contribute three more stanzas to the wealth of sub-Symbolist love poetry on the album, but they are so wholeheartedly supported by the musical motifs which underpin them—slogging, soggy power cadences out of which delicately picked arpeggios fall like water-drops—that you don't actually register the infelicity of the words: you hear *song*. "I am a changeling, like the wind across the waves / Though in the end, there will be nothing left to save..." Well, quite. But somehow it doesn't matter that this is wanky doggerel. It didn't matter to me in 1975, and thirty-five years on, though resoundingly callow, it still contrives within the frame of the recorded song to sound like a pretty authentic assertion of a moment's feeling. Real feeling. Damp and chilly feeling.

I got stuck on "Sister Seagull" this week, as I did back then. Kept playing it over and over again, to the exclusion of the rest of *Futurama*, on which there are another five twisty, turny, showy-offy songs about the other clutter in the poet's unruly mind. Tin aeroplanes. Caskets of silver and sea-jade. Siamese twins. All the baloney in Bill's oddly optimistic suburban-futurist love-closet (presumably the same one in which he used to hang his suits and ties). So come on: the rest of the album is okay: it's chilled Euro-intellectual Art Rock power-trio ham of some technical accomplishment, and no rhythmic excitement whatsoever, only departing from the model momentarily to Lady-Grinning-Soul its way through the abominable "Jean Cocteau," which I disliked at the time and feel really quite queasy over now.

But then again, it's a basic requirement of Euro-intellectual Art Rock, surely, that occasionally it should make you feel sick.

And as for Harlequin and the Ticktock Man—well, they were the antagonists in a Harlan Ellison Sci-Fi story from the mid-sixties. Thompson and I read it in our own decade because...well, because we were hip. Ellison was not well known in the U.K., which was a precious quality as far as we were concerned; and at the age of fifteen there is nothing more enthralling than a narrative which pits the vaulting spirit of Cocteau's Harlequin against the regulatory totalitarianism of your average clock-watching Ticktock Man. And lo, there, on the reverse sleeve of *Futurama*, you'll find Bill Nelson dressed in a Harlequin's ruff and lozenges, cuffed and restrained by Simon Fox and Charlie Tumahai in, you guessed it, Nazi uniforms.

Nelson once insisted, and probably still does to this day, that he did not read the story until long after making the record. And we must believe him.

ON THE RELEASE DATE of Be-Bop's next album, *Sunburst Finish*, in February the following year, Thompson was dispatched from school to the record stall on the market square in town to bring back a bundle of four copies for distribution among the renegade posse of Be-Bop fans in our class. Thompson and I had made two new converts to the cause.

But that moment of hasty dispatch was to be the high noon of our contentment.

The cover of *Sunburst Finish* featured an inferno-orange photograph of a naked, slick-haired chick in a glass tube waving a flaming Gibson ES-345 around like a burning brand. We decided, with mustered authority, that this was not really in keeping. It felt like a cheapening of the vision, somehow. The image seemed, if truth be told, a little provincial, a little *heavy metal*. Thompson and I weren't that enamored of the music within, either, which had lost the sense of penitential chill and over-elaboration which had made *Futurama* so special to nervous Prog evacuees. This Be-Bop frothed and fizzed and popped and sizzled and, inevitably, had a minor hit after appearing on *Top of the Pops*.

And then they came to the Corn Exchange for the first time as headliners. The support act were the Doctors of Madness, a kind of proto-Punk Art Rock gang-stallation fronted by an epically gaunt individual called Kid Strange, who wore a white duster and a single sequin on each of his eyelids; he was supported to the hilt by a bassist who had evidently been dug up only that morning from a shallow grave on the municipal dump. The Doctors were fast and ugly and apocalyptic, as if they'd read all of Harlan Ellison and none of Jean Cocteau. They were exciting.

Be-Bop, on the other hand, were not. They slogged through note-for-note simulacra of songs from the three albums, with a particular emphasis on the contents of the new one. They showed off their rather ordinary keyboard-playing new recruit. And then, in the middle of something long, dramatic and conclusive-sounding, a roadie walked onstage with a lighter and a charred-looking Gibson ES-345, and tried to set fire to it while squatting like a monkey behind the drum riser. Ignition did not take place. The guitar refused to flame.

Downstage, Bill Nelson squinted anxiously over his shoulder for the duration of a few choruses, rolled his eyes, refocused on his fretboard and carried on with the song, as if this were all in a day's work. And that, dear reader, was for me the day the Be-Bop died.

Nick Coleman has been a journalist and broadcaster for more than twenty-five years. He wrote briefly for NME in the mid-eighties before becoming Music Editor at Time Out London. Between the mid-nineties and 2006 he was Art and Features Editor at The Independent newspaper. He has written for The Guardian, Times, Daily Telegraph, New Statesman, U.S. Vogue, GQ, and a variety of other publications. His first book, The Train in the Night: A Story of Music and Loss, was published in the U.K. by Jonathan Cape in 2012. It is scheduled for publication in the U.S. by Counterpoint, fall 2013. It partly concerns Nick's considerable debt to Progressive Rock.

Set An Open Course For The Virgin Sea
by Jeff Gordinier

...and ohhhh, what an entrance.

—Norman Mailer, *Ancient Evenings*

BEFORE I GET AROUND to talking about the night that I ended my fling with Prog Rock, I think it makes sense to talk about the night, several years later, when I lost my virginity. Or didn't lose my virginity, as it were.

Even then, as a teenager in Southern California, I was predisposed to romantic grandeur. I was a sucker for sweeping gestures, which probably explains why I had been temporarily susceptible to a mode of musical expression that often involved castles, elves, and oceanic voyages. When it came to sex, I really did want to wait until I felt sufficiently in love with someone, and then, when that love was confirmed and reciprocated by the other party, I wanted to make sure that our consummation took place in very special—very grand—circumstances.

Which is another way of saying that I wanted us to fuck on a mountaintop.

In my memory, my girlfriend, whom I'll call Sophia, had the beseeching brown eyes and the lanky, languid curves of a French film star. She wasn't French, but neither was she entirely American in the traditionally peppy sense. Her father was British and her mother came from South or Central America—Ecuador, maybe— and Sophia had an air of quiet, foreign mystery, which naturally I found impossible to resist. As was her style, I don't think she registered much of a protest when I suggested that, since we were truly in love, we should drive up into the mountains overlooking the San Gabriel Valley and find a dramatic place to have sex. She just fixed those big brown eyes on me and whispered, "Okay."

It didn't take long for us to learn that mystic alpine defloration was harder to achieve than we thought. For one thing, mountains get cold at night, even in the summer in California. I parked my family's Oldsmobile station wagon near a secluded perch where we could fool around while gazing upon the humming, electrified bowl of Pasadena. I placed a Navajo-style wool blanket on the ground. We took off our clothes. We got down on the blanket. We kissed. I saw goosebumps up and down Sophia's long, slim legs. She was freezing. So was I. I soon realized that my wild adolescent lust for Sophia was locked in a cosmic battle with a frosty mountain breeze that hit my equipment with all the delicacy of a sack of ice cubes. Meanwhile that Navajo blanket was itchy, and sharp twigs and stones were poking into my knees, and into Sophia's beautiful spine, from beneath it. No matter where we rolled, or how much we wanted to make this thing work, it felt like we were kissing on the floor of a dried-up riverbed. Sophia, in her wisdom, was the one who first accepted that our rustic coupling was not to be. She fixed her cocoa-colored high beams on me and whispered, "It's okay."

So how, you might ask, does any of this tale of erotic disappointment relate to the realm of songs that involve Icarus and fifteen-minute synthesizer solos?

Here's how. The night when I attempted to lose my virginity felt a lot like the night when my father had taken me to see Styx at the Long Beach Arena. In the sense that both nights totally sucked—and both nights changed me.

When people start telling me about their first concert experiences, I usually get envious. Like them, I too could have pogo'ed to the Ramones or The B-52s. I could have caught Led Zeppelin before John Bonham died. Hell, I could have been a stowaway in a van full of hot, sticky-haired, glitter-nosed girls going off to squeal to Duran Duran. But I did not. Instead I went to check out Styx at the Long Beach Arena.

Styx represented a weird hybrid that I now see, in retrospect, probably reflected some corporate cokehead's master plan to push that Prog Rock shit farther into the mainstream and milk it for all it was worth. The guys in Styx ventured into the bombastic, Tolkien-tinged territory of Prog—"a gathering of angels appeared above my head," etc.—but they did so with the chromium studio gleam that you got from bands like Foreigner, and they made sure that all the sylvan-glade, dwarves-on-horseback, "Come Sail Away" stuff was counterbalanced by a commensurate supply of what we'd now refer to as "power ballads." When, as a birthday gift, my father took me and two junior-high friends to see Styx, the band was dominating radio with a gloopy, electric-piano-blanketed mash note, called "Babe," that would not have been out of place on a Michael McDonald album.

I didn't really want to hear "Babe." I mostly wanted to hear "Renegade," Styx's tribal-thumping, man-on-the-lam roof-raiser. Even as a kid, I could tell that Styx was drifting inexorably toward the dreaded Sea of Cheese, and that Tommy Shaw, the group's perceived Torchbearer of True Rock and the guy behind "Renegade," was losing a power struggle with Dennis DeYoung, the man responsible for "Babe," who seemed determined to turn the whole Styx enterprise into a Broadway spectacle.

Still, "Babe" suggested that Styx's arranged marriage of Prog and Pop had the potential to open up a whole new target market, the one generally referred to as "women."

Alas, I did not see many women as we took our seats at the Long Beach Arena. Beards abounded. The concert hall was full of thousands of dudes who looked like pot-bellied versions of Richard Branson. Behind us sat three or four sullen, lumberjacky Bransons, and when the lights went down, they took out a paper plate covered with white powder.

I don't want to be here.

I don't belong here.

I want to leave.

I don't think Styx got three songs into their set before such thoughts became insistent in my mind. Styx had been named after a mythical river into hell, and that seemed like an apt encapsulation of my experience. (And my father's: for the duration of the show he sat as immobile as an Easter Island statue, unable to mask his massive sneer.) I can't pretend to recall the set list, but I do remember smoke bombs. Smoke bombs and lasers, spinning drum sets and choreographed guitar solos that conveyed the overall message that not a single moment of this show would be organic or spontaneous. Or maybe what happened is just that my teen brain exploded with embarrassment. I recall a wave of Holden Caulfield-like contempt washing through me—an unshakeable conviction that Styx was phony to the core. As the opening chords of "Babe" began to burble and the beardies went apeshit, I turned to my father and pleaded,

"Can we go now?" He looked as though someone had just passed him a perfectly executed martini. Within ten minutes we were on the freeway back to San Marino. My friends were pissed.

A few days later I got down on my knees in my bedroom and subjected my record collection to a radical purge. I took out all of my Styx albums. All of my Kansas albums. All of my Yes, Genesis, Pink Floyd, and Emerson Lake & Palmer albums. In my mind, any band that betrayed even the slightest hint of extraterrestrial exploration or medieval minstrelsy was toast. (That said, not even "The Battle of Evermore" could get me to part with Led Zeppelin.) I placed all those now-sullied epics into a basket attached to my motocross bike. I rode up to Poo-Bah Record Shop, which was then housed in an actual bungalow on Walnut Street in Pasadena, and I sold the lot. I traded them in. The guy at the cash register hinted that this bounty wouldn't necessarily net me a fortune, but I didn't care. I just wanted to divest.

I had the vague idea that Punk Rock was afoot, and that it represented some kind of gutter rebuke to the pompous excesses of Prog. I'd heard that Johnny Rotten of the Sex Pistols had been spotted on the streets of London wearing a t-shirt that said, "I Hate Pink Floyd." That was good enough for me. Who knows exactly what I went home with, in the great Prog-for-Punk swap that would turn out to be an oddly pivotal point in my life. I'm pretty sure it included the first Ramones album, Elvis Costello's *This Year's Model*, and *Never Mind the Bollocks, Here's the Sex Pistols*.

And a few years later, on the afternoon following our frosty misadventure in the mountains, Sophia and I slipped into my bedroom, with the help of a wrought-iron balcony, and managed to succeed at having sex, which came as a great relief to both of us. A lot more sex would follow. We kept it simple. We learned that it was best to avoid the mountains. Sometimes you have to know where you belong.

Jeff Gordinier is a staff writer for The New York Times *and the author of* X Saves the World. *His work has appeared in a variety of publications, including* Details, Outside, Esquire, *PoetryFoundation.org,* Creative Nonfiction, Fortune, GQ, Elle, *and* Entertainment Weekly.

In The Court Of The CrimsonKing02
by Charles Bock

One of the cornerstone ideas of the subgenre of music known as Prog is that when a note or chord or idea is introduced, it will be followed to its logical, maximalist conclusion.

—Charles Bock

L ET'S HEAD BACK TO the late nineties, when apartments had what are now referred to as land lines, and every incoming call to my land line cut off the dialup feed and disconnected my fragile internet service. Days, I was trying to write a novel. Nights, I was trying to write as well, although I also worked as a freelance, third-shift legal proofreader—this meant anytime between six and midnight I might get paged to work, and that I was fairly accustomed to working until eight in the morning. On one such night, I hadn't been paged, and was in my apartment at some godforsaken hour, most likely working on the third draft of a novel with a finish line that always seemed to be moving further out of reach, taking breaks at designated hours to walk my dog. I often listened to a fair amount of classic Metal on my shitty Coby knockoff stereo. Logic suggests this listening prompted a web search. Which is most likely how I found a ridiculous website.

No. Not a Prog website. Sweet, kind reader, I know it's a collection of essays about Prog Rock. But if you are reading this, it can be assumed you are either a friend—*Hi Howie!*—or you understand, at least in a generally cloudy manner, that one of the cornerstone ideas of the subgenre of music known as Prog is that when a note or chord or idea is introduced, it will be followed to its logical, maximalist conclusion. In keeping with that notion, I'm taking some room here, setting things up then blowing them out as completely as possible. Which is to say, sit tight. The Prog stuff kicks in on the back end. Also, get ready for some thick-ass paragraphs.

Sweet, patient, loving reader, you most likely have tried to wipe this from your memory, but in the late nineties, the landscape for musical culture was fairly brutal: Metallica—once the band championed by those tape and LP collectors who also happened to be the angry weird guys living in sketchy houses with peeling paint and dying lawns—had brought a lawsuit against the music file sharing site Napster, and this was indicative of a giant betrayal that seemed to dominate the rock scene. Talentless bands that were simultaneously aggressive and over-processed—and as an added, moron-friendly bonus boasted of horribly spelled names (Limp Bizkit, Korn)—owned commercial rock radio in part because their labels actually paid the stations to play their shitty singles, and the new mutant genre known as Rap Rock had done away with Grunge pretty much the way Grunge had flushed away Hair Metal at the turn of the nineties (the only difference being that much of what we call Grunge was, you know, good). This, at a time when commercial rock radio and what we now think of as the old media, no matter how corrupt and smelly it may have been, still actually mattered. When a Southern Cal Hard Rock magazine called *Metal Edge* wouldn't give any press to a tone-deaf afterthought from the sunset strip named Tuff, Tuff's lead singer (a balding, self-promoting idiot infamous for routinely unloading crates of obscure discs at Hollywood used record stores) and one of his buddies (a comedic actor who sometimes ran video equipment for the Orange County band Lit) took matters into their own masturbation-calloused hands, and started a GeoCities site. Don't laugh, millenials. Before blogs, and long before Twitter, GeoCities is pretty much what there was in the way of taking matters into your own hands. That and 'zines. (These guys probably weren't allowed near staplers, though.)

By the time I discovered MetalSludge.com, with its crude black background and screaming red logo (replete with umlauts and barbed wire—any hetero teen from the eighties would recognize them from Mötley Crüe), it was apparent that I was not the only one idling through a shift at work, taking a break or what have you, who occasionally typed into a search engine the name of a lead singer whose heyday addiction to Aqua Net had resulted in a reliance on bandanas so he could cover up a bald pate, who checked up on guitarists whose appetites (be it for destruction or double stuffed cream puffs) had burst them out of their leather pants, drummers whose Bonhamesque excesses had left them half-witted, addled, and sometimes working in the kitchens of restaurants. As many as ten thousand visitors a day came back for the musings of MetalSludge's own frontman, Jani Bon Neil, whose name was an amalgam of hair band frontmen and whose face always appeared mangled via Photoshop. Other contributors included Ozzy Stillborne, Bastard Boy Floyd, and Donna Anderson, the phenomenon of jumbled internet names still novel to come off as original.

Sludge's missives may have been sneering, badly punctuated, and grammatically abominal, but they were also acidly funny and knowledgeable. Sludge delivered updates on the original members of Ratt suing one another, as well as first person accounts from the sad little clubs where each of the two bands named Ratt happened to be parking their Econoline vans to play gigs. ("*Click here to see photos of Pantera when they still looked like Hair Metal poofs and had not yet made the turn to badass death rockers.*" "*Click here for the latest tantrum, complete with annotations, from former Skid Row singer Sebastian Bach...*" "*...for twenty questions with one of the brothers from Enuff Z'Nuff,*" "*...with the bassist from Danger Danger.*")...I should stop now; you get the picture, except I am obligated to mention Donna's Penis Chart, where one might learn that the lead singer of Slayer "fucks exactly like he plays guitar...too fast & plenty hard..." and/or that Flea had a "beautiful, extremely rock hard cock of well-proportioned length and width."

Kissinger's famous line about academic politics goes that the fighting is so vicious because the stakes are so small; MetalSludge not only attracted men and women nostalgic for—and still quite enraptured with, and with a prurient curiosity about—the music of their teen years. There were music lifers as well: roadies, radio types, concert promoters, other never-weres and would-have-beens, and—yes—former rock stars.

Long denied the attention they'd once taken for granted, the former Real Deals gravitated to this obscure corner of the net like, well, like aging rockers in need of attention. Sometimes the check-ins were classy and adult and cleared the air on something (Dan Spitz writing in to the guestbook—er, hatebook—to explain why he'd left Anthrax and defend his religious beliefs), often a performer was a good sport, played along, and promoted themselves in the process (Faster Pussycat's Brett Muscat doing a tour diary, Poison's Rikki Rockett contributing a recurring advice column). Almost inevitably, though, an entertainingly large number of arrivals still took themselves seriously, or hadn't aired old grievances, or couldn't help but reveal the train wrecks that were their true psyches: Sebastian Bach, for example, refused to be photographed by anyone in a Sludge shirt and had tantrums if the site's name was so much as mentioned; many, many others checked-in with badly spelled complaints that ended with threats to the anonymous site owners. And who can forget Donna D'Errico? Former *Playboy* centerfold and *Baywatch* babe? The now ex-wife of Mötley Crüe's Nikki Sixx? Still nothing? Well, in answering a question about Pamela Anderson (who just happened to be an ex-Playmate who'd also run on the beach in a bright red onesie, married a member of Mötley Crüe, and was *way* more famous), D'Errico caps-locked out the following: "IF SHE HAD AS MANY DICKS STICKING OUT OF HER AS SHE'S HAD STICKING IN HER, SHE'D LOOK LIKE A PORCUPINE."

Of course Sludge also had message boards. We're all familiar with boards and how they work by now, their flame wars and ridiculous arguments that never end. Who hasn't been sucked into an hours-long typing marathon, exchanging impassioned essays and crotch-shot insults with someone whose frothing soapbox-like corner preacher views you, in real life, would cross the street to avoid? The Sludge Gossip Board was my introduction to message boards, and I was hooked. I trolled for a while and jumped in and posted before I should have, checking the site every ten minutes to see if anyone had answered my witticisms.

I'd been twelve or so when an older brother had gotten me involved with Metal. And while I'd taken to it with the enthusiasm of any younger brother following his big brother's footsteps, I was also five feet tall, scrawny, prepubescent, and bookish. And no matter how deeply unhappy and alienated I may have been inside my stringy, shitty body, no matter how many Metal magazines I read through alone at the 7-Eleven, no matter how tuff or alpha-doggish I tried to act in compensation, I was obviously different than all those larger kids who stalked the hallways and lunch tables of Las Vegas's Cashman Jr. High in their concert tees. Part of it was physical, naturally, but there was more. Being aware of the differences further put me outside the circle; observing and obsessing over the rituals and still not being accepted created—or exacerbated—a self-consciousness, I think, and with it, whether I liked it or not at the time, the sinking feeling that I could never be wholeheartedly Metal. I was traveling a different road. This was true half a lifetime later as well. Even at twenty-eight or twenty-nine, though I humbly considered myself to be able to hold my own about more than a few subsets of rock music, I found myself to be a lightweight in comparison to the majority of Sludge Board posters, for I would never have possibly imagined how intricate or nuanced the discussion concerning a band named Sleeze Beez could be.

It was not long before I learned to choose my battles: shutting up, logging in, and appreciating the untold geniuses of the boards—tech support guys who needed something to keep them awake and entertained during overlong and sedate shifts, late night data punch entry clerks needing the exact same thing, graphic artists, beauty school students, nursing aides... Who were they? Well, I vaguely remember a bony stripper from Texas who called herself Heavy Metal Lust Queen. Using a photo of herself in a bikini as her avatar, she posted almost around the clock and by all indications was on some kind of speed.

There was a self-aware, droll southerner named Arkansas Cracker who seemed to understand how absurd being on the site was, but nonetheless posted every five seconds. This pudgy goth guy from Buffalo called himself IggyPopWillEatItself, and quickly gained a rep for his encompassing musical knowledge and giant blue font. A tall, over-pancaked beauty school student named Ette made monthly excursions from San Bernardino to Los Angeles and seemed to have made her way onto any number of tour buses. Scads of people crushed on her and followed up or commented positively on anything she posted, and soon word spread that she was a drag queen (naturally and true to form, she embraced the rumor). I seem to remember, and research confirms, that when *Spin* did an article about rock groupies, all five of the women they followed and featured were members of Sludge's groupie board. I remember that my all time favorite message board name, Sharon Kneadles, belonged to a former rock journalist from the Midwest who checked in rarely, but always had smart and knowing posts.

My favorite poster, however, was an antisocial misogynist nutjob, The Electric Snow Gorilla, his name an obscure reference to the big dumb stop-action villain from the *Rudolph, the Red-Nosed*

Reindeer Christmas special. ESG was relentlessly, brutally negative, to any and all; he held grudges, distorted opposing viewpoints, created and burned to the ground straw man arguments, never pretended to so much as care about fairness or feelings, specialized in bizarre and filthy Photoshopping, as well fictional legal documents and court filings as responses to those who disagreed with him, and had at his disposal any number of other Snow Gorilla identities, including Dan Spitz Snow Gorilla, a mentally challenged, screeching monstrosity whom Anthrax's original frontman gave props to in an interview, labeling DSSG "fucking hilarious."

Following September 11th, 2001, the board turned bloodthirsty, and the collective enthusiasm for war in Iraq was one of the things—along with the commitments of marriage—that slowed my visits. I was long gone three years later, after faulty flash pots at a Great White show prompted a tragic, fatal fire in a Long Island nightclub, and the Sludge board became an online gathering place, undoubtedly the high point of the site's existence. A year after that, the two site founders had an ugly fight that resulted in lawsuits (the comic actor thought Sludge had run its course and wanted to shutter its doors; the CD selling singer wanted to ride it for every last dime). The result was an out of court, non-disclosure agreement. By then Sludge had sold untold t-shirts and hoodies, a fifth anniversary CD, had put a summer tour on the road, been featured in a few magazine articles, and was referred to with bemusement and admiration by more music boards than I care to track. VH1 even commissioned a pilot that never aired. The site's still up today, a shell of its former self, its longtime posters having abandoned it, its owner hanging on to the scraps, a washed-up website covering the washed-upedness of a subset that itself is twenty years beyond expiration date.

ONE FINAL POSTER FROM the board is worth mentioning, though, for even compared to the rest of the screen junkies who seemed to live on Sludge, he always seemed to be on there. Three in the morning. Two in the afternoon. No discernible pattern for it, and I am not exaggerating when I say he put up dozens, perhaps even a hundred comments a day. Not particularly nuanced views; more like a guy who'd post *HA!* just to let you know he was alive. He thought that kind of thing was funny. He posted in the same way that modern teens text one another. He called himself CrimsonKing02.

His screen name, obviously, came from King Crimson, a band that started in the late sixties and which helped to define the genre this book is commemorating. King Crimson was notable for winding, melodic songs, few of which were less than six minutes in length. "Larks' Tongues In Aspic (Part 2)"—a not quite random example of their work—clocks in at seven minutes fifteen seconds, and is an accumulating, momentum-building classic considered influential, by people who care, in the development of early Metal, although very little of what they did we'd think of as hard or heavy now. One of their best-known songs, "21st Century Schizoid Man," was not that unusual for them in that it featured a horn section and extended horn solos, and wasn't far from something Mingus might write. Their 1969 album, *In the Court of the Crimson King*, is considered by many a genre-defining example of Prog, replete with sword and sorcerers title.

Though almost every single King Crimson song—as I am sure you, dearest reader, are aware—sounds phenomenal in the background while firing up a spliffie, it remains a stretch for someone on Sludge to use that handle. I say this because of the obvious dissonance between Prog and Hair Metal. We all know one of the things Prog is most defined by is its exact, wonky, R&D nature; the stereotype of Prog fans being pimply, string bean virgins who spend their afternoons memorizing chord progressions; the joke about Prog music as girl repellent.

By contrast, Hair Metal is the anti-Prog: sloppy, for the most part popishly remedial in terms of musical sophistication, basically existing because hot dumb guys had to have songs to play in order to attract nubile women. So yeah, why would anyone name himself CrimsonKing02 on a Hair Metal board? The name wasn't clever, funny, or even self-deprecating; rather, here was something nondescript as toast, workmanlike even, with the 02 at the end suggesting that the larger network of boards Sludge belonged to already *had* a CrimsonKing. Again, what the shit?

Thankfully, the inclusive nature of what is pleasing to the ear, the malleable boundaries of what defines Hard Rock, as well as the truth that most of us go through a number of musical phases, allowed a solid tenth of Sludge's thousand-plus posters to show appreciation for more than one genre's narrow corridor or subset. CrimsonKing02 was one of them, blasting out his caffeine-jacked two- and three-sentence posts about a range of bands (he favored The Misfits, King Diamond, and GnR) with a frequency that suggested the guy had some variety to his tastes, sure, but that he also couldn't let any subject go by without comment. Again, it's almost impossible to overstate how constant a presence he was on Sludge boards, and how often those posts weren't didactic or venomous, so much as typing just to type. I see him in retrospect less as an OCD freak or know-it-all than someone who just wanted to be in on the carnage and fun, who maybe spent way too much time by himself and had a format that now allowed him to try and push beyond his loneliness.

I also choose to think musical minutiae, and the weird hours we kept, created the minor connection that got me and CrimsonKing02 zipping occasional, short emails back and forth. It would be naïve to believe my own isolated life at the time did not contribute as well. Sometimes we commented on one another's comments, or some heated thread. (I didn't keep the emails, so I cannot quote from them.) I know I learned he was single, trying to support a teenage daughter to whom he was very close, and that he kept his ridiculous hours because he made at least part of what passed for his living buying and selling crap on eBay—rock memorabilia, burned CDRs of live performances, that kind of stuff. Not exactly the career you choose because you're holding aces. And while raising a teenaged daughter.

At some point I posted about some bootlegged disc of some band I'd come upon, offering copies to other board members. He promised to send me demos of Mötley Crüe's first album in exchange. Today, either of them could be downloaded from Pirate's Bay in minutes; but back then, at 26K bbps, it would have taken five years, and my connection would have been interrupted ten million times. I sent the discs to Philly; he emailed thanks when he got them, promising to send the demos ASAP. This was the extent of our connection. I never asked about the screen name.

Also in my memory banks is that at some juncture, CrimsonKing02 had troubles with another poster. Boundaries of privacy and safety were apparently violated. Afterwards, he was no longer welcome on Sludge. My antenna was up enough to learn that another Philly poster talked about seeing him at local shows, asking what had happened, and not receiving an answer.

On April 30th, 2008—about three months after the publication of the same novel I'd been writing when I'd accidentally discovered MetalSludge—both *The Philadelphia Inquirer* and *Philadelphia Daily News* ran short obituaries for a man (who happened to have been born the same year as me) named Christopher J. Paulos. By then, a smattering of tributes had already sprouted online, bemoaning the death of the CrimsonKing02, aka Kriss Vicious, aka Chris Sixx, the beloved son of shopkeepers in Philadelphia who'd left behind a younger sister and a teenaged daughter to whom he was quite close. Sudden death. No cause given. Age thirty-eight.

From every account I was able to find, and what I've learned from a few emails, Chris was exactly what you'd expect, an average blue collar guy who had hair to his shoulders and a fleshy face, a big guy who wore jeans and black t-shirts, leather trenches and jean jackets with patches of his favorite bands. In pictures he looks both massive and friendly. Though in more than a couple of shots, he looks like he's tossed a few back and could perhaps be scary if things went the wrong way. Apparently, Chris went to lots of shows at local bars in Philly that played Hard Rock—Northstar and the like. And if a friend's band was there, he tried to show up. He not only went to lots of pro wrestling shows in Philly, but also hung out afterwards at the bar where the wrestlers hung out, and may have worked for a local wrestling outfit for a while.

Many of Paulos' friends were longtime buddies, and for eighteen years he was pals with a pro wrestler named The Blue Meanie, who for a time worked with the WWE. Their friendship was strong enough that the Meanie once organized a tribute fundraiser for Chris and his daughter. There are also a number of pictures of Chris online where he's hugging friends, or his parents. The ones where he's happily dancing with his teenaged, gothed-out daughter are my personal favorites.

THE WHIMS OF LIFE and its unpredictable roads have dictated that I am presently a widowed single father who happens to be raising a three year old girl; it therefore follows that I can't help but look at those photos and think about this guy and think there but for the grace... So, yeah, the ones of Chris dancing with his daughter are my favorites.

One other photo is worth noting, though. An older shot, probably from his twenties. He's caught in profile, and beneath a backwards mesh hat and a bandana, his hair flows in dark curls. His head is raised slightly and his eyes are closed, and it looks as if he is raising his face into a cool, nice breeze. He's wearing a sleeveless jean jacket of light blue and a black t-shirt with short sleeves hugging his bronzed huge arms, which are crossed in front of his chest. He looks contemplative. Regal. A king in his court. He looks at peace.

Charles Bock is the author of Beautiful Children *(Random House),
which won the Sue Kaufman award for First Fiction from the American
Academy of Arts and Letters. His work has appeared in* Harper's, The
New York Times, Esquire, *on NPR, and in various anthologies. He lives
in New York City with his daughter, Lily.*

There Is No Rush

by Joe Meno

What about the voice of Geddy Lee?
How did it get so high?
I wonder if he speaks like an ordinary guy
                              —"Stereo," Pavement

1

THE BAND RUSH ALMOST killed me; their 1981 single "Tom Sawyer" was playing the first time I ever got in a car accident. It was New Year's Eve and I was driving dizzily from one party on the south side of Chicago to another one way out in the suburbs because I had been told there was a girl there who would kiss me. So desperate was I to mate with a female of my own species—any female, really, as she could have been Vulcan, Klingon, or one of those blue-skinned Andorians from *Star Trek: The Next Generation*—that I was willing to drive an hour off into the unknown, passing many, enormous, protean mansions, admirable front lawns, and inestimable cul-de-sacs, all the while borrowing my older sister's car without asking. It was 1990, around 11:15 P.M., less than an hour until the year 1991, less than an hour until the future world of unkempt promises, a future world where I, and so many like me, would inherit the earth, or so we had been told time and time again in so many dystopian novels, comic books, and science fiction shows on television. I was sixteen. I had had my driver's license for less than five months. I was an idiot who did not think he was an idiot. I did not know that rock music could be played at anything other than the loudest possible volume.

On the car stereo Rush's Prog Rock anthem "Tom Sawyer" was blaring, with its monolithic-sounding, bass-heavy, moon-crawler lick. My friend Brian in the passenger seat tomahawked the air along with the space-age, syncopated rhythm. Somehow we were exactly like Tom Sawyer in the song, whoever he was, fleeing the places we had known for something exciting and new. There was an unspoken feeling that—listening to Rush and driving at breakneck speed along the abandoned suburban streets—we were hurrying off to our future destinies.

Then the unthinkable happened, just as it almost always does: only a few miles from the party I blew through an unmarked four-way intersection and collided with a hatchback traveling in a perpendicular direction. The last thing I heard was Geddy Lee's ridiculous exclamation, "He knows changes aren't permanent, but change is." Fender met fender amidst the sound of collapsing metal. The airbag did not deploy, as there were no airbags in my sister's early-eighties Volkswagen. Brian in the passenger seat—who had been playing a wicked air drum solo only moments before—stared wide-eyed at the crumpled hood before us. White smoke poured out from the engine. Then the battery went dead, then the stereo, then the music died all around us.

2

Needless to say, I never made it to the party. I never met the girl. I had to call my dad from a payphone and cop to borrowing my older sister's car without asking. All that winter, I had to work doing some bullshit landscaping job just to get my sister's car fixed. All because I was sixteen and did not know any better. All because my frontal lobe had not fully formed. All because I had very little impulse control and did not want to listen to music at a rational level. All because I had been listening to Rush.

3

Then again, Rush always sounded like a future I could not clearly comprehend. There was always something distinctly foreign, something kind of off-putting about them. First there were the synthesizers—and since when did rock bands have synthesizers? There was Geddy Lee's comically/tragically high voice, the odd breaks from 4/4 time to 7/8. There was the masturbatory, band-nerd instrumental solo sections, their relentlessly incomprehensible lyrics: "Catch the mist / Catch the myth / Catch the mystery / Catch the drift." Was this sixteenth century poetry? Why did it feel like something I was supposed to be studying in A.P. English? Also, where was the mention of girls? Girls, their heart-shaped faces, their wet, luminous eyes, their endlessly long hair, the subtle mystery of their mouths, their long, tawny legs, their soft, yielding hands, the tiny blonde hairs on the back of their arms, their daring, impossibly firm breasts? How could there be a Hard Rock song that did not—in any way as far as I could tell—allude to sex? Did Rush misunderstand the most basic premise of rock and roll? Why, when I was so, so horny, distracted at all hours, trying to find someone, anything to mate with, why was this band singing about "mist?" Unless "mist" was some strange euphemism for male or female ejaculate—which it very well may have been, as the extent of my sexual knowledge rested firmly between the borders of soft-core Cinemax porn and the treacly sex scenes of Stephen King novels—how was this band going to get me laid? Wasn't that the job of rock and roll in the first place?

4

In the end, Rush made me feel the way trying to do calculus always felt; only the hardest of hardcore nerds could possibly enjoy it, and hopefully, only in the privacy of their own homes. Rush was unrelenting in its out-and-out nerdiness, like the guys who worked at the comic book store at the mall, with their oddly sculpted facial hair, premature bald spots, and all-too-realistic Green Lantern rings. The members of Rush seemed totally unwilling to hide their dorkiness, to feel shame for what they were. It was like they had totally given up on the idea of social acceptance. For me, as a nerd trying to pass as a normal human, this was a terrifying concept, something akin to becoming a eunuch or priest, which as a young man at a Catholic all-boys school was not just some abstract fear. It was something I faced every day, staring through the wire fence out at the Catholic all-girls school on the other side of the football field, trying to catch a glimpse of anything remotely female. Leaning against the fence, I would wonder: did that girl have two arms and two legs, a head? Wouldn't she be a perfect candidate for coupling? Was that a supple sophomore or a middle-aged security guard? At this distance, who could tell?

I would stand at that fence and stare until the morning bell rang and then march off to school, left to consider Rush, eunuchism, self-imposed vows of chastity. Why? Why, if given the choice, would someone say no to sex? Unless you were Oedipus Rex and happened to have the minor bad luck to sleep with your own mother—why would someone purposefully castrate themselves? (A side note here: there was a long, secret discussion, one that took up weeks and weeks at the nerds-only lunch table where I ate, in which we argued whether sleeping with one's own mother could actually be considered a tragedy. On one hand, there was the obvious question of incest, the embarrassment of that rumor getting around, etc. On the other, it was still sex. For a group of philosophical virgins and seminal outcasts, the debate was never one that was completely settled.)

It seemed like Rush had, like so many nerds that I knew, completely given up on sex. And why would I want to align myself with that?

5

AT THE RECORD STORE, I'd spend hours flipping through record album after record album, searching for some clue, some telltale sign, something in the visages, in the apparel of various bands to help me become cool, to transform my puny body and acne-speckled face into something attractive, something mysterious, something worthy of the act of sexual reproduction. Here was Richard Marx with his longish hair. Was longish hair sexy? It didn't matter as my Catholic high school had a strict dress code outlawing long hair. Here was Axl Rose. Was a leather jacket and tight leather pants sexy? It didn't matter. I couldn't afford either one of these items as all the money I was making at my low-wage job was going towards repairs on my older sister's car. Here was Mötley Crüe, here was Ratt, here were the members of Poison, prettier than most girls on the southside. Did having ridiculous, poofy, bleach-blond hair, and dressing like a lady make you attractive to females? Could this be? It really didn't matter. My father was a former Green Beret and dressing like a girl was possibly the worst thing I could do as a human. He was already suspicious about all the time I spent alone, all the video games, all the books I read.

Then there was Rush. Flipping through their record covers, searching for some sort of model of attractiveness, something that would win over the conceptual female population that I knew existed but barely ever interacted with, I came across their 1981 album *Moving Pictures*. What the fuck? It was literally a photograph of some movers in red jumpsuits carrying some gold-framed pictures into a gothic-looking museum. It was not sexual, it was not rebellious, it was not even coded in the weird confusion of transvestism. It was a Monty Pythonesque joke. It was despicably, unapologetically nerdy. It looked like an advertisement for a television show on PBS, something narrated by some wanker with a highfalutin British accent.

At the time, I assumed that Rush's lack of interest in carnal matters was because they were from the future, a future where humans had evolved beyond sex and furthered the species through artificial insemination or telepathic mind-melds, thereby freeing up more energy to consider things like visual double entendres, 7/8 time signatures, and "mist," whatever the heck that was. The future, apparently, was a world without sex, a world dominated by castrated male singers and forty-piece drum kits, where instrumental solos filled the void once held by an interest in sex. If so, this was not the future I had so often imagined. Like the escapees in *Logan's Run* or the whistle-blowers in *Soylent Green*, this was a future I did not want any part of. Although some of my friends were mesmerized by the phenomenal musical talents of Geddy Lee, Alex Lifeson, and Neil Peart, I shied away from Rush altogether, seeing something in them that was fiendish or otherworldly. If "Tom Sawyer" or "Fly By Night" was playing at a party or in some friend's bedroom, I would walk away. It was like Geddy Lee's voice was a threat, an admonition, a warning as to what would happen if I did not get laid soon, issued several decades from the future.

6

THE SECOND TIME I got into a car accident I was also listening to Rush. This time their music didn't happen to be playing on the radio. I had a friend, Thierry, with his suspicious Quebecois-sounding name, who was way into Rush at the time. He was also into bands like Primus and the Red Hot Chili Peppers, any group that eschewed conventional lead guitar dramatics in favor of a more bass-driven sound. He himself was learning how to play bass. The bass guitar, he believed, was "seminally underrated." He was some sort of aficionado in training, a future record store snob, or elitist video store clerk. At the time, Rush's 1991 album *Roll the Bones* had just been released. Thierry carried a cassette tape of that album with him everywhere. He was always jamming it into a boombox or car stereo without asking.

That summer afternoon, we were pulling out of a Wendy's parking lot, French fries and Frosties jammed between our legs. I was driving, trying to eat and pilot the shitty Chevy Cavalier I had bought for three hundred dollars. The head gasket in the car had been blown, which meant the vehicle would frequently overheat. The cabin of the car always smelled like coconut oil; I imagined the previous owner as some kind of professional, fake-tanned, bodybuilding contestant. Worst of all, the cassette tape player only ever worked sporadically; all I wanted when I was six-teen was to drive as fast and as far from the world I knew, my exodus accompanied by the triumphant sound of loud music. But the car stereo was uncooperative, even in this most lowly teenage delusion. Sometimes the tape player would eat tapes; sometimes it just spit the tapes out. The feeling was like trying to masturbate while some stranger kept knocking at the door; it was impossible to get any kind of worthwhile fantasy going because the sound sys-tem was so unwilling. Regardless, that afternoon Thierry popped the Rush cassette in the stereo and cranked the volume to ten. A repetitive arpeggio built to divide the air with a tense-sounding flourish. Was this rock music? This wasn't rock music. Was it? It couldn't be rock music. It sounded like science. Or math. Some-one honked from behind me as the first track, "Dreamline," built; when the synths and drums came in, I panicked and turned right without looking. I immediately plowed into a cute sporty red car, driven by a sporty teenage girl. For a brief second, I thought may-be the girl and I would exchange insurance information, decide to go to a high school dance together, and then fall madly in love. But she only glared at me, as we inspected the gash in her car, the Rush song still blaring somewhere behind us, with its pathetic, off-time rhythms. Apparently, switching insurance information while Rush played in the background was not cool. It was dorky, it was the soundtrack to awkwardness, social humiliation, and ultimate defeat. There couldn't be a better, more clear sign. It was like we were announcing it to everyone with our music: *Here we are, world! We will remain virgins forever! We will drive around in our run-down cars, listening to dorky music, forever sealing our fates! We will only find comfort in the arms of imaginary she-elves playing* Dungeons & Dragons! *This! This is what it sounds like to be a loser! This is what it sounds like to be a nerd!* When I got back to the car, I quickly shut the stereo off and laid my head down against the steering wheel. Thierry asked me if I was okay. I don't think I bothered to answer. I spent the next several months working at an ice cream store paying to have the girl's rear bumper replaced. It seemed like the sensible rule: after that there was no more Rush in the car, no more Rush anywhere.

7

ONLY YEARS LATER, DID I find out that Rush was Canadian. Rush being Canadian explained a lot about their unmitigated, unrepentant nerdiness. Only a country with socialized medicine could produce such proud weaklings, or so I felt. In America, Rush would have had their noses broken, their homework stolen, their eyeglasses smashed. Canada has always seemed to be the land of the future, the land of progress, a nation were the *Dungeons & Dragons* kids, band nerds, and student council kids ran the show. As a nerd myself I've always been a little envious of Canadians, with their politely sonorous accents, their unabashed approval of science, their government-subsidized art programs, their love of classic turtlenecks. It is the future so many books and movies promised, a utopia where man has conquered his animal instincts, where the national symbol is a peaceful maple leaf, where popular music is detached from the throbbing, harmful hustle of sex and violence, its vague, free verse lyrics set to 13/16 time; a future of absolute safety, synthesizer solos, and hormone-less musical pursuit.

8

HAVE YOU EVER SEEN the music video for Rush's "Tom Sawyer?" If not, you really owe it to yourself to go check it out. The trio is in some kind of recording studio/snow-bound lake house. The background is a glassy window looking onto the Canadian winterland, framed by faded wood paneling. Geddy Lee, with his dark oval glasses and center-parted, long black hair—he actually looks more like an old lady who teaches Sunday school than some kind of rock musician, wearing the requisite turtleneck sweater—stands beside a keyboard and some bongos. Bongos? Yes, bongos. I don't even think there are bongos in the song, but the sight of them, the possibility of bongos ought to give everybody pause. After this single shot of Geddy—and what in the world could the nickname Geddy be short for? Gedric? Geodore?—after this single shot of Geddy singing the first verse into a down-pointed microphone, we cut to a full band shot. There is drummer Neil Peart obscured by his fortress of cymbals and toms. There is guitarist Alex Lifeson, wearing headphones, trying not to be noticed, sitting off to the side in a chair—because really shouldn't all rock and roll be recorded sitting down? Suddenly in a new wide shot you notice Geddy Lee playing bass. But what is this? Wasn't he just singing, playing the keyboards, contemplating the bongos a moment ago? Where did this bass-playing Geddy Lee come from? Are there actually two Geddy Lees in our universe? Have the Canadians with their infallible, Progressive, scientific brains found a way to clone their musicians? If so, who could think of a better use for this particular technology? Of course, this explains how Canadians—in the future—reproduce.

The video continues, cutting between these two clones, and after a few moments, it becomes clear these two Geddy Lees are dressed exactly the same—the turtleneck sweater, dark blue sweatpants, red socks, (yes, red socks), and cream-colored, lace-up saddle shoes. Half a minute into the song, any sane viewer has to ask, *why?* Why is the lead singer of this rock band dressed like somebody's grandma? Is this what happens when capitalism is reined-in? When nerds rule the land? When the law of the jungle is finally subverted? Did the concept of coolness, of sexual attraction just dissolve? The video is about as harrowing as any science fiction climax—the one where the wizened scientist stares off into the mushroom-clouded distance and asks, *What? What have we, in the name of civilization, in the name of humanity, in the name of Progress, what have we done?*

This four-minute and thirty-second video is enough to swear off the proposition of Progress altogether. It makes the threat of a country run by bullies, a nation overseen by sneering, high-fiving fraternity brothers seem like an entirely viable prospect. Because with the frat guys there is at least the possibility of a somewhat decent party, the distinct probability that there might be girls there who will get a little tipsy and dance with you out of pity. At least with the frat bros you won't be forced to dress like a retiree, cordoned off in same-sex, wood-paneled encampments, far off in the wintry northern snow. Given the choice between a future of sexless, synthesizer-driven, deep woods noodling and an obnoxious national frat party, who could fight against the oldest, irrational human instinct and choose the former? Even in my darkest, most tortured teenage moments, I knew I was a follower, a pack animal, a nerd by circumstance and not by devotion, a wanna-be beta-male desperately waiting for his chance to dance with somebody..

9

FOR MORE THAN TWENTY years I have not listened to Rush. Until this very moment, I'd forgotten they'd even existed. That world, those far-off moments of 1990, 1991, they feel like yesterday and then nothing like yesterday. Those people, those places, that music, it's all like a re-run of some unpopular television show, part sci-fi, part family drama, part teen comedy. To be honest, I try to do myself a favor and not think about it for too long.

10

BUT THEN SOMETIMES YOU hear a song, see an old friend, drive past a place where you got in a car wreck. Sometimes it's hard not to ask: *Where did the future go?* Today, in the futuristic-sounding year of 2013, I drive a Prius around Chicago, listening to modern bands desperately trying to sound like they're from the late eighties. Synthesizers, digital beats, No Wave artwork on their album covers. I listen to new music and, for a few moments, feel like a teenager again. Last week an old man driving a Ford Escort yelled out his window, "Hey, faggot. That's a faggot car." It's beautiful and kind of upsetting how little anything changes at all.

Now I drive my two kids to school, to birthday parties, to parks, to art museums. We like to listen to loud music whenever their mother is not in the car. My son does the same moves my friend Brian used to, but from the confines of his car seat. My daughter rolls the window up and down in time to the beat. I glance at them in the rear view mirror and think: *Why don't I feel like a grown up? Why don't I feel any older? Why do I still feel like a kid myself?* Somehow, miraculously, I now have a wife. I am married. I have procreated. I have reproduced. I have had sex at least twice. Considering the burden of my teenage years, this feels like no small feat. Still, the future is nothing like I would have ever imagined. It is more mundane and more wonderful than anything I would have ever conceived. In 2013, nobody lives on the moon. Nobody teleports anywhere. Nobody has jetpacks. Instead, we communicate via miniature consoles. We send our thoughts over the airwaves. We have sex with computers. Robot planes rain down fire from the sky. Record stores and bookstores have disappeared; all the places I spent my formative years are now entirely "virtual." It is a sci-fi geek's paradise; so much like *Star Trek: The Next Generation* that sometimes it feels like the only thing we're missing are the people with blue skin.

Still some things haven't changed. We still love books and music. We still try to get up and dance. We still worry about being cool, about being attractive, about how good we look. Instead of acne, instead of braces, we glance at our bald spots, at our wrinkles, at the weird Illinois-shaped moles. We still drive around in cars, along the street, out in the city. We go fast whenever we get the chance. We play records as loud as is humanly tolerable and speed down alleys like fools. We think about the future as something far-off, something impossibly distant. We dream ourselves as something greater, forgetting for a moment who we truly are. We give high fives to each other when a song we love comes on. We still do not listen to Rush in the car.

Joe Meno is a fiction writer and playwright who lives in Chicago. A winner of the Nelson Algren Literary Award, A Pushcart Prize, a Great Lakes Book Award, and a finalist for the Story Prize, he is the author of six novels: Office Girl; The Great Perhaps; The Boy Detective Falls; Hairstyles of the Damned; How the Hula Girl Sings; and Tender as Hellfire. His short story collections are Bluebirds Used to Croon in the Choir and Demons in the Spring. His short fiction has been published in McSweeney's, One Story, Swink, LIT, TriQuarterly, Other Voices, Gulf Coast, and broadcast on NPR. He was a contributing editor to Punk Planet, the seminal underground arts and politics magazine. His nonfiction has appeared in The New York Times and Chicago Magazine.

Acknowledgments

MANY YEARS HAVE LED to this moment, and I couldn't be more inspired by the work in this book. Thank you so much to all of the contributors, bands, musicians, and those of you who supported this along the way. Obviously, our work isn't even close to being done. There's still a ridiculous amount of Prog to cover. Our hope, though, is that the world will enjoy this book as much as we loved compiling it. And, if possible, we'd love to keep the tradition going until the Prog legacy has been restored to its proper balance of respectability and embarrassment. Of course, I mean that in the best possible way.

This is more of a passion project than I can go into explaining here, but there are key moments that I would like to address, if you don't mind. I guess they could have been elaborated on more formally in the context of the actual essays—or my own—but it feels fitting to lay them out as if they're a life-flashing-before-my-eyes montage of cosmic Prog memories: listening to the sound of Peter Banks trading off an eclectic range of different guitars nearly every bar on the first side of *Two Sides of Peter Banks*; driving up the Malibu coast at night with Greenslade's "Chalkhill" at full volume (I highly recommend it); defending Yes's Tormato, even the production (just listen to "On The Silent Wings Of Freedom" and we may not need to have that argument); sitting next to Steve Howe on a Rhodes beach for nearly two hours and being too nervous to even say hello; rehearsing Yes and King Crimson songs for twelve weeks with Voyager in preparation for Prog Angeles; driving from Minneapolis to Chicago for only one reason: to trade for a mint condition bootleg double LP of Peter Gabriel live at Rockpalast, 1978. I could go on and on.

Thank you, as well, to Scott Shriner and Jillian Lauren, Jay Terrien, Abbie Huxley, and Alexander Rossi, Ray Hartman, Julia Callahan, Alice Marsh, Kevin Votel, Elise Cannon, Adrian Belew, Dave Naz and Oriana Small, Sam Benjamin, Jamie Zimlin, Mike Einziger, Liz Garo, Alex Maslansky, Joseph Mattson, Mike Fleiss, Cinefamily, Marina Dundjerski, Whitney Backman, Nathan Popp, Elise Gochberg, Chip Jacobs, Dave Krizan, Bernard Radfar, Charles and Lily Bock, Lita Weissman, Richard McNeace, Robert Sobul, 826LA, and Billy Sherwood.

Also, I couldn't have done this without my Prog partner, Marc Weingarten: thank you for either being as crazy as I am or kind enough to indulge me with politeness. You're a true friend and co-conspirator.

Most importantly, though, I would like to thank my beautiful wife, Alexandra. Prog is, no doubt, the annoying presence that hovers over our lives on a daily basis. Please believe me when I say that I'm sorry for what you have to put up with, and I'm forever grateful that you do. I love you.

—Tyson Cornell, March 2013

Acknowledgments
by MARC WEINGARTEN

A hearty flick of the Bic to all the brilliant writers who contributed to this book. It was a pleasure working with you all. My Prog love really began with Spectre, my high school band, which was heavy on Focus covers. So thanks to Dave Levin, Jack Schorsch, and Joe Raposo for playing music that no girls ever wanted to hear, ever. Thanks to Rick Moody, Barney Hoskyns, Jeff Gordinier, and David Browne for the writer hook-ups. Thanks also to Jay Terrien, Adrian Belew, Chuck Dukowski, Jess Rotter, Mike Fleiss, Mike Einziger, Voyager (Abbie Huxley, Alexander Rossi, Scott Shriner, and T.C.), Liz Garo, Joel Arquillos, and 826LA.

An extended Moog solo, please, for my partner in Prog, Tyson Cornell, whose hard work and passion made this project a delight. I couldn't and wouldn't have done it with anyone else. Finally, a shout-out to my favorite supergroup: Lynn, Sam, and Allegra.

There is no end to my life,
No beginning to my death:

DEATH IS LIFE